Eleanor

Also by Alice Loxton

UPROAR!: Satire, Scandal and Printmakers in Georgian London
Eighteen: A History of Britain in 18 Young Lives

Eleanor

A 200-Mile Walk
in Search of England's
Lost Queen

ALICE LOXTON

MACMILLAN

First published 2025 by Macmillan
an imprint of Pan Macmillan
The Smithson, 6 Briset Street, London EC1M 5NR
EU representative: Macmillan Publishers Ireland Ltd, 1st Floor,
The Liffey Trust Centre, 117–126 Sheriff Street Upper,
Dublin 1 D01 YC43
Associated companies throughout the world

ISBN 978-1-0350-7694-9

1 3 5 7 9 8 6 4 2

A CIP catalogue record for this book is available from the British Library.

Map artwork by Hamesh Alles
Chapter illustrations by Belinda Roberts

Typeset in Minion Pro by Palimpsest Book Production Limited, Falkirk, Stirlingshire
Printed and bound in the UK using 100% Renewable Electricity by CPI Group (UK) Ltd

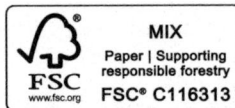

MIX
Paper | Supporting
responsible forestry
FSC
www.fsc.org
FSC® C116313

Visit www.panmacmillan.com to read more about all our books
and to buy them.

To those whom in life we dearly cherished
and in death we cannot cease to love.

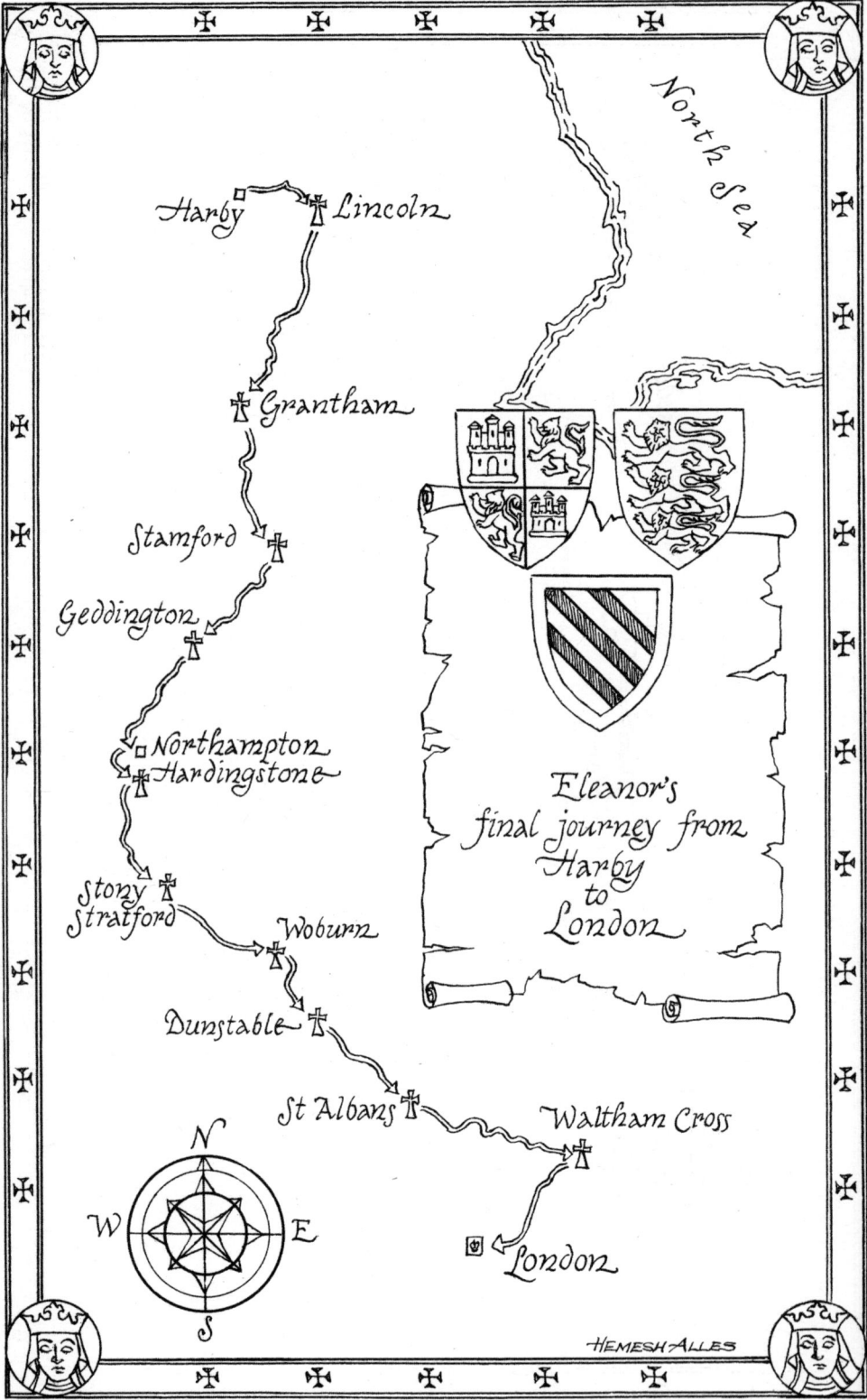

Harby

Lincoln

Grantham

Stamford

Geddington

Northampton
Hardingstone

Stony
Stratford

Woburn

Dunstable

St Albans

Waltham Cross

London

North Sea

Eleanor's
final journey from
Harby
to
London

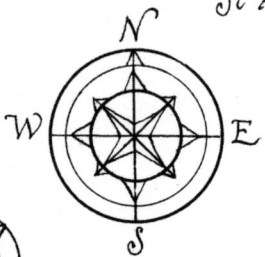

N
W   E
S

HEMESH·ALLES

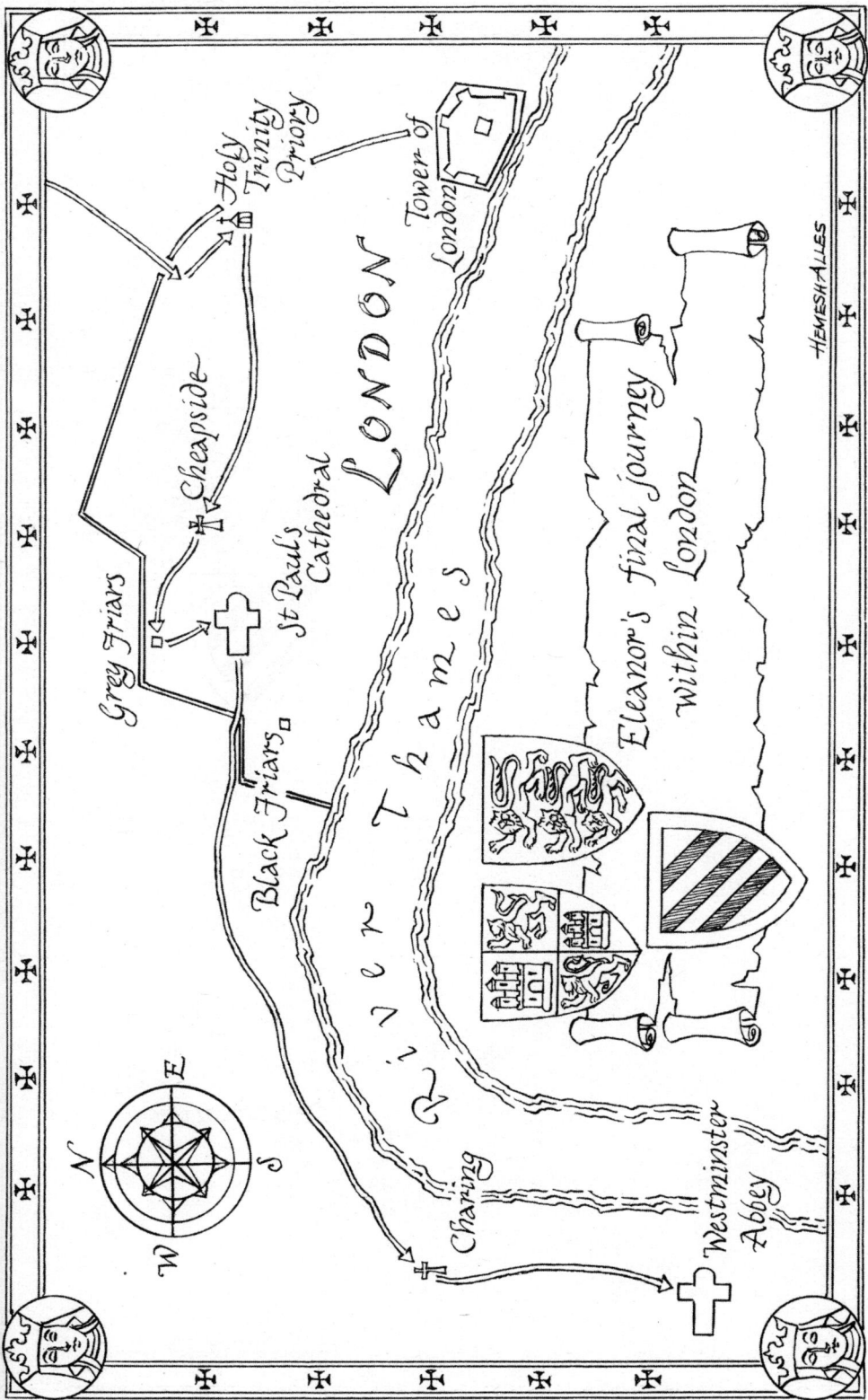

Eleanor's final journey within London

LONDON

Holy Trinity Priory

Tower of London

Cheapside

St Paul's Cathedral

Grey Friars

Black Friars

River Thames

Charing

Westminster Abbey

HEMESH ALLES

N E S W

CONTENTS

Introduction: Searching for a Lost Queen   1

1.   Pomegranates and Purgatory   19

2.   Diary of a Church Mouse   33

3.   The Past Is a Foreign Country   49

4.   Perseverantia Vincit   67

5.   Breakdown on the B1176   89

6.   A Geddingtonian Welcome   115

7.   The Tree of Happy Things   131

8.   The Queen Eleanor Interchange   147

9.   A Five-Legged Tansy Beetle   167

10.   Trapped 'Twixt Marsh and Lake   185

11.   A Pilgrimage to Dunstable   203

12.   Purple Frogs for Dinner   221

13.   Sacred Monuments and Anti-Scrapes   243

14.   Warerite Makes History   263

15.   The Forgotten Women   285

16.   In Death We Cannot Cease to Love   299

      A Note of Thanks   313

      More to Explore   315

      The Journey Continues   319

      More Photos   325

INTRODUCTION: SEARCHING FOR A LOST QUEEN

'Unable are the loved to die, for love is immortality.'
Emily Dickinson

IN SEPTEMBER 2022, A CURIOUS spectacle played out in the streets of London. Over the course of six days, 250,000 people gathered in an extraordinary, 10-mile-long queue. It started at the doors of the Palace of Westminster then stretched out like a snake, winding through the city. Along the River Thames, past the National Theatre, London Bridge and out towards Southwark Park in the east. The country was captivated: 'How long is the queue now?' was the highest trending Google search in the United Kingdom that week.

What caused this phenomenon? Were these people queuing to grab music tickets or audition for a TV show? Nothing of the sort. These were mourners – ordinary people – deeply moved by an unprecedented event: the death of a beloved queen, Elizabeth II.

After a record-breaking seventy years on the throne, Queen Elizabeth died on 8 September 2022, at Balmoral in Scotland. In the days that followed, her body was taken to Edinburgh, where a vigil was held at St Giles' Cathedral, after which, she was brought

1

400 miles south to London. First to Buckingham Palace, then to Westminster Hall. Here, the public were welcomed to pay their respects.

On Thursday 15 September 2022, at 10.12 a.m., I joined the throng. I took a day off work and became part of 'The Queue'. My companions were Len, a smartly dressed octogenarian veteran who travelled up from Cornwall that morning; Rachel and Jane, two beauticians from Merseyside; and Leo, a French student from UCL, with a large flop of black hair.

For eight hours we shuffled along the riverbank, leant against railings and fetched food for one another (though Len, the Cornish veteran, had ham sandwiches packed by his wife). We watched the Thames rise and fall with the tide, chatted about everything and nothing and zig-zagged through fencing. All of this, to spend time in the presence of the late Queen's body. To inhabit the same space – for just a moment – before being ushered out the door and back into the streets.

But why?

For Len, the Queen had been a constant comfort over his long life: 'I remember watching the coronation as a boy,' he laughed, 'and we all piled into the only house in the village that had a television. It was one of the most exciting days of my life.'

For Rachel, it was Queen Elizabeth's values – duty, faith, optimism, humility – that she so admired: 'She felt like a kind of distant grandmother, a woman of real conviction and character. She always did what was right, not what was easy – unlike me!'

Leo was fascinated by the history: 'We don't have the royal family in France. So it is very cool for me to see all the royal ceremony and traditions continue in Britain.'

By the time we arrived at Westminster Hall, it was dusk. We were ushered in and suddenly – after hours of anticipation – I was hovering on those famous stone steps and gazing upon one of the most important, oldest rooms in British history, built in the eleventh century. Under this immense hammerbeam roof, King Charles I was put on trial and condemned to die. Here, tables had groaned with the feasts of coronation banquets and the great and good had listened with anticipation to the speeches of world leaders.

We split into two lines. The Queen's coffin lay ahead in the centre of the hall, draped with a Royal Standard and surrounded by an armed guard wielding swords. The room wasn't noisy as such, but there was an eerie, unearthly sound as hushed whispers and shuffling steps danced around the great stone walls, writing their own mournful lament as they went. It seemed to come in waves, a crescendo in volume that naturally lulled, as if we – this body of mourners – were breathing in and out together.

In 'The Queue' opposite the Palace of Westminster. Photo taken by Rachel, the hairdresser from Merseyside.

The Queue outside the Palace of Westminster.

After tentatively descending the steps, I arrived at the coffin. How strange it was to think that Elizabeth II was in there. This wasn't her image on a postage stamp or on a £10 note, but the woman herself. This was her very flesh and blood, just metres from me – and in that fleeting moment, I was one of the closest to her in the whole world.

Out of Westminster Hall, I bade goodbye to Rachel and Jane and helped direct them to Westminster tube station. 'Goodbye, Len!' I cried, seeing his frail figure shuffle into the distance, swallowed by the crowd. 'Safe journey home!' I didn't see Leo again.

And just like that, after eight hours together, our little group disbanded, carried in different directions like leaves in the wind. I sometimes think of them. Are Rachel's daughters through university yet? How is Len getting on with his garden, with a view of the sea? Would he remember me? Is he still alive?

It was an intimate thing, to share this experience with strangers. To be united in camaraderie by this slightly odd process of memorial. The day was like a dream. After centuries of hibernation, the ways of the medieval world – with vigils and sacred shrines – had been awakened. It was as if the clock had been wound back and I'd walked arm in arm with the pilgrims of Chaucer's day. It was a surreal, strange blur – and one that called for a drink.

I sauntered in a daze along Whitehall, through Trafalgar Square and settled into the Lamb & Flag in Covent Garden. As I recounted my experience to a friend, Alex, we watched the live stream of mourners on a fuzzy TV screen. We considered how the history books might remember The Queue and how it would be written up during the passage of British history.

Of course, Elizabeth II is not the first royal woman whose passing provoked an outpouring of public grieving. Princess Diana's sudden death in 1997 sent many into a frenzy, verging on mass hysteria. For days and days, mourners gathered to lay a sea of flowers near the palace. One million people gathered in London to line the route of the funeral procession.

Almost a century earlier, on 2 February 1901, the funeral of eighty-one-year-old Queen Victoria unfolded at Windsor Castle. Pretty much every member of European royalty travelled to be there, many of whom would soon be fighting one another in the First World War. Or what of the funerary procession of sixty-nine-year-old Elizabeth I in 1603, to Westminster Abbey? The chronicler John Stow reported that there was 'such a general sighing, groaning and weeping as the like hath not been seen or known in the memory of man'.

There was one queen, however, whose death was commemorated

with more extravagance than any other British royal: Eleanor of Castile, the Queen Consort of King Edward I. When Eleanor unexpectedly died in a Nottinghamshire village on 28 November 1290, her body was taken to Lincoln, where it was embalmed, before being carried to Westminster Abbey in London. It was an epic procession, almost 200 miles long, through rushing rivers and along icy roads, where overnight vigils were held at towns like Grantham, Stamford, Dunstable and St Albans.

Eleanor's husband, King Edward I – one of the most formidable warrior kings of British history – was beside himself with grief. As he withdrew into isolation in the weeks that followed, he wrote the heartfelt words of his late wife: 'who in life we dearly cherished and who in death we cannot cease to love'.

Following this, Edward set out to commemorate her and her funerary journey with an extraordinary gesture. Twelve glorious stone monuments – the Eleanor Crosses – were erected in each town the procession stopped, from Lincoln to London. The final cross was at the hamlet of Charing (now central London), giving us the name Charing Cross. These were revolutionary in their scale and design, pioneering the new Gothic style in Britain. Never before or since have we seen such an ode to love, marked in stone.

Edward and Eleanor's marriage was famed for Arthurian tournaments, Crusades, castle building and fighting the Welsh. But it was forged – unusually for royal medieval marriages – by deep, respectful love and acts of true devotion. It is the great unsung love story in the history of the British monarchy, and the Eleanor Crosses – an architectural tribute to that – are England's answer to the Taj Mahal, the magnificent mausoleum in Agra, India, built by Mughal Emperor Shah Jahan in memory of his favourite wife, Mumtaz Mahal.

But what can you tell me about Eleanor of Castile? I wouldn't be surprised if your answer is 'not much' or 'nothing' or 'never heard of her'. She's pretty D-list when it comes to Britain's historical figures and is probably confused with an earlier queen, Eleanor of Aquitaine (to clarify, this is *not* a book about Eleanor of Aquitaine). Our Eleanor of Castile has never been honoured with a bodice-ripping TV drama, a place on the history curriculum or even a fridge magnet (something to look into, @EnglishHeritageGiftShop?).

Eleanor was one of England's most remarkable queens and most strikingly overlooked – perhaps because there are few contemporary sources that give us a clear sense of her character. Luckily – by pulling a few strings – I've managed to secure an interview (the first for more than 700 years). Here is Eleanor, from the horse's mouth. The transcript is as follows:

ALICE: *Eleanor – s-sorry – Your Majesty – thank you so much for your time. I know you're incredibly busy.*

ELEANOR: *No problem. I've only got a few minutes, so keep it short, please.*

ALICE: *Of course! Your childhood, tell me a little about that.*

ELEANOR: *My father was the Castilian king, Ferdinand III, and my mother – a fabulous woman – his second wife, Jeanne. It was a joyful childhood, all in all, but quite a difficult time for my parents. It was the 1240s, you see, the time of the Reconquista, the military conquest of Al-Andalus – now in Spain. The Christian north had been fighting the Muslim south for years and years, so my father was away, always on campaigns, always fighting. I can't remember him much.*

ALICE: *And what about your marriage to King Edward, in 1254?*

ELEANOR: *Well, I was twelve years old, almost thirteen. He was fifteen. I didn't know anything about him, except he was Prince Edward of England and one day he'd be King. And I'd never been to England before. The marriage was a political arrangement between our parents – a diplomatic precaution for both England and Castile against France. Luckily for me, turns out we were a good match.*

ALICE: *An understatement, I think – you were the love match of the century! The new Arthur and Guinevere, as people often put it. Do you have any tips for a successful marriage?*

ELEANOR: *Teamwork is key. Edward and I have always been a partnership. And we've had to overcome some really difficult times. In our early marriage, civil war was raging – the Barons' War, they called it – and Edward and I were both taken captive. There was a low point where I had just suffered the terrible loss of my first child and I was alone and imprisoned in a foreign land. It was really tough.*

ALICE: *It must have been incredibly difficult. Presumably you found some solace in your new family in England. Did you get on well with them?*

ELEANOR: *Old King Henry, I was fond of. He was a good man, no doubt, but a terrible king. I mean, an actual civil war broke out – doesn't that tell you everything you need to know? Then there's Edward's mother, Eleanor of Provence. Well . . . where to start. Between you and me . . . she was always jealous of Edward's devotion to me. We never got on, unfortunately. Every family has its drama, you see.*

ALICE: *Indeed it does – but you seem to be incredibly resilient. You've travelled the length and breadth of Europe on royal business, on Crusade, and all the while you've been managing a property portfolio in England that has made you financially independent. And throughout all this, you were pregnant sixteen times, which is over a decade total. Asking for a friend . . . how do you do it?*

ELEANOR: I'm hard-working – always have been, always will be. That St Albans monk once said that I was 'by sex a woman, but in spirit and virtue more like a man', which I rather like.

ALICE: And do you ever have time to relax? To switch off?

ELEANOR: Absolutely. People misunderstand me, I think. They think I'm unfriendly or aloof – but I'm just being professional. I'm at work. Behind the scenes, when I'm with the royal court, I'm quite different. We once had a party where we danced so much the floor collapsed. But, listen, I must go – I've got to read this tenancy agreement before noon.

ALICE: Of course, and I'll send a copy of the book when it's out.

ELEANOR: Thanks. If you need help with printing, get in touch with my household. You can use my scriptorium. Goodbye – BEEEEEEP

Today, she'd be winning prizes for Women in Business, photographed in a no-nonsense power suit surrounded by her brood of children. She'd write books like *How Women Really Can Have It All*. She'd be a judge on *Dragons' Den*, throwing out snappy remarks like, 'Your numbers are off, the presentation is sloppy. For that reason, I'm out.'

The Victorians liked to remember her as 'Eleanor the Faithful', the devoted wife of King Edward, but perhaps 'Eleanor the Feisty' or 'Eleanor the Formidable' or 'Eleanor the No-Nonsense' would be a better sobriquet.

More importantly, for you and me, Eleanor introduced some basic daily necessities within her court: carpets on the floor, tiles in the bathroom, forks at dinner. She adored gardening and was an enthusiast for water fountains and courtyards, like those of her Castilian youth.

She also loved to read. Eleanor was an early devotee of the Romantasy genre, particularly tales of King Arthur. Taking this obsession to new levels, in 1278 she and Edward took part in the reburial of (what was thought to be) King Arthur and his beloved Guinevere. Just imagine the scenes in the candlelight of Glastonbury Abbey, as the ancient bones of Arthur and Guinevere were wrapped in silken cloth and placed in a tomb of black marble.

Despite being immensely capable, perhaps it's not surprising that Eleanor's story has been all but forgotten. For centuries after the medieval period, write-ups of the womenfolk of Britain's past were largely overlooked. History was seen as a series of grand narratives of war, dynasties, bishops, kings and crusading knights of the day – like watching a succession of Russell Crowe films, one after the other.

It was only in the nineteenth century – perhaps inspired by the advent of eighteen-year-old Queen Victoria's reign – that things began to change. In light of Victoria's ascension to the throne in 1837, the sisters Agnes and Elizabeth Strickland began writing a collection titled *Lives of the Queens of England*. In the decade that followed, the historian Mary Anne Everett Green published *Letters of Royal and Illustrious Ladies of Great Britain*, shining a light on medieval noblewomen. Next, she compiled short biographies of princesses: *Lives of the Princesses of England, from the Norman Conquest.*

In the twentieth century, some historians began to explore women's social history, such as Eileen Power, author of *Medieval*

English Nunneries, published in 1922. It's only since the 1970s that medieval women's history has really kicked off as a major field of study.

Despite this, our perception of medieval women is still skewed. Sometimes, we view them through the lens of Victorian Pre-Raphaelites: tragic, passive, fairy-tale figures. Damsels in distress, who dangle long hair from tower windows and befriend twittering forest birds. On the other side of the coin, a focus group helping the British Library prepare their exhibition 'Medieval Women' were asked what they supposed such an exhibition would include. The results were a picture of domestic drudgery: 'cooking, linen clothing, witch trials, housewives, basket-weaving and modesty'.

In reality, the lives of medieval women were neither the stuff of romance nor never-ending housework. And these women were far from sidenotes to the story of their husband, father or sons. Though women were at a disadvantage – for example, married women were legally forbidden to own land – some commanded castle garrisons, negotiated international trade agreements and managed great estates.

By her eighteenth birthday, Empress Matilda had been in charge of Italy and, had the throne not been snatched by her cousin, she would have become the first queen regent some 400 years before Mary I. In 1190, Eleanor of Aquitaine took the helm of England when her son, Richard the Lionheart, joined the Third Crusade. Margaret of Anjou was a leader of the Lancastrians in the Wars of the Roses. And Eleanor of Castile . . . well, you'll soon find out.

All of this ran through my mind as I waited to pay my respects to Elizabeth II. And I wanted to know more. Who was Eleanor? And what kind of woman was it that inspired these crosses to be built? As I considered this, a thrilling idea came to mind and a plan began to form.

Two years later, in the final weeks of 2024 – more than seven centuries after Eleanor's death – I walked the route of Eleanor's funeral cortège: almost 200 miles from Harby, the village where she died, to London, on the corresponding dates in November and December. It was an epic adventure that ended up being one of the most fascinating experiences of my life.

In doing so, I was following in the footsteps of Edward's grief. I hoped, on this journey, to get to know Edward and Eleanor. I wanted to discover why her death provoked this flowering of memorials and I wanted to make sense of what these memorials meant, not just to Edward, but to ordinary people. I also wanted to know why they had been forgotten. By experiencing the same physical challenge, I hoped to catch a glimpse of the most elusive and thrilling of things – the innermost workings of the medieval mind.

This book is a record of that journey. It is – as far as I know – the first of its kind. There have been cycle rides in the summer, such as the Queen Eleanor Cycle Ride each August bank holiday, which raises money for homeless charities. But this is the first time someone has completed the journey by foot on the exact dates of the medieval procession and written up an account of it. An historic moment!

Retelling this is no simple task, however. It is a complex story and there are several lines of investigation interwoven throughout each chapter. As we travel from Lincoln to London, here are the threads we'll pull together:

- The life of Queen Eleanor (1241–90), the Castilian princess who married King Edward I.
- The procession of December 1290, when Eleanor's body was carried from Lincoln to London. We can't be sure of the exact

route of the cortège, step by step, but it was probably around 170 miles long, although if you consider the possibility of unrecorded diversions and pit stops then the likelihood is that it was a few miles longer.

- The construction of twelve stone crosses, commissioned by Edward and erected within five years of her death (1291–95). It's important to remember that when the funeral cortège passed through the towns in December 1290, the crosses were not yet built. The crosses were a later commemoration of the journey – not a guide.

- The dramatic lives of the crosses in the centuries since. Though twelve were built, only three still stand; the rest were destroyed during the turbulence of the Reformation and Civil War. They became such potent political symbols of royalism or Catholicism that mobs rushed to pull them down and others desperately resisted.

- My own experience of walking from Harby to London in November and December 2024. Though I set off with a route that was about 180 miles long, factoring in winding footpaths, the occasional retracing of steps and lunch stop detours, this ended up at almost 200 miles and half a million steps along tarmacked roads, winding paths and waterlogged fields.

- Along this route, the ways in which the points above have been commemorated afresh, by artists and craftsmen in our own time.

- I've also visited a few interesting figures and historic sites in relation to Eleanor's incredible story, which I will share with you.

So you'll understand that this is no dusty biography of Queen Eleanor, nor an architectural record, nor a classic walking book with anoraks and blister plasters. It is a mix. This is a tapestry of a life and its legacy. Along this journey, we will meet artists and stonemasons, funeral directors and schoolchildren, roofers and deans. They are a varied bunch, united by one thing: they do their bit to keep Eleanor's legacy alive.

This legacy comes in many surprising forms. Exquisitely beautiful stone monuments created with utmost care, which were later subject to vicious iconoclasm. The walls of a tube station, adorned with woodcut prints. A statue in a shopping centre, later used to promote dental hygiene. An enormous mural, painted by a local artist. A grand painting violently cut out of its frame in the dead of night, never to be seen again. A roundabout, romantically named 'Queen Eleanor Interchange'.

Talking of roundabouts, another message I hope you take from this book is the immense richness of history to be found in Britain, hidden in plain sight: obelisks surmounted by teapots, strange lumps and bumps in fields, yew trees growing in churchyards. This journey is not a curated walking tour, designed to max out on picturesque views and picnic stops. This is a warts-and-all route, through pretty villages and industrial estates, past stately homes and high-rise office blocks, across green fields and deafening motorways. But there is history every step of the way and it is this random cross-section that makes it all the more exciting.

One of the towns we will visit is Dunstable. In 1821, a history of Dunstable was published, titled *Dunno's Originals*. It opens with this pertinent question: 'If men of talent will not write/Shall our old Towns be buried quite/In dark Oblivion's gloomy shade?' I am not a man and my talents are questionable, but I hope these observations may do just that: bring history out of the gloomy shade and inspire you to uncover the stories that lie in *your* town, wherever in the world that may be. These are stories to be celebrated, cherished and passed down through the generations.

As we untangle the history that awaits, slashing through the brambles of mythology and legend, we will trace the shadows of a bygone, medieval world. One where churches were adorned with brightly coloured paintings. Where the tolling of bells sounded across vast fields, devoid of hedges or walls. A landscape peppered by priories and monasteries, abbeys and cathedrals. A world that only leaves a few clues – peeling wall paintings, crumbling ruins, strange earthworks.

But it was also an alien, wacky place, where a book was more valuable than a house. Where accidently eating a purple frog, then throwing it up, was considered a miraculous blessing.

As we peel back the layers of time, there are many curious questions to answer. How did medieval people navigate without a map? How did travellers keep their feet dry? Was the climate different from today? Where does the word 'medieval' come from? What about 'Gothic'? How did embalming work? Did our medieval ancestors feel love and grief in the same way as us? How can a man be two opposing things at once – to some, a tyrant who 'troubled the whole world by his wickedness', but to his wife, a kind, devoted husband? Stay tuned to find out.

I hope this might also inspire anyone who is hiking-curious. I'm not a serious walker – more a rambler from pub to pub. To prepare, I paid a few visits to Mountain Warehouse, subscribed to Ordnance Survey Maps Premium and (I can hear the sharp intake of breath from keen walkers, for this is the cardinal sin of walking) walked most of the route in brand-new boots, not yet worn in.

Perhaps this was wholly irresponsible. It certainly made it exciting. Things were touch and go, believe you me. I had no idea if I would make the 200 miles from Lincoln to London. This was testing the limits of my ambulatory potential. I was venturing into the rambling abyss.

Along the journey, I was struck by how uplifting it all was, even in bitter winter. It wasn't just the fresh air that was so invigorating. While walking over fifty hours through unfamiliar territory, I began to think with increased clarity. Lightbulb moments became more regular, spurred on by being curious about the changing surroundings.

Small, surprising details – a tombstone, an information sign hidden in the reeds, a clank of a gate – began to jump out at me. Step by step, the threads of history emerged, forming a rich tapestry. It was only by walking, by travelling at the natural human pace, that these unexpected revelations arrived. I saw so many things that I wouldn't have done from a bike, car or library desk.

Many of these threads tell the stories of ordinary people. Because that's what history is. University lecturers might analyse great movements and monarchies, rebellions and regimes. Podcast hosts will debate whether bad weather or rusty ammunition was a greater contributing factor in terrible wars. But it all comes back to the same thing – people. The common denominator is the human condition. Protagonists are motivated by innate emotions, deep within us: fear, hunger, jealousy, love.

I find this comforting. The past is full of ordinary people like you and me, driven by the same emotions. Have you ever felt the desperate ache of unrequited love? Or the deep humiliation and sorrow on realising a partner has been unfaithful? Perhaps a particular scent catches you off guard, bringing memories of a loved one, no longer around. All these emotions we share with ancestors past. These are moments of vulnerability that bind us across time.

Remember this, as we consider the story of King Edward I and Eleanor of Castile, and consider them in the context of their own time, too. They may have lived a life of royalty, within a world that seems alien to us, with strange customs and uncomfortable values. But they were also people: fragile and raw and vulnerable, who were thrust into unprecedented situations. Eleanor still felt pangs of sadness for the children she lost in miscarriages, stillbirths and neonatal death – little Katherine, Joanna, John, Henry, Alphonso, Berengaria and those children who were never named. King Edward – though a powerful, sometimes cruel man – wasn't the two-dimensional baddy that *Braveheart* would have us believe. He still carried the deep, heavy burden of grief after the loss of Eleanor. In the Eleanor Crosses, we see his 'action-focused' grieving process immortalised in stone.

The adventure we are about to embark on is one of twists and turns, highs and lows, and plenty of surprises. On one level, it is a joyful saunter through the English countryside. On another, it is an elegy to the great passion in my life: history – and a history that isn't a distant, bygone, irrelevant thing, but alive and changing and something that we all play a part in.

So this book is also a celebration of love, in all its glorious forms. Whether that be a warrior king who writes a mournful letter about his late wife or a stonemason who devotes care to carve a memorial of immense beauty or a stranger who offers a rambling walker a welcome cup of tea.

It is also a tale of loss. But this is uplifting – comforting, even. It is moments of darkness in our lives, of grief, that make the light shine brighter. As Queen Elizabeth II once wrote: 'Grief is the price we pay for love.' Such lights and shadows are the contours of our humanity, of what it means to be human.

1. POMEGRANATES AND PURGATORY

'Our dead are never dead to us until we have forgotten them.'
George Eliot

THE START OF MY VENTURE into Eleanor's world – but not yet the walk itself – began at King's Cross train station. Thursday 28 November 2024. It was a crisp winter's morning and London sparkled in the sunlight. I arrived half an hour early with a ticket to board the 08:06 on a London North Eastern Railway Azuma service of five coaches. The destination was a magnificent medieval city, 140 miles north: Lincoln.

King's Cross is not a bad place to wait, cup of tea in hand. It is an impressive building: a marvel of the Victorian age, with iron-ribbed glazed roofs and London stock brick. The new Western Concourse – which opened in 2012 – has a striking 'diagrid' roof, akin to a giant beehive. And inside, every day, 150,000 humans pass through, buzzing about from place to place.

As I began my mission to untangle Eleanor's story, I headed for the platform. Platform Number . . . 0. Zero! Nought! How could a platform have no quantity or number? I was entering into nothingness! Disappearing into a black hole!

The reason for this is one of mundanity, I'm afraid. To increase station capacity, a new platform was added and numbered Zero to avoid renumbering the rest. Nonetheless, I stepped into the time-travelling void, lost in the mists of time.

The adventure had begun.

As the train left King's Cross far behind, the urban sprawl thinned into open countryside, where fields glistened with frost, melting in the morning sunlight. We whizzed past the rolling hills of Hertfordshire, then the marshy fenland of Cambridgeshire. Over the coming days, all this land, field after field, I would retrace. Somewhere, in that mass of brown and grey and green, would be a small figure in a purple anorak, battling the elements.

About an hour into the journey, I caught a glimpse of Peterborough Cathedral. One of the highlights of this Gothic masterpiece is the tomb of Katherine of Aragon. Like Eleanor, she was born a Spanish princess and, through marriage, became an English queen.

As I thought of Katherine, I tucked into my breakfast. The Pret fruit salad in front of me felt like an auspicious choice. Among the tropical fruits of mango, kiwi and blueberries were – of course! – pomegranate seeds. The pomegranate was Katherine of Aragon's emblem, as an ancient symbol of fertility and regeneration (a cruel irony, when only one of her six children survived to adulthood). On my journey up to Lincoln, this was – I felt – Queen Katherine's blessing. Her way of saying 'Good luck!' (or *Buena suerte!*).

Though an exotic luxury to most people of medieval England, for Eleanor, the sweet tang of the pomegranate seed was a taste from childhood, which she had spent in Castile – a powerful kingdom that covered most of modern Spain. Her father was the Castilian king, Ferdinand III, and her mother, his second wife, Jeanne, Countess of Ponthieu.

As a young girl – when Eleanor went by 'Leonor' – she enjoyed the luxuries of the Castilian court. There she would skip through exquisite palace gardens and splash in the fountains of cool water, which no doubt offered a welcome relief in the scorching heat, before feasting on oranges, lemons, figs and pomegranates. Sometimes she played boardgames with her older brothers – perhaps Henry or Sancho – or else studied under the wary eye of her governor, who oversaw a rigorous education fit for a prince. She was also taken on visits to the beautiful towns of Cordoba and Seville, dazzled by the beauty of buildings, with columns built of jasper, granite and marble.

Outside this luxurious bubble, however, Eleanor's childhood – and her parents' lives – was dominated by war, when Catholic kingdoms in the Iberian Peninsula sought to recover regions lost to Muslim control. For little Leonor, this meant visiting her parents in campaigning tents or running through the halls of great defensive castles (castles that were the namesake of the Kingdom of Castile).

So, from the very start, Eleanor was exposed to a model of monarchy that lay hand in hand with the rigours of warfare. It was also one where royal women – such as Eleanor's mother, Jeanne – were known to join military campaigns and stay in military camps. A habit that Eleanor would continue with enthusiasm in her adult years.

When Eleanor was eleven, her father, King Ferdinand, died. The crown passed to Eleanor's half-brother, who became Alfonso X. Soon after, Alfonso made negotiations with King Henry III of England for Eleanor to marry his son and heir, Prince Edward. It was a diplomatic precaution to bolster England and Castile against a mutual adversary, France.

On 1 November 1254, at the monastery of Las Huelgas, in

Burgos, a tiny figure – twelve-year-old Eleanor – processed through the vast stone arches. Within the church, a fifteen-year-old boy – lanky, confident and with a slight lisp – awaited her. Was Eleanor scared of Prince Edward as she gazed up at his mop of tousled blonde hair?

In October 1255 (still only thirteen years old), Eleanor arrived in England for the first time. With Edward fulfilling his new duties as the Duke of Gascony, she travelled without him. Sailing towards Dover, with white cliffs looming ever closer, the sea breeze whipping at her hair and saltwater spraying on her face, Eleanor set eyes on the land that would become her new home. As she stepped down on the shore, wrapping thick furs around her, local fishermen whispered among themselves: 'You really think that little thing will be up to the task? Of being Edward's queen?'

The fishermen need not have worried. England was in safe hands. Over the coming decades, she proved to be eminently capable: a trusted advisor and devoted wife to King Edward, a caring mother and hard-working queen who took her duties seriously.

So it was uncharacteristic – in the 1280s, with Eleanor in her late forties – that this powerhouse seemed increasingly frail. As she gave commands, her voice – usually so firm, so authoritative – quivered. As she signed documents for the transfer of lands, her hands wavered. Her ladies noticed a difference in her behaviour. She slept a little longer and found it harder to sit upright.

There are a few clues that hint at Eleanor's declining health. From April 1289, a silver vessel was provided for her household, 'wherein to place the Queen's syrups' (the equivalent of a pill organiser). The following year, in 1290, her regular hunting expenses – costs of feeding and entertaining the hunting party, of paying the huntsmen and hawkers – suddenly stopped. Had the rigours of the sport become too taxing?

By February 1290, a court goldsmith was making images of the Queen for intercessions – an aid for those praying for the Queen's health. Perhaps most tellingly, Eleanor made arrangements for her own death, giving £100 to the Dominican priory of the Black Friars, in London, to prepare for the burial of her heart.

That year she also visited Thurrock, in Essex. Here lived a man named William Torel, a skilled goldsmith who would make the bronze effigy on Eleanor's Westminster Abbey tomb. Did she drop in to Torel's house, perhaps, to firm up arrangements for her own memorial? Giving instructions like: 'Whatever you do, don't mess up my nose!'

Even so, Eleanor soldiered on. 'Don't fuss!' she might have snapped, if anyone suggested she take a break. In the summer of 1290, she was busier than ever. In light of her worsening condition, weddings of her children were hastened, their futures secured.

The royal brood was made up of twenty-year-old Eleanor, eighteen-year-old Joan (known as 'Joan of Acre', as she'd been born during Eleanor's crusading years), fifteen-year-old Margaret, eleven-year-old Mary (who had become a nun at Amesbury Priory), seven-year-old Elizabeth and six-year-old Edward (the future King Edward II).

With five royal princesses and only one little prince, Eleanor's brood was certainly girl-heavy. Think the Bennet sisters, if a younger brother was added to the mix. What did those princesses think, knowing that little Edward would one day rule over them all?

In April, the royal sisters were in a flurry of excitement, as Princess Joan prepared for her wedding. She was betrothed to Gilbert de Clare, a powerful English noble thirty years her senior. That spring, the betrothal – which had taken five years to negotiate – was abruptly put into action. There wasn't even time for new dresses to be made – much to the disappointment of the princesses, no doubt. But why the rush? Was it Eleanor's impatience to see Joan's marriage completed, knowing her own health was failing?

The wedding took place on 30 April in Westminster Abbey, the glittering new church built by Edward's father, King Henry III. A fortnight later, the same King Henry took his final position among the stones.

Though he'd been dead for two decades, on 11 May, his corpse was transferred from his temporary burial to a permanent resting place, beside the shrine of the Anglo-Saxon king and saint Edward the Confessor. This was common practice: monarchs were temporarily housed in crypts or vaults, while an elaborate tomb was created.

How strange it must have been for Eleanor to see the body of her father-in-law again (and apparently with a healthy beard still intact). As she gazed on – perhaps stifling her own cough or clutching the arm of a daughter for support – it would likely have been a reminder of her own imminent fate. 'Will it be my body in the coffin', she must have wondered, 'in months to come?'

A second wedding came not long after, on 8 July. This time, Princess Margaret to the Duke of Brabant, who been betrothed to Margaret since she was three years old. Finally – suddenly – they would tie the knot. The wedding was a splendid affair (and in an extra snub to Joan, rather glitzier than the first wedding of the summer). Princess Margaret arrived at Westminster Abbey glittering with pearls, rubies and sapphires. Her sister, Princess Eleanor, dazzled in an outfit with 636 silver buttons. Their little brother Edward attended with eighty knights. The groom had two outfit changes.

As parties thronged the streets, the young royals continued with an after-party at the palace, where minstrels, harpists and trumpeters fuelled the cheer. But amid such revelry, a dark cloud sullied the merriment: the sad reality of a dying mother.

In the final weeks of Eleanor's life, she pushed on with a tour of the country: Buckinghamshire, Bedfordshire, Northamptonshire, Nottinghamshire, Rutland, Derbyshire, Cheshire. In October, she was at Clipstone, the old hunting lodge of King John, nestled in Sherwood Forest. Here, a parliament took place and great men of the realm gathered with the King, as they did twice a year. Though parliaments were held across the country, Westminster was the usual location. Was it Eleanor's ill health that prevented further travel?

During the Clipstone parliament, one of the foremost issues on Eleanor's mind was the prospective marriage of six-year-old Prince Edward. His bride-to-be was Margaret, 'Maid of Norway'. By strange circumstance, Margaret – the seven-year-old daughter of a Norwegian king – was the rightful inheritor to the Scottish crown, through her mother, who had died giving birth to her. As such, she was a perfect match for the heir to the English throne. The betrothal would have effectively united the Scottish and English kingdoms some 300 years before the Union of the Crowns under King James VI and I, in 1603.

In the autumn of 1290, a Norwegian fleet brought Margaret to Scotland. The Scottish magnates assembled at Scone, in anticipation of their new queen. Meanwhile, the Clipstone parliament expected to receive news of her safe arrival. But the good news never came. Instead, a messenger arrived reporting that Margaret had fallen ill on the crossing and had died at Orkney, no doubt sending shockwaves rippling through the royal court.

It was in light of this omen – the death of a future Queen of England and Eleanor's successor – that the October parliament closed and Eleanor weakened further. The royal party left Clipstone and headed for Lincoln, perhaps with the intention to pray for the Queen's recovery at the cathedral. As Princess Joan headed to London, going her separate way, it must have struck Eleanor that – if things turned for the worse – she might never see her again.

The 20-mile journey to Lincoln – usually a day's ride – proved taxing. Eleanor – accompanied by Edward and probably her eldest daughters, Eleanor and Margaret – travelled at a snail's pace – sometimes 2 miles a day, with a day in between to recover. Seven miles from Lincoln, near a village called Harby, the Queen's condition took a serious turn for the worse. On the evening of Monday 20 November 1290, a messenger was sent to the largest house he could find: a stone building surrounded by a moat.

This was the manor house of a knight, Sir Richard de Weston. As Sir Richard dozed off and considered the day ahead – 'I must sort out that leak in the moat' or 'I mustn't forget to order the boar's head for Christmas' – he was interrupted by a loud, urgent rapping at the door. Imagine the dramatic scene . . .

Hurrying downstairs, with only the flickering of a candle to light the room, the locks were unbolted and the great oak door creaked open. In whipped the freezing November air. Through the blast, Sir Richard squinted to see a pink-cheeked man dressed in royal livery. 'Sir, I bring a message from the King,' he announced breathlessly. 'Queen Eleanor is gravely ill. She will be here imminently. You must prepare her room. Make haste, sir, make haste!'

As Sir Richard's household scrambled to prepare for this unexpected visit, in piled a retinue of royal servants: almoners and yeomen, dairymaids and clerks. They carried furniture and chests, wooden spoons and copper pots. Next, an enormous figure filled the threshold, silhouetted in the moonlight. Sir

Richard gasped, knowing immediately who it was. He bowed as the terrifying figure of Edward Longshanks thudded into the hall, his face ashen, his brow furrowed.

In Edward's arms was a large bundle of fur, oddly shaped, from which came a cough. On realising this was the formidable Queen Eleanor, Sir Richard's jaw dropped in disbelief. She was desperately frail – far from the mighty queen he had heard so much about.

Over the following days, Eleanor lay in Sir Richard's bed, weakening by the day. The question historians have long grappled with is this: why was Eleanor so ill? Some have pointed to tuberculosis, which was a big killer in medieval England. You could get it from drinking infected cow's milk or the bacteria could spread through talking, coughing, sneezing or singing. It might settle on dust, remaining infectious for several weeks.

Perhaps it was tuberculous cervical lymphadenitis – better known as scrofula. This was an infection of lymph nodes, which makes your neck balloon. Symptoms included the usual suspects – coughing up blood, fatigue, weight loss, fever and, for the unlucky ones, death. It would have been ironic had Eleanor perished so, for the disease was known as the 'King's Evil', believed to be cured by the touch of a monarch.

Another possibility was some kind of malarial infection. Though you might associate malaria with tropical climates, throughout English history it was endemic. In low-lying marshlands in Essex, Kent, Sussex, Somerset, Yorkshire and Lancashire, the dangerous *Anopheles* mosquitoes lurked. Malaria went by the name of 'marsh fever' or 'ague' (from the Old French word meaning 'severe fever').

Plenty succumbed to agues over the years. King James I died

of a stroke and an attack of dysentery, complicated by malarial infection. It's thought Oliver Cromwell may have suffered from marsh agues after visiting the Fens in the summer of 1658; he died the following year. Even as late as 1877, the newspapers reported the terrible effects of 'swampy undrained land' that formed a 'malarious atmosphere' and 'hotbeds of pestilence to both man and beast'. The modern term, malaria, arrived in the nineteenth century – *mala aria* in Latin is 'bad air'.

The disease was incurable, but herbal potions and bark from ash trees could bring some relief. Opium was widely considered 'the antidote to the effect of the noxious vapours' and, in Fenland areas, patches of poppies were a familiar sight in cottage gardens, where they were harvested for poppy tea. Alcohol was another alternative – to the detrimental effect of congregation numbers, as one Kent clergyman vexed: 'the poor do not attend church from the use of spirituous liquors which the bad air seems to render necessary as a protection from agues.' (You've got to admit, it's a great excuse – 'I'm not an alcoholic, I'm just batting off marsh fever.')

Another factor to consider relates to Eleanor's family medical history. Both her father, Ferdinand III of Castile, and her grandfather, Alfonso IX of León, had coronary problems, which would mark them as high risk today.

We can't be sure of the cause of Eleanor's death, but it may have been a combination of factors. A heart problem made worse by malarial infection – picked up at home or on Crusade. Or a nasty bout of tuberculosis, which became deadly with underlying coronary weakness.

Either way, by Friday 24 November 1290, she had 'become infirm'. It wasn't now a question of *if* Eleanor would die, but *when*. Messengers rushed from Lincoln and London, 'on account of the

Queen's illness'. For days, Eleanor tossed and turned, while Edward paced up and down, praying for some sign of her recovery.

Whatever treatment was dispensed at that manor house in Harby was a far cry from A&E today. In the thirteenth century, medical practice derived from theories of ancient physicians – the likes of Hippocrates, the Greek philosopher, or Galen, a Roman surgeon who learned about anatomy from treating injured glad-iators. Their works – after being translated by Islamic scholars – survived the centuries and filtered into the medieval world.

Their medical understanding revolved around one idea – that the universe is made up of four elements: fire, earth, water and air. There were, they posited, four corresponding humours of the body – yellow bile, black bile, phlegm and blood – and the four qualities of hot, cold, wet and dry. Though it was thought everyone has a natural excess of one of the humours (and this created character), an excessive imbalance of these – perhaps caused by old age – caused illness.

The four humours theory was believed to alter mental state, too. Too much yellow bile (also known as choler) and you'd become 'choleric'. Too much phlegm would make you 'phlegmatic', while too much black bile gave you 'melancholia'. Too much blood and you'd be 'sanguine'. Choler gave courage, but phlegm produced cowards. Women's bodies were cold, weak and moist, while men's were hot, strong and dry.

If Eleanor was deemed to have an excess of blood, she might have endured bloodletting – cutting into a vein or applying leeches to her flesh. If an overabundance of phlegm was deemed to be the culprit – demonstrating characteristics that were cold and wet – she would have been given a treatment that was hot and dry, such as eating a spicy pepper. Alternatively, if the diagnosis was a high level of yellow bile, which was hot and dry, she might have been balanced out with some cold water: 'Sir Richard!' the physician would have called. 'Fetch me a bucket of icy water from the moat!'

One of the best ways to keep track of humour balances was examining urine. Before the seventeenth century, when William Harvey recognised circulation of the blood, it was believed that food converted into blood during digestion. This blood was always running out, so had to be constantly replenished by a supply of food. Mothers of the medieval period might have said to their children: 'Eat your greens, young man – you don't want to run out of blood.' Urine, it was believed, would indicate the balance of humours and the status of digestion.

If the royal doctor believed Eleanor's illness was caused by miasma or poisoned air, Sir Richard's house may have been adorned with bunches of sweet-smelling herbs and flowers. They might also have brought birds into the house, whose flapping wings would circulate the air.

'She's not got long to live,' some of the household might have murmured, looking at the night sky, 'not with the planets as they are.' Indeed, astrology was another point of reference, as it was believed the movements of planets provoked changes to bodily organs. Mercury was attached to the brain, Jupiter the liver. In 1348, the University of Paris wrote a report on the Black Death, concluding: 'The distant and first cause of this pestilence was and is the configuration of the heavens.'

On the following Tuesday, it was clear the end was nigh. A priest was present, William de Kelm, as was the Bishop of Lincoln. The room, filled with the scent of incense and the soft glow of candlelight, became a sacred space. Day waned and night set in. Eleanor's breath slowed and her heartbeat softened to a quiet thud.

Antiphons and psalms were chanted: 'Lord,' the verses ran,

'come down to heal my daughter before she dies.' With this mournful accompaniment, Eleanor received her last rites and a final chance to confess any wrongdoing before her eternal fate was decided. She took her final communion and extreme unction was performed: a blessing with holy oil.

With the prayers complete, it must have been a moving scene: Edward sitting at Eleanor's bedside, holding his beloved's hand for the final time. He looked down upon the face he knew so well: her rounded chin, her upturned mouth, that slim, long nose and those large, almond-shaped eyes with arched brows. He caressed her long greying hair and traced the lines of her olive skin – lines formed from years of laughter.

He remembered their life together, how they'd first met in adolescence, when they had adult responsibilities, but were still children in their hearts. The happy days hunting, when Eleanor's eyes lit up as the falcon swooped down on her arm. Her delight at exploring new gardens, of tasting the first fruits from her orchard.

There were moments of difficulty, moments of adventure – the thousands of miles they'd travelled together, criss-crossing Europe, Africa and the Middle East. There were also moments of deep sadness, when, time after time, another of their beloved children died.

But at every point, Edward had coped, for Eleanor had been there by his side. How was he to survive without her? This great and terrible king would now – for the first time in thirty-six years – face the world alone.

And what of the royal children? The records don't give us their whereabouts, but it's tantalising to think: were her daughters, Eleanor and Margaret, in the room, sitting beside their mother in those final moments, sobbing at the unbearable prospect ahead?

As darkness fell, Eleanor's breathing slowed. A candle flickered and she took her final breath. Her body was still, her eyes blank. '*Decessus Regine*', it was recorded in the household account: 'Death of the Queen.'

As Eleanor's soul departed this life, the chants continued, to pray for her journey through purgatory: 'Hurry, saints of God,' the quivering lament cried. 'Make haste, angels of the Lord, who are taking her soul and offering it in the sight of the Most High.' A bell tolled to mark Eleanor's departure. As it sounded throughout Sir Richard's manor and across the fields, the people of Harby held still, their hearts heavy, their prayers offered up in mourning.

There was another mourner who joined them, many years later. On 28 November 2024, 734 years since Eleanor passed away, a woman arrived at Sir Richard's manor to pay her respects. That woman was me.

2. DIARY OF A CHURCH MOUSE

'A human being does not cease to exist at death.
It is change, not destruction, which takes place.'
Florence Nightingale

AFTER TAKING A TAXI FROM Lincoln station, I arrived at All Saints' Church in the village of Harby. The church is set back from the road, surrounded by a couple of houses and open fields. In these first moments in the Nottinghamshire countryside, which seemed so serene, so calm, I didn't expect to be confronted with violence. Yet within seconds, I became unexpectedly embroiled in a fight.

The gate of Harby churchyard has a mind of its own and I spent some time wrestling it open, only for it to become entangled in the tassels of my brand-new National Gallery bicentenary scarf. Thinking I was extracted from the metal work, I stepped forward, only to realise I was still in the gate's clutches. My scarf was yanked back by the strands still attached, now unravelling at speed. Luckily, I became aware of my situation at an early stage, or else I'd have lost my scarf altogether and left Harby churchyard covered in a strange cobweb of thread.

Despite the terrors of ThreadGate, nothing could dampen my excitement at starting the investigation. With eyes wide, I scanned the view. There! On the church wall! I spotted the very first clue. Thrillingly, Eleanor was waiting to greet me. She stood in a small niche, beneath the clock – and, rather embarrassingly, had a good view of the church gate. Beside her are four coats of arms and the words '1290 ELEANOR', just to make things clear.

Excited to find more clues, I zig-zagged through the graveyard, where there were plenty of interesting headstones (among them Thomas Arthur Bingham, 'Hard working farmer returned to the land'). On the far side, marking the church boundary, I arrived at a crooked metal fence.

From there, I looked out upon a field with rough brambles and hedges: the site of Sir Richard de Weston's house. There are no surviving records of what Sir Richard's house looked like, but we can make a good guess.

A classic English manor house had two or more buildings, set out like an 'L' and surrounded by large ditches. It was a kind of mini-castle, complete with mini-moat and centred around a hall, which would have had an open fire and a raised dais for the lord's table. This served as a gathering place for eating and a spot for the servants to sleep. At the other end of the hall, separated by wooden screens, was a kitchen for preparing food.

On the first floor was a private room – the 'solar', where a lord could be *'seul'*, the French for alone – which is probably where Eleanor died. Outside was a moat, the earthworks of which are still visible today, and there may also have been a gatehouse and drawbridge, for extra security and – more importantly – to impress the neighbours.

As I came to a stop at the crooked fence – and realised the implications of what I was looking at – the hand of history was upon me. Here it was, the very spot where Eleanor had died, 734 years before.

The field in Harby where Richard de Weston's manor house once stood. (Note my scarf, bottom right-hand corner, carefully folded and resting on the fence.)

What a strange thing that after a lifetime of travelling the length and breadth of Europe, staying in grand castles and sumptuous palaces, it was here where she took her final breath, in a humble manor house, now reduced to a few strange bumps in the ground.

Of course, the medieval perception of death is quite different from that of the modern world. When someone dies today, those of the Christian faith tend to think of their soul going to heaven. Straight up. No stops. No detours. In traditional medieval Catholic belief, heaven was still the presumed destination, but it wasn't a direct flight. First, you were going to purgatory – a kind of divine waiting room.

Derived from *purgo*, meaning 'I purge' or 'I cleanse' in Latin, here your soul would be purified in a 'cleansing fire'. Your length of stay in purgatory was variable and depended on how well you had behaved, which meant the lives of many medieval people were driven by investing in their spiritual future – by doing good deeds in life, you could reduce your time in purgatory and hasten your journey to heaven. For Eleanor, this would have meant the years spent on Crusade or giving alms to the poor or visiting the great cathedral shrines with her family.

But these heavenly brownie points could also be obtained *after* you died, by good works carried out on your behalf – more prayers, masses for your soul, donations to the poor and payments to the church.

All of this radically changes the relationship with the dead, keeping you connected with loved ones even after they've left the earthly realm. It was no different for royalty and so, when Eleanor died, Edward had work to do. Of course, there was the usual commemoration to arrange – moving the body, arranging the funeral – but also the matter of Eleanor's soul. Operation Get Eleanor Out of Purgatory began.

At Harby, in the years after Eleanor's death, a chantry chapel was built, commissioned by Edward and consecrated by the Archbishop of York in 1294. 'Chantry' derives from the Latin *cantare* ('to sing') and these chapels were endowed so that a priest could perform masses and anniversary funeral services for the soul of their founder. A kind of fast-track service to get souls – in this instance, Eleanor's – through purgatory. The chantry chapel stood somewhere in Harby churchyard and no longer survives.

There are plenty of Eleanor clues inside the current church, however, which I went back to explore. Whenever I enter a village church, Philip Larkin's poem 'Church Going' springs to mind: 'I step inside,' he writes, 'letting the door thud shut.' He lists familiar features to look out for: 'matting, seats and stone/And little books; sprawlings of flowers, cut/For Sunday, brownish now'.

Though rebuilt in the Victorian period, Harby's church ticks off the features that Larkin describes. There is the central space, the nave, which is derived from the Latin word *navis*, meaning 'ship' (probably because the roof sometimes resembles the hull of a ship). Beyond this and its pews and pulpit lies the chancel, which contains an altar. This is – as Larkin put it – the 'holy end' with 'some brass and stuff' and possibly 'the small neat organ'. But the overall atmosphere? A 'tense, musty, unignorable silence/Brewed God knows how long.'

Another poem I rather like, John Betjeman's 'Diary of a Church Mouse', captures the life of a regular church inhabitant. 'Here among long-discarded cassocks,' he writes, 'Damp stools and half-split-open hassocks/Here where the vicar never looks/I nibble through old service books.'

Why was the church rebuilt, you might be wondering? The truth is, it had become shabby. By 1872, it was deemed 'the most unsightly place of worship in the diocese' and a new church was required. This was easier said than done – the building manager was described as 'quite an impossible man' and his workers were apparently 'a worthless drunken lot and not to be trusted'. After plenty of 'sharp words', however, the building works were completed. On 2 August 1877, the new All Saints' Harby with Swinethorpe Parish Church – in which I was now standing – was consecrated.

The *Nottinghamshire Guardian* reported it as 'a great day in the history of Harby' – one that was 'observed as a general holiday by all classes'. There were processions, strings of bunting, church bells and an offertory hymn that raised 'the handsome sum of £140 10s' – some £14,000 today!

It was in Vicarage Field – the site of Sir Richard's manor – that an enormous tent was erected. Here, 800 hungry villagers sat down for tea. But – as several papers reported – disaster struck. Preparations had only been made for 600 and 'there was at one time a prospect of the provisions failing'. Another paper reported 'a panic rumour that the butter was getting short, then that the plum bread was gone and next that there was no white bread'.

As the brass band struck up, 'the three village shops were emptied, private houses yielded up their supplies and a basketful of cut bread and butter attested to the victory of the Harby ladies over the hungry crowd'. A victory indeed. The newspaper reporter delighted at the 'enthusiastic assistance' of the people of Harby – a willingness to help in a moment of crisis, which the royal family were privy to in Eleanor's illness all those years before.

And now, I was on the receiving end of Harby's enthusiastic assistance. By good chance, as I stood in the nave admiring the chancel arch, the door creaked open. In strolled the local church warden, a cheery man named Paul, accompanied by his wire-haired Jack Russell, Percy.

Paul and Percy gave me a whistle-stop tour of the church, pointing out every Eleanor clue. On the nave wall is a framed photograph of Harby villagers at Westminster Abbey. Bedecked in high-vis and helmets, it shows a group of eight cyclists who rode from Westminster to Harby across five days in September 2007, covering 226 miles. 'We raised £11,000 for the church roof,' Paul told me with pride. 'When we were at Westminster Abbey, we gifted them a wooden cross, which they placed on her tomb. And they gave us one, too, which you can see in the frame.' Beside the photograph was the Westminster memento in question, a permanent link to the place where Eleanor was buried.

Nearby was a window commemorating Eleanor's death. It was installed in 2008 to mark the millennium of 2000, a bold design of vivid blue, full of swirling lines and curved shapes – reminding me of those whirls you see in a marble. On the left is Eleanor with a furrowed brow, looking sternly towards visitors as they step in from the porch. On the right are her heraldic arms – an indication of her pedigree.

These shields are handy to remember, for they pop up on all the Eleanor monuments and tombs. In the centre is the shield displaying the heraldic arms of England: three gold lions passant ('passant' meaning they are walking, with a paw raised up, instead of 'rampant', where they are rearing up).

The Millennium window in All Saints' Church, Harby.

Then, above it, another shield that nods to Eleanor's father, Ferdinand III of Castile: the arms of Castile (a yellow castle) quartered with the arms of León (a purple lion rampant). At the bottom is a third shield with blue and yellow diagonal stripes (a 'bend' is the technical heraldic name). These are the arms of Ponthieu, derived from Eleanor's position as Countess of Ponthieu, which she inherited from her mother.

Among this, sparkling in deep blue, like stars in the firmament, are twelve golden crosses: the twelve memorial crosses built by Edward. Above the window is a roundel, showing a carnation and narcissus, the symbols of true love. In the right-hand window, an inscription states: 'A GIFT FROM THE PEOPLE OF HARBY TO COMMEMORATE 2000 YEARS OF CHRISTIANITY AND TO THE GLORY OF GOD'.

There was plenty more to explore in the church, but time was of the essence and the winter days were short. No more dilly-dallying. I signed the visitors' book, bade goodbye to Paul and Percy, stepped out of the church, clanked shut the churchyard gate (scarf tucked in this time) and opened the Ordnance Survey Maps app, which plotted my route.

After Eleanor's death on 28 November 1290, her body was taken to Lincoln, about 6 miles away, where it was prepared for the journey to London. As I turned left at the church gate, I was now following in the footsteps of that medieval journey. The first leg of the Eleanor pilgrimage had begun.

Harby is a pleasant village, where I discovered all kinds of curiosities – an old cobblers' cottage, a Methodist chapel, a Methodist school. I walked with caution, as black ice threatened my footing while enormous tractors, with wheels much taller than me, hurtled past. I passed the Queen Eleanor Primary School and, not much further along, a village sign. Above 'WELCOME TO HARBY' and 'PLEASE DRIVE CAREFULLY' was an image of the great seal of Eleanor, about 20 centimetres high.

If you ever see an important medieval document – say, Magna Carta, created twenty-six years before Eleanor's birth – you'll probably see the mark of a seal. When we talk about the leases and contracts Eleanor managed, they were written upon a large piece of parchment (a material made from the skin of animals, most commonly sheep, goats or calves), at the bottom of which, beneath rows of text, was a rounded piece of flattened wax. This was about the size of a large coin, imprinted with a portrait or heraldry. The metal tool that created these imprints was the 'seal' – though the wax itself is now commonly described as a seal, too.

The sign for Harby village, with Eleanor's seal.

The idea was to provide a kind of signature. The seal proved the document was genuine. So you should really say Magna Carta was sealed rather than signed (and, while we're here, it's Magna Carta, not 'the' Magna Carta). It's amazing how many of these seals survive. The National Archives alone holds over a quarter of a million, dating from the eleventh to the twentieth century.

Eleanor's seal was in an oval shape, containing a full-size portrait, a castle (the symbol of Castile and León) and the lions passant of England. As I walked out of Harby, I was delighted to see it on the village sign, printed in sheet aluminium with retro-reflective plastic coating. A nice touch, I think.

The walk to Lincoln was straightforward. For most of it I followed a disbanded railway line, now a cycle path. It was a friendly place, where runners and cyclists would trickle through, offering a nod as they went. The path took me past traces of the old railway dotted around – benches made from old sleepers, brick arches the trains once chugged through. There was an ancient woodland, too, 'Old Wood', with trees of oak, lime and hazel.

At some point I crossed a county border, leaving Nottinghamshire and entering the mighty county of Lincolnshire. This is England's second largest county, which spreads from the shores of the North Sea, westward to the Midlands and north to Yorkshire. Here are the towns of Boston, Bourne, Cleethorpes, Grimsby, Scunthorpe and Spalding and the rivers Trent, Welland, Ancholme, Witham, Brant, Glen, Bain and Steeping.

Lincolnshire is largely flat, which is good news for the amateur walker – and the farmer, for this is England's largest producer of potatoes, wheat, cereal and poultry. The exception to this pancake-like topography is the high central limestone ridge – the Lincolnshire Edge – upon which the city of Lincoln perches.

By Eleanor's day, Lincoln was England's third largest city. It had become wealthy from cloth and wool exports to Flanders and famed woollen cloth dyed Lincoln green (modelled by local folk legend Robin Hood). In the heart of the city is Lincoln Castle, which has the best-preserved example of Magna Carta. But it is the cathedral that is the star of the show.

From 1311, Lincoln Cathedral was the tallest building on the planet – the Burj Khalifa of the medieval world. After more than 3,000 years, it knocked the Great Pyramid of Giza off the top spot. What an incredible achievement for Lincoln's medieval masons, to create what was the tallest structure mankind had *ever* built.

Pride comes before a fall, of course, and the accolade lasted until a terrible, stormy night in January 1548, when the great wooden and lead spire collapsed, crashing to the ground. As Lincolnites watched on in horror, once again, the pyramid retained the title, not to be surpassed for another 300 years, when the Eiffel Tower was completed in 1889.

The magnificent west front of Lincoln Cathedral, with Christmas tree and tiny man for scale.

Spire or no spire, when I arrived at the cathedral on that sunny November afternoon, gazing up at the west front, I was stunned by the magnificence of it all. It makes the cathedrals of Salisbury or Winchester look like parish churches. I felt like a tiny ant, looking up at the house of a giant. Towering over me stood an enormous stone screen of arches, rose windows, tracery, carvings – all of which would have originally been brightly coloured, with white, yellow, blue, green, red and black. How did our medieval ancestors – without modern technology – build something so enormous, so powerful, so absolutely *epic*?

Inside, the wonders continued. I was transfixed by the Tournai font, an enormous block of blue-black carboniferous limestone brought over from Belgium. In the chapel, I blushed at the healthy display of pert buttocks on the murals made by Duncan Grant, a member of the notorious Bloomsbury Group. I visited the 'cathedra' – the bishop's seat – which gives us the word 'cathedral'. It is an enormous canopy of carved wood, topped with stalagmites of Gothic detailing.

One of the highlights is the chapter house, with its perfectly formed star-shaped vaulted ceiling, like an enormous Victorian jelly mould. It was thrilling to think that Edward I had been here, in 1301, holding parliament. I sat on the benches and imagined his towering figure in this space, barking instructions across the room.

But it was at the Angel Choir, located at the east end of the cathedral, beyond the altar, where I spent most of my visit. Named for the angel sculptures that adorn the walls, the choir is also home to a cheeky, cackling character with teeth bared, horns and ears like a goat, sitting amid the angels with one leg balanced on his knee.

This is the Lincoln Imp, now a symbol of the city. Lincoln City Football Club are nicknamed 'The Imps', while at Oxford University's

Lincoln College (founded by the Bishop of Lincoln in 1427), the quads are decorated with statues of imps and the undergraduate newspaper is named – you guessed it – *The Imp*. The Angel Choir was completed and opened in 1280, with Edward and Eleanor present as guests of honour (so there's every chance Edward whispered to his beloved, 'Look, darling, up there! The imp!').

After Eleanor died in Harby, her body was brought to Lincoln, where it was treated to be buried. Her viscera – her internal organs, the stomach, lungs and intestines – were removed and buried here in Lincoln Cathedral, in what was known as a visceral tomb. The rest of her – her heart and embalmed body – were prepared to be taken to London and buried separately.

So, by the late medieval period, there were three important monuments in Lincoln Cathedral: the shrine of St Hugh of Lincoln (a French-born Bishop of Lincoln, who died in 1200); the shrine of Little St Hugh of Lincoln (a nine-year-old boy, who became a Christian martyr); and the visceral tomb of Eleanor of Castile. Today, none of the originals remain. The shrines were smashed up during the Reformation and Eleanor's tomb destroyed in the Civil War.

You'll notice already the amount of medieval culture – buildings, paintings, monuments, tombs – that was destroyed in later centuries. Estimates put the loss at up to 97 per cent. There were two waves of destruction. The first was following the Reformation. Due to Henry VIII's lust for Anne Boleyn and the need for a male heir, a chain of events unravelled that led Henry to break away from the Catholic Pope in Rome. Over the century, England became a largely Protestant country.

During this period, in the 1540s, the wonders of the Catholic medieval world – which had taken immense skill and patience to create and were held sacred by ordinary people up and down the country – were viciously destroyed by the state. Sacred shrines – the holy sites of miracles – were smashed to pieces, while monasteries – valuable real estate – were sold off.

A century later, in the 1640s and 1650s, came the second wave of upheaval: Civil War and Interregnum. It was a turbulent time, during which King Charles I was executed in 1649, then Oliver Cromwell ran the Commonwealth, before King Charles II returned in 1660.

During the English Civil War, roughly 4.5 per cent of the population died (a greater proportion than that of the First World War). But there was a cultural cost, too. Any images of royalty were smashed and slashed by Parliamentarian troops. Great castles and houses – which had taken centuries to build – were deliberately slighted, to prevent the opposition from reaping their benefits.

Lincoln Cathedral was ransacked. Wielding axes and hammers and barring the doors, soldiers seized every piece of metal they could find, 'so hellish an avarice possessed them'. In the north aisle, you can still see the damage. On the ground are stone memorial slabs, where the brass figures are missing. These were prised off by the soldiers and melted down to make weapons.

Despite the destruction of Eleanor's original viscera tomb, a Victorian replica stands in its place. A large stone rectangular structure, it is painted with the heraldic shields we saw on the window in Harby church. The tomb is topped by a bronze effigy of Eleanor. She wears flowing robes, her hair is loose and her crowned head rests on two soft pillows.

When I visited the cathedral on 28 November, the anniversary of Eleanor's death, a candle was alight – a small flicker to mark her departure, 734 years before. As I stood beside her effigy, I felt a wash of sadness. Even though it had been only a day, I already felt so rooted to her story. Not only her life, but her legacy. I considered the care others had taken, years before me, to rebuild this replica tomb. From this, I took comfort. Here was that long thread – this queue of mourners, if you like – who did their bit to keep the memory of Eleanor alive.

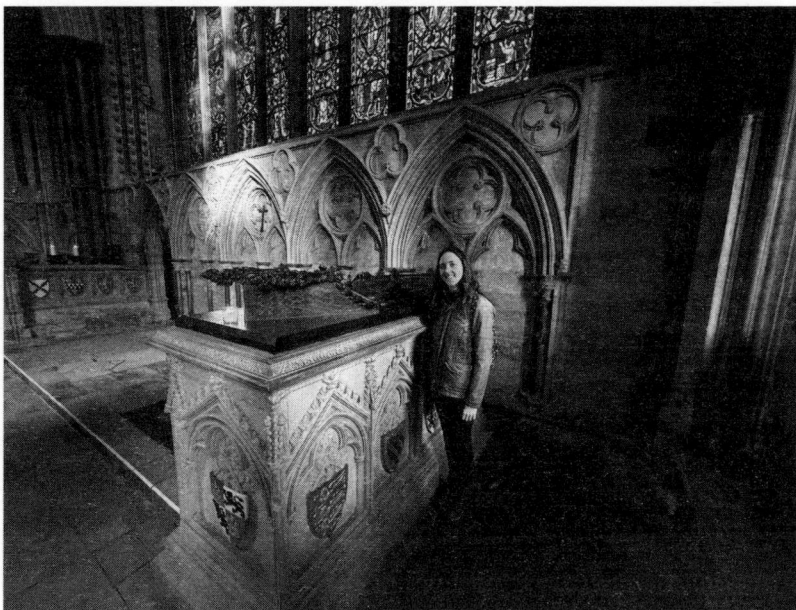

Eleanor's visceral tomb in the Angel Choir of Lincoln Cathedral
(though this is a Victorian replica).

After a moment of quiet reflection, I headed to another shrine of the cathedral: the gift shop, where I bought a Lincoln Imp chocolate lollipop. Then, onwards, for some proper sustenance. Nearby is the Wig and Mitre pub. Like many a weary traveller before me, I settled into a leather armchair, unlaced my walking boots and ordered sausage and mash. Delighted in the knowledge that the first day was complete, I settled into a gripping read: the Lincoln Cathedral guidebook.

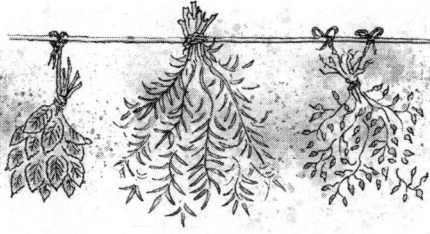

3. THE PAST IS A FOREIGN COUNTRY

'In the midst of life, we are in death.'
The Book of Common Prayer

FOR MOST PEOPLE OF THE thirteenth century – the *hoi polloi* like you and me – burial was a straightforward matter. For Christians, when someone died, their body was washed, anointed with holy oils, wrapped in a shroud and perhaps placed in a coffin. You were buried in the consecrated ground of a churchyard and the earth was marked with a cross. Jewish people were laid to rest in burial grounds usually built beyond town or city walls.

Your body was laid with feet pointing east and head to the west – the idea being that you were looking east towards Jerusalem and, on the event of Jesus' second resurrection, the Second Coming, you could easily sit up and watch it all unfold. So everyone in the churchyard was ready to sit up, where they'd be facing the same direction, like theatre stalls. No swivelling required. It's worth keeping this in mind – if you want to make the front row, make sure you're buried in the east corner of the churchyard. And make sure your plot isn't near someone who coughs.

Things were quite different for the crème-de-la-crème of medieval society – the likes of Eleanor and her family. First, she'd planned her burial herself and had arranged an elaborate effigy for her tomb in Westminster Abbey. Second, as we know, her body was split up and buried in separate locations: her embalmed body at Westminster Abbey, her heart at Blackfriars in London.

This was not uncommon practice. For those who travelled a great deal – on tour, campaigns or Crusades – there was a high chance you'd die far from home. As the entrails decompose first, they needed to be removed and buried quickly. Sometimes, the body was embalmed and sent home, perhaps along with the heart, as a memento. In other cases, the body was boiled down to the bones, leaving nothing but a skeleton.

There are some peculiar jobs in history, among them leech collectors (who collect leeches for medical use), Grooms of the Stool (who help the monarch go to the toilet), knocker-uppers (human alarm clocks), whipping boys (children who took punishment on behalf of an aristocratic child) and gong farmers (collectors of human excrement). But perhaps a royal embalmer should be up there, too.

Consider, for a moment, how bizarre this job must be. In front of you is a man or woman, believed to be appointed by God. While alive, people fawned to be in their presence, their physical form believed to be imbued with divine healing powers, able to cure scrofula. This was a figure so powerful, the point of a finger could condemn a man to death. But now, they lie before you – lifeless, cold and cut open. Not only do you touch their holy body, you see parts that have never seen the light of day: the liver, spleen, heart and brain. What must those embalmers have thought, as they were tasked with rubbing salt on the inside of the late Queen's ribs?

There were hiccups in the process, of course. Eleanor was no doubt aware of the fate of King Henry I, who died in 1135 and whose body was embalmed at Rouen Cathedral. As his innards were removed, there was such a 'strong, pervasive stench', the man tasked with removing the stinking brain passed away. To stop the corpse rotting further, salt was applied and it was wrapped in ox hides. But that wasn't the end of it. When the body was returned to England, the journey was delayed by bad weather and, as the crew waited at Caen for winds to change, the ox hides containing the King's body began to leak, seeping black fluid. There's another of history's horror jobs – to scrub the deck of a ship stained by the foul juices of a rotting king.

Considering these snags, it's surprising such practices continued. Yet, many centuries later, the Romantics – romanticising the morbid reality, as was their habit – pushed for a revival. When Thomas Hardy died in 1928, his body was buried in two places: his ashes in Westminster Abbey; his heart in Dorset. According to legend, when the surgeon was preparing Hardy's body, he popped the heart in a biscuit tin for safekeeping. When the doctor returned, he found the tin opened, empty, and a cat licking its lips. The story goes the cat was killed, to be buried alongside what remained of the heart it had snacked on.

The heart of another poet, twenty-nine-year-old Percy Bysshe Shelley, who died in 1822, was also prised from his corpse. After drowning in a shipwreck, he was cremated, according to the account of Captain Edward John Trelawny:

The fire was so fierce as to produce a white heat on the iron and to reduce its contents to grey ashes. The only portions that were not consumed were some fragments of bones, the jaw and the skull, but what surprised us all was that the heart remained entire. In

*snatching this relic from the fiery furnace, my hand was severely
burnt . . .*

Perhaps it was an earlier bout of tuberculosis that had calcified
Shelley's heart and prevented it burning. Either way, his wife, Mary
Shelley (author of *Frankenstein*), kept it on her desk in a box – the
perfect paperweight.

Eleanor's body was embalmed in Lincoln, being just 7 miles from
Harby. It was a good place to end up, given the city was chock-a-
block with churches and religious houses. Here were parish clergy,
cathedral clergy, monks, nuns, lay brethren – the works. Five of
Lincoln's churches and monasteries were friaries: the Greyfriars,
Blackfriars, Whitefriars, Austin Friars and the Friars of the Sack.
Friaries were a type of monastery: friars were like monks, but did
more outreach – they went into the city to preach and hear confession and they helped out at funerals with prayers and processions.

It's thought that Eleanor's body was cared for by the Blackfriars.
This house no longer stands, but it was located five minutes from
the cathedral, at the corner of Lindum Road and Monks Road.
Had you been a visitor to this friary in early December 1290 and
wandered the halls, you'd have been confronted with a sombre
sight: friars walking mournfully in black capes over white tunics,
adorned with a leather belt and a rosary. Had you pushed open
a large wooden door and stepped inside a stone chamber, you
would have stumbled upon an extraordinary scene: the cold body
of Queen Eleanor, covered with cloth, waiting to be embalmed.

As most medieval monarchs were buried in consecrated ground
– and it's not the done thing to go poking about their tombs – it's
near-impossible to access the forensic evidence that might tell us
about how they died. But there are a few exceptions that give us
valuable insight into medieval burial customs.

Take the example of King Richard I (nicknamed Richard the Lionheart, supposedly from having torn out and eaten the heart of a lion to obtain its courage). When he died in 1199, his viscera were buried in Châlus, near Limoges in central France. His embalmed body was entombed further north, in Fontevraud Abbey, alongside his parents, Henry II and Eleanor of Aquitaine. But his heart was buried elsewhere, in the cathedral of Notre-Dame in Rouen. In 2012, the remains of his heart – now a grey-brown powder – were tested. A microscopic examination, toxicological and pollen analysis were applied, with astonishing results. More than 800 years later, this tiny sample shed new light on Richard's life and death.

For centuries, it was suspected the deadly crossbow bolt that struck Richard was poisoned. But the toxicology report dispelled this, as no arsenic or any other metals were discovered. What they did find was pollen, including grains from poplar and bellflower. This gave credence to the traditional date of Richard's death being 6 April 1199, in late spring, when such plants are in flower.

But, importantly for our story, this analysis gave us a pretty handy insight into habits of embalming in the century leading up to Eleanor's death. King Richard's heart was wrapped in linen and pickled in a concoction of spices and vegetables, including myrtle, daisy, mint and lime. Mercury was also in the mix, to stop the heart from decomposing. Were these the methods used on the body of Eleanor?

There is no record of how Eleanor's viscera were packaged, but an object discovered at Kirkham Priory (a twelfth-century priory not far from York) might give some clues. In 1931, a viscera casket was found among the ruins. It is a rectangular stone box with a thick stone lid – the kind of object within which Eleanor's stomach, lungs and intestines would have been carefully placed.

It's likely her body was simply disembowelled, stuffed with medicinal herbs and wrapped in cerecloths – strips of fabric covered in wax, which created an airtight package. The goal was to slow decomposition long enough to display the body during a funeral, which, in Eleanor's case, would be three weeks later. So her body was in three parts: the entrails in a mini stone casket, to be buried in Lincoln Cathedral; her heart in a small pot or silver vessel, to be carried to London Blackfriars; and her embalmed body, probably in a wooden coffin, to be carried to Westminster Abbey in London.

But could a few herbs really keep a body in good shape? Would Eleanor survive travelling some 200 miles? Sceptical of this process, I went to see Rodney, a funeral director, who possessed a font of funerary knowledge, having been making coffins since the age of six. 'We would buy the boards in and steam them and bend them and pitch them inside,' he told me. These were the same techniques practised in Eleanor's day and perhaps used for her coffin itself.

'If you embalm a body with herbs,' I asked Rodney, 'and carried it two hundred miles, what kind of condition would it be in?' Rodney gazed at me with unblinking eyes. Why, he wanted to know, was I asking such questions about disposing of a body? After being reassured this was for research purposes only, he talked me through the process. Though embalming is rare today and not generally recommended, he told me, it is all chemical. These days, blood is pumped out of the body and a chemical mixture – pink dye and formaldehyde – is pumped in. Sometimes small stitches are used to close someone's jaw, and eye-caps are put in place to keep the eyelids shut.

We discussed Eleanor's treatment. From the sounds of things, a few bunches of herbs wouldn't have done much to help discolouration and decomposition. But, Rodney reminded me, it was December, so the low temperatures would have helped enormously. These days, if a body is kept at around 2°C (36°F), it would be OK – and considering Eleanor's body was either carried outside or kept in churches, it probably stayed chilled.

'Three weeks is the cut-off time,' Rodney explained, when it comes to preserving bodies. Eleanor died on 28 November and was buried on 17 December – so with two days to spare, she was in the nick of time! As we'll discover, there were also a couple of days dilly-dallying in London at the end of the journey, suggesting there wasn't a pressing need for burial. In which case, the body might have stayed in good shape . . . and so perhaps . . . the medieval embalmers knew what they were doing.

In the early days of December 1290, as Eleanor's body was readied for burial, the royal household busied themselves in preparation for the mammoth task ahead – the journey to London. Horses were washed, food supplies replenished and winter clothing patched up to tackle the poor roads and cold winds. Messengers were sent ahead to stop-off points – to Grantham, Stamford, Geddington and the rest – to inform of King Edward's imminent arrival and make preparations to accommodate Eleanor's body for a night.

And what of Edward in all this? In the days before and after Eleanor's death, the royal household ceased to operate as a machine of statecraft. Letters were sent without being copied into official registers, and the King refused to deal with daily paperwork.

Between 28 November and 4 December, I, too, made preparations, spending many industrious hours in Lincoln's pubs, plotting the course for the days ahead and noting locations to be aware of – historic landmarks, roads that might be unsuitable, shops to buy lunch, bakeries worth diverting to. There were logistics, too, as I arranged for belongings and bags to be transported between each stop.

I also invited a few companions to join along the route, so made a WhatsApp group and informed them of the dates and timings. There were some words of warning – firm but fair, I'd say.

A few points to note:
- *Some days are quite long and not for the faint-hearted. This is no Bronze D of E! On long days we will have to leave at daybreak (perhaps 6 a.m.) as the days get dark around 4 p.m.*
- *You might want to consider booking a place to stay the night.*
- *It's very important I complete the route on time, so we won't be able to stop or wait for people, if you are late or pull a muscle – sorry! I think all the areas have Uber, so you could easily get back to a station nearby.*
- *The book idea is a secret, so please don't tell anyone!*
- *At the moment I'll just be joined by Mum (I think). But whoever is around on any days – it would be great to have you with us. A motley crew very welcome, à la Canterbury Tales.*
- *Most importantly, it will be really epic and perhaps magical – a wonderful December walk to celebrate a forgotten medieval queen!*

Aware that I may not have all the essentials I needed, I trotted down the hill – via Lincoln Waterstones, where I signed a pile of books – and visited the local Mountain Warehouse to stock up. I became the proud owner of a high-vis waterproof backpack cover, a woolly hat with an in-built torch, and many, many pairs of socks. I spent a small fortune in Boots, piling a basket high with every variation of muscular relief treatment – Deep Heat, Tiger Balm – as well as the complete range of Compeed Hydrocolloid Blister Plasters. Modern luxuries the medieval cortège could only dream of.

Alice
invites you to
hunt out your sturdy boots
& walk with her
in the footsteps of history
one day or more,
on the extraordinary

Eleanor Walk
Lincoln - London

start date in December	Lincoln Cathedral	miles to walk each day
4th	✝ Lincoln Cathedral	
	✝ Grantham	28
5th		23
6th	✝ Stamford	
		20
8th	✝ Geddington	
	✝ Hardingstone	20
9th	✝ Stony Stratford	13
10th	✝ Woburn	13
11th	✝ Dunstable	10
12th	✝ St Albans	13
13th	✝ Waltham Priory	19
14th		14
15th	✝ Westcheap	1
16th	✝ Charing end	1
17th	Westminster Abbey	

The invitation to join the Eleanor Walk.

57

One street I became reluctantly familiar with was Lincoln's notorious Steep Hill, named as such because of the 14 per cent incline. Not the kind of place you want to drop anything, for it will go rolling off into the distance, never to be recovered. In 1909, a scheme was proposed for an 'underground tramway scheme to obviate the difficulties of ascending Steep Hill'. The tramway was never built, but the incline has been put to good use for adventure training. In 1999, the *Lincolnshire Echo* reported that twenty-seven-year-old Rachel Friend prepared for an epic Himalayan hike by 'walking up and down Lincoln's Steep Hill'.

Despite the incline, it is a lovely street to explore. On the corner is Lincoln Antiques and Collectables, a true treasure trove. Inside I found two floors of swords and rare vinyl, copper kettles and silver candlesticks, and glass cases teeming with row upon row of historic coins.

Kneeling down for a closer look at this mini-museum, I inspected a tiny silver denarius, from the time of Septimius Severus (a Roman emperor who died in York in AD 211). On another shelf was a large assortment of medieval coins, minted by hand. Then, much larger, heavier coins from the Georgian and Victorian periods.

Edward and Eleanor played an important part in England's coin history. When Edward became king in 1272, the only coins in use were silver pennies. But there was a serious problem that threatened to undermine the entirety of England's trade. The illegal practice of coin clipping – the act of shaving off the silver edges – was devaluing the coinage and caused a lack of trust in the currency.

Fearful of the potentially devastating repercussions on the economy, Edward acted with a heavy hand. Those who were found guilty of coin clipping were hanged. Then, in 1279, Edward collected all the existing coins and replaced them with ones that were harder to clip. As well as the old coins, new denominations were issued, including the groat (4p), the halfpenny (½p) and the farthing (¼p).

In the medieval period, mints were similar to blacksmiths' shops, often operated by a part-time moneyer who travelled town to town to meet the local demand. Coins were created by placing a square piece of blank metal between two engraved dies – a pile and trussell. Just as today, they were stamped with the face of the monarch, which back then was the only glimpse most people ever had of their king or queen (so one mistake could have massive repercussions – say, the whole county of Norfolk forever thinking the King had a double chin or a pinched nose). The pile and trussell were struck with a hammer to imprint the design, after which the coin was trimmed by hand to make it circular.

In 1279, Edward and Eleanor oversaw a Royal Mint installed within the Tower of London – a new, centralised hub of coin making that would remain in situ for more than 500 years. The area became known as Mint Street and produced the nation's coins until 1810, when it was moved to a new building on nearby Tower Hill and then, in 1968, to its present home in Llantrisant, Wales.

As I browsed the antiques shop, I spotted an original Edward I penny for sale. It was a small, silver coin, with the face of Edward on one side and a cross on the reverse. In honour of the journey ahead, I bought it – paying just £24. How incredible that the people of Lincoln – while nipping to the shops for a pint of milk and a newspaper – could also pick up a centuries-old slice of history. Delighted with this medieval memento, I opened the blue door and stepped out onto Steep Hill, back into the winter sunlight.

As I did so, a curious house on the street opposite caught my eye. It is a two-storey building with walls of neatly squared lime-stone, two round-arched windows and a beautifully carved

Romanesque doorway. As it dates from around 1170, Eleanor might well have glanced at the house, as I was now. In Eleanor's day, it's believed this was the dwelling of a wealthy Jewish woman called Belaset of Wallingford and it is now known as the Jew's House.

Though a prosperous, hard-working businesswoman, Belaset – as a Jewish woman – had a difficult life. She was ostracised, persecuted and, as she walked up and down Steep Hill, jeered at.

Antisemitism was ingrained into the society of thirteenth-century England and was two centuries in the making. Jewish people first settled in England after the Norman Conquest in 1066. They came mainly from Rouen, in Normandy, and established themselves in major towns such as London, York, Lincoln, Norwich, Bristol and Oxford.

They had a unique status – different from both the new Norman aristocracy and the native Anglo-Saxons. English Jews were 'royal serfs', legally under the jurisdiction of the King, who offered them protection in return for economic benefits. The King considered Jews and their possessions to be his property; they were allowed to stay in England only with the King's permission. For the two centuries that followed, Jewish people built successful lives – but were only able to stay in England if they were financially useful to the Crown, through loans or taxes.

Over the twelfth and thirteenth centuries, they were increasingly persecuted. Some were resentful that Jewish people could lend money with interest, while Christians could not (as it was considered a mortal sin). Others held Jews responsible for the death of Christ, believing this a legitimate excuse to inflict violence.

In 1190, one of the worst antisemitism massacres of the Middle Ages took place. The Jewish people of York – some 150 people – were trapped by an angry mob inside the tower of York Castle (now known as Clifford's Tower), which was set alight. It is a shameful episode of York's – indeed Britain's – story. Today, on the anniversary – 16 March – the massacre is commemorated. Daffodils are planted on the tower mound, whose six-pointed shape echoes the Star of David.

Though Jewish people were mostly welcomed into English society, moments of Blood Libel hysteria – false accusations of Jews of murdering Christians – continued throughout the thirteenth century. On 29 August 1255, the body of a nine-year-old boy was discovered in a well in Lincoln. The rumour spread that the Jewish people had tortured and killed him, and Little Saint Hugh of Lincoln became a child martyr, with a shrine in Lincoln Cathedral.

Things became increasingly difficult. Take the example of Licoricia of Winchester (whose name meant 'sweet meat'), who was perhaps the most important Jewish woman in England in the medieval period. She was a major businesswoman, financing clients such as King Henry III and nobles like Simon de Montfort, 6th Earl of Leicester. When her husband David died, Licoricia paid thousands to help build Westminster Abbey.

Despite playing this important role, in early 1277, Licoricia was found murdered inside her house. Though three men were indicted for the murders, none were convicted and the crass murder of Licoricia was never solved. Was this because she was a woman? Or Jewish? Perhaps both? Today, a beautiful statue stands in the streets of Winchester to remember Licoricia's life, her contributions and her plight. The words on the plinth read: 'Love Thy Neighbour As Thyself'.

When Edward I came to the throne in 1272, this habitual cruelty to Jewish people was ingrained in English society. Edward – driven by financial needs – was happy to exploit it. Jewish people faced arbitrary imprisonments, punitive taxations and increasingly violent religious intolerance. In 1278, nearly 300 Jewish people – including one of Licoricia's sons, Benedict – were accused of coin clipping and hanged.

By 1289, facing vast debts, Edward I needed Parliament to grant him funds of around £100,000. Parliament agreed to do this, on the condition that Jewish people were expelled from England. So, in 1290, Edward signed the Edict of Expulsion, forcing them to leave the country or convert to Christianity.

In autumn of 1290 – the final weeks of Eleanor's life – Jewish people were no longer able to reside 'freely and honourably' in England. They fled and their properties were seized. This meant that many, including Edward, avoided repaying the money they owed to them. Parliament duly granted Edward a tax of £116,000 (around £113 million today), the largest single tax of the Middle Ages.

From a twenty-first-century perspective, Edward's cruelty towards the Jewish people, which Eleanor was complicit in, is a black mark against his name. But it's important to consider the actions of historical figures within the standards of their own time. For Edward I's contemporaries, the expulsion was wildly popular and a crowning achievement of his reign.

For 366 years after their expulsion from England, no Jewish people lived in England. Jewish visitors were required to obtain a special licence to set foot in the realm. An unlikely hero came in the form of Oliver Cromwell, who readmitted Jews in 1656, based on theological reasoning and trade incentives.

Sadly, such expulsions weren't uncommon. In 1231, Simon de Montfort drove the Jewish people from Leicester. In 1275, Eleanor of Provence ordered their removal from her lands and towns. In 1306, King Philippe IV ordered that all Jews must leave the kingdom of France.

I stood for a while outside the antiques shop, holding my new

Edward I penny and looking across to the Jew's House. All those years ago, Belaset, the owner, would have held these coins in her hand – perhaps the very penny in my hand now.

The coin I bought at the antiques shop.

What was her life like in this lovely house? Did she shed tears, in the autumn of 1290, the final time she walked out her front door and glanced up at those rounded windows, as I was now? Looking at the life she had created, thrown away? Where did she go?

As it turns out, Belaset was never expelled from England. Tragically, she never made it that far. Earlier in 1290 – as Eleanor was enjoying the luxuries of royal weddings in Westminster – Belaset was accused of coin clipping and hanged. Was she dragged from the house in front of me and paraded in front of a braying mob? I envisioned her lifeless body swinging from a rope as crowds mocked and jeered. How strange: Eleanor and Belaset – both wealthy women in England, both died in 1290, near Lincoln, in such different circumstances.

It was evident that Eleanor's legacy was to be more complex to untangle than I first realised. As we learn about famous figures in history, there is always another side of the coin, where lives of luxury go hand in hand with the terrible persecution of people whose voices we will never hear. If Eleanor was to be revered with stone crosses and ceremony and grand tomb effigies, this beautiful stone house on Steep Hill in Lincoln was to be Belaset's enduring memorial and a reminder of the lives and sufferings of the Jewish people of medieval England.

The Jew's House, Lincoln.

On the evening of 3 December – the night before I set off south – I visited Lincoln Cathedral, once again, for evensong. The stone facade was lit up in purple to mark the season of Advent. Inside, hundreds of seats were laid out.

'Is this for an Advent service?' I asked an usher.

'No,' she replied, 'we've got a Michael Bublé tribute act tonight.'

I didn't hear the sonorous tones of Bublé that evening, but evensong in St Hugh's Chapel was a performance enough for me. I took a pew near the bishop's seat and flicked open the worn paper booklet. It explained the origins of the service that was about to unfold – one designed by Archbishop Cranmer in the sixteenth century, but 'contains text and melodies which are much earlier, many of which would have been familiar to St Hugh, the rebuilder of this cathedral at the end of the twelfth century and to Remigius who founded it in 1072.'

As the service began and these ancient melodies echoed off the vaulting, I considered the events that had taken place on this day, 734 years before: a chest containing Eleanor's internal organs was placed at the altar and a vigil held.

I also pondered – with excited anticipation – the monumental journey ahead. In just a matter of hours, the great march to London would begin. All my preparation would be put to the test. There was excitement, but apprehension, too. Would anything go wrong? What if the route was flooded or I pulled a muscle or – God forbid – my resolve crumbled in the face of the endeavour?

After the service, I returned to the Angel Choir and stood beside Eleanor's visceral tomb. The cathedral was quiet and empty. The dean of Lincoln, the Very Revd Dr Simon Jones, shared a prayer of blessing to wish me well on the journey. I thanked the dean and departed from the cathedral by the north door. Outside, high up on the facade, on the most south-easterly corner of the cathedral, are two statues. It's believed this couple are Edward and Eleanor. I bade them goodnight, happy in the knowledge that as I walked the 28 miles south the following morning, they would be watching over me from afar.

I stayed the final night at the White Hart Hotel, a handsome Georgian building, built of brick with fine sash windows, located just beside the cathedral. I prepared my backpack and laid everything out in an orderly fashion – boots, socks, spare socks, thermals, hat, waterproofs and a Lincoln Imp lollipop. I charged up my battery packs and double-checked the route. I set my alarm for 5.30 a.m., 5.32 a.m., 5.45 a.m. and 6 a.m. and – though darting between feelings of immense excitement and utmost dread at the task ahead – I was soon asleep, lulled to a slumber by the tolling of Lincoln's bells.

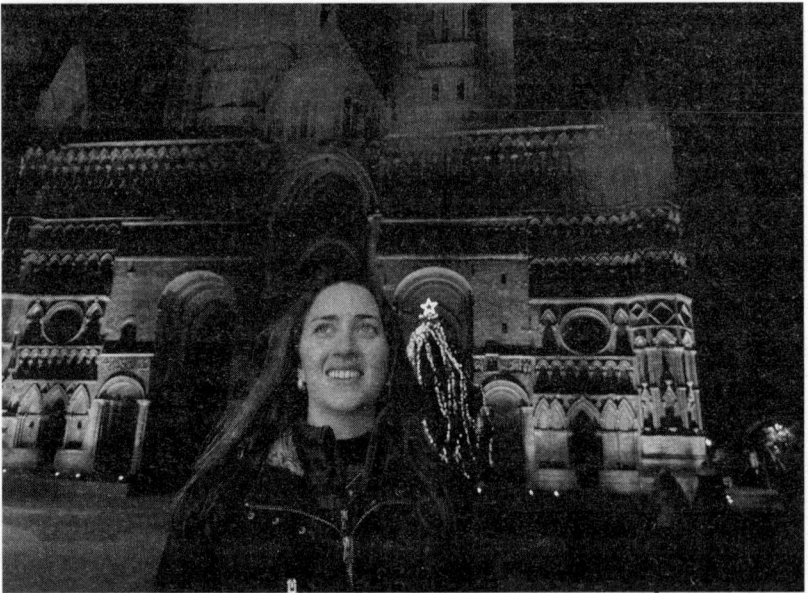

Outside Lincoln Cathedral, the night before the great march south.

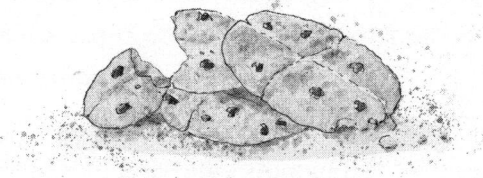

4. PERSEVERANTIA VINCIT

"Tis very true, my grief lies all within;
And these external manners of laments
Are merely shadows to the unseen grief
That swells with silence in the tortured soul.'
William Shakespeare

IN THE EARLY HOURS OF 4 December 1290, the people of Lincoln were woken up to the clatter of steel, the clip-clop of horses' hooves and the soft trample of hundreds of footsteps. Peeping out their windows, they saw the source of this strange symphony: an enormous procession snaking its way through the streets.

At the front was the bier upon which Queen Eleanor's body lay, probably carried by the strongest knights, before being transported in a cart. As she passed the city walls, she departed Lincoln for the final time, never to return. Behind her, high on a horse, was the heartbroken King Edward, eyes red and heart heavy.

Following him were perhaps a hundred figures dressed in royal livery. These were the people who knew the Queen personally – physicians, tailors, messengers. Among all this there were, it's thought, the royal princesses, Eleanor and Margaret. With the cathedral's towering spire behind them, they traversed the narrow streets with great wagons of feather beds, linen sheets, rugs and furs, tapestries and hangings. The long march to London had begun.

Seven hundred and thirty-four years later, more alarms disturbed the quiet of Lincoln's cathedral quarter. This time, the loud, honking noise of my iPhone's Old Car Horn. No more slumbering and no time to snooze. Minutes later, I stood in the threshold of the White Hart Hotel wearing pristine walking boots, a thin Barbour jacket, a purple waterproof and headtorch.

I had three good-luck charms. First, I was joined by my mum, the ultimate morale boost and a much-needed one. The day ahead was a long one: 28 miles, from Lincoln to Grantham. Second, around my neck I wore the King Edward I penny – which I'd had made into a necklace. Third, divine assistance was provided by the dean of Lincoln, who shared a prayer from the thirteenth century written by St Thomas Aquinas, an Italian Dominican friar and priest. It is a prayer that Eleanor would have known and Edward might have thought of as he travelled.

In the soft glow of the White Hart's Christmas lights, we read the prayer aloud, echoing the words of pilgrims for hundreds of years:

Give me, O Lord, a steadfast heart, which no unworthy affection may drag downwards; give me an unconquered heart, which no tribulation can wear out; give me an upright heart, which no unworthy purpose may tempt aside.

Blessings complete, spirits were up as we set off from mighty Lincoln. No conquered hearts here! No tribulation would wear us out! With the digital OS Maps for guidance, we triumphantly took the first steps of our trip, passing the city highlights as we went.

Goodbye, Lincoln Cathedral! Farewell, Steep Hill! Adieu, little antiques shop! In high spirits we cheerily greeted a few early birds: a black Labrador exercising its elderly owner; a construction worker rolling a cigarette; a man in a sharp suit speed-walking to catch the first commuter train to London.

Twenty minutes after setting off, at the outskirts of the city, we came to a busy road junction: the intersection of the A1434 and A607. As an endless stream of cars beeped and swerved and indicated their way through the junction, I examined the map and exclaimed with delight: 'Look, Mum! How exciting! We've arrived at the site of the first Eleanor Cross!'

Bewilderment crept across her face, then disappointment – then dread. She'd been given the whole spiel about the crosses, these exquisite examples of medieval architecture – but here we were, gazing at a scruffy assortment of metal railings, traffic lights and concrete. Was this . . . it? We were walking 200 miles, just to stare at . . . tarmac?

The cross at Lincoln was 'a very fair crosse and large', completed by 1293. For three centuries, it was a major marker of the Lincoln landscape. But by 1624, the cross was in bad condition – perhaps bashed about by carts and wagons – and it was 'Ordered the Queen's Cross . . . be repaired'. But the repairs were in vain, for not long after, in 1643, the cross was destroyed by Order of the Common Council of Lincoln, another victim of the Civil War – and the reason there is no cross to be seen today.

The original stones disappeared – probably seized by anyone who could carry them home, to patch up walls or lay the foundations for a new conservatory. But, in the Victorian period, one original piece reappeared: 'a mutilated female figure which had lain as a footbridge over a neighbouring ditch'. This is believed to be the bottom half of one of Eleanor's statues, now kept at Lincoln Castle.

We must have been a strange sight that December morning, taking photos of one another on a busy road junction. Passing motorists must have wondered: are those women traffic-light enthusiasts? Local surveyors? Or just plain lost?

The Lincoln cross raises an important question. How was a location chosen for each of the crosses? Did they mark a stopping point for Eleanor's body? At the spot we were standing on, we would have been close to the Gilbertine priory of St Katherine, where some have suggested the Queen's body was eviscerated or stayed for a night. The priory no longer remains, but an old church, St Katherine's (now restored as a parish hall and events venue), stands in its place.

Alternatively, perhaps the crosses were built at busy junctions, where the maximum number of travellers and pilgrims would pass by and be inspired to pray for Eleanor's soul. It's impossible to conclude, as we don't know the precise location of all twelve crosses, but we can be sure of one thing: Eleanor's body was carried across each of the dozen sites, even if it didn't stay the night on the exact spot.

With only one mile down and twenty-seven to go, we pressed on. We were keen to make progress early on in the day. Mum and I are both reasonably fit, having ticked off a smattering of half marathons (and coming in around the two-hour mark, which seems to me perfectly respectable). But this kind of walking wasn't just about fitness. It was about resilience and a determination not to give up. Time would tell if we had it in us.

As we departed Lincoln, we pushed up Cross O'Cliff Hill and

zig-zagged through the housing estates of Bracebridge Heath. One by one, homes became lit by a warm glow as households woke up to this frosty December morn and switched on the kettle. We weaved between gardens, along passages of brick walls, neatly trimmed hedges and rickety fences.

With every step, the sky turned from inky black to a cornflower blue, softening into creamy pink on the horizon – or as Charles Dickens put it, the 'white face of the winter day came sluggishly on'. These are the skies you'd see in a Turner painting: washes of yellows and bluish grey, light refracted through the early morning mist. We could make out stark silhouettes of leafless trees, of enormous electricity pylons shrouded in fog.

For several miles, we followed a pavement beside the A607. We walked intensely and with purpose, keenly aware of the distance yet to cover. Though the landscape seemed totally flat, we travelled parallel to the Lincolnshire Edge, the 50-mile straight escarpment that runs north–south, from the River Humber down to Grantham. It forms a natural divide between the two sides of Lincolnshire: the fenland of the east, which stetches far out to the North Sea coast; and in the west, the farmland merging into the Midlands.

Along this route, we passed several 'cliff villages', as they are known: Bracebridge, Waddington, Harmston, Coleby, Boothby Graffoe and Navenby – which we arrived at by 9 a.m. We'd been walking for around three hours, at a speed of more than 3 miles an hour. Ten miles down, seventeen to go – legs a little shaky, but still in good working order.

Triumphant at this early progress, I took an executive decision: a break was needed. Navenby is a charming village and the perfect place to stop. Here was Welbourne's Bakery, situated in a stone building with a red door, which has been serving bread and pastries since 1896.

Thank you, Welbourne's Bakery, for a delicious iced bun! Yum!

I bought an iced bun – a classic treat from childhood, which has long both delighted and bemused me in equal measure. How can two such mundane foods – a cheap bun and thin, runny icing – come together to form a snack of unparalleled deliciousness? Navenby's offering was no exception and tasted all the sweeter as a reward for our endeavours.

As we pressed on south, enveloped once more by vast Lincolnshire skies, we passed a strange tower standing tall and alone in a farmyard. This unusual building was somewhere I had longed to visit for a while, having read about it beforehand. Up the steps we went, through the rounded doorway. 'Knock knock,' Mum called, 'anyone home?'

Inside was a single room, empty apart from a weathered coffin slab in the corner. The walls were covered in extraordinary decoration, a carpet of ancient markings and graffiti. Some were the marks of a stonemason, which acted as a kind of signature to mark the work completed. Some were the names of local people and visitors, left for posterity. The circular shapes – the kind you often find on old doorways and beams – were symbols to offer protection from witches and evil spirits.

Though seemingly inconspicuous today, the tower is of immense historical significance – and it stands in a location Eleanor would have been familiar with. This is all that remains of a preceptory, a kind of regional headquarters of the Knights Templar, a military and religious order founded to protect pilgrims on their way to and from Jerusalem. It was a base to manage fundraising and property and to generate income for the more important work in the Holy Land.

The Knights Templar owned preceptories and churches across Europe, and this one – the Preceptory of Temple Bruer – was the second most important in England, second only to Temple Church in London. Like the London HQ, here was a church with a round nave, designed to echo the circular Church of the Holy Sepulchre in Jerusalem, built over Jesus's tomb.

Of course, Eleanor was well acquainted with Europe's religious conflicts, having spent a childhood embroiled in the Reconquista, where Christian kingdoms of the Iberian Peninsula – Castile, Aragon, León and Portugal – fought to reclaim Al-Andalus (Islamic Spain). Then, at the age of twenty-nine, Eleanor accompanied Edward on a formidable military expedition: the Crusades.

In a nutshell, the Crusades were a series of violent religious wars in Europe's High Medieval Period (spanning the eleventh to thirteenth centuries), where Christians (largely from Europe) and Muslims (from the Middle East) battled for control of the Holy Land. Millions perished as a result.

For English kings and queens, this meant combining forces with Christian leaders, journeying to cities such as Jerusalem, Constantinople, Antioch or Damascus, laying siege to cities and defending castles. The First Crusade began in 1096 and the Crusades came to an end with the fall of Acre in 1291, a year after Eleanor's death.

Though the vast majority of those involved in the Crusades were men, there were a handful of women who played their part. In 1147, Eleanor of Aquitaine accompanied her first husband, King Louis VII, on the Second Crusade (which was such a failure, it probably led to their divorce).

While some women came along for the ride, others fought alongside men in battle. In 1187, Margaret of Beverley helped defend Jerusalem against Saladin's army, even wearing a cauldron on her head as a makeshift helmet. Then there were those women who stayed at home and held up the 'home front'. While their husbands were away, they acted as regents, managing estates, leading prayers and processions in a PR push or raising money and acquiring lands for religious-military orders, such as the Knights Templar.

In 1270, while still prince and princess, Eleanor and Edward set off to join King Louis IX of France on the Eighth Crusade. They travelled south, through France, Sardinia and Tunisia. But before they arrived, a spanner appeared in the works: King Louis died of dysentery. From that point onwards, Edward took control, leading a force to the Holy Land. The Crusade then became known as the Ninth Crusade or Lord Edward's Crusade, lasting from 1271–72.

On 9 May 1271, Edward and Eleanor arrived in the blistering heat of Acre, in modern-day Israel. They were accompanied by a fleet of more than thirty ships and a force of 1,000 soldiers, including 225 knights. Over the following year, Edward captured Nazareth, launched raids with the support of the Templar, Hospitaller and Teutonic Knights, and clashed with the Egyptian Mamluks under Sultan Baibars. At this point, the Mamluk empire controlled most of what is now Egypt, Israel, Palestine, Jordan and Syria – apart from the tiny Crusader kingdom of Acre.

Eleanor – then pregnant with little Joan – sat in the cool shade of a campaigning tent, probably managing Edward's accounts and sending letters home to England. But being Edward's trusted advisor, it's hard to believe she wasn't more involved. Did she ride out with Edward's knights to assess the city walls of Nazareth? As Edward's knights pored over maps, did Eleanor – remembering tales of her father's campaigns from childhood – offer advice: 'These walls will be impossible to scale – we must attack from the north'? Did she help Edward into his chainmail, never knowing if he was to return? Did she watch on as her husband galloped along the lines in a cloud of dust, rallying his men for the fight ahead?

It wasn't just acts of war that threatened their safety. Danger lurked in every shadow. One evening, while Edward and Eleanor relaxed in their private tent, an assassin – supposedly a member of the Syrian Order of Assassins and under the command of Baibars – emerged from the darkness and drove a poisoned dagger deep into Edward's flesh.

Reeling in pain, Edward tackled the assassin to the ground and killed him. But he, too, was in mortal danger: poison was seeping through his veins. The legend goes that, in this moment, Eleanor sucked the poison from Edward's wound, willing to risk her own life for that of her husband. Whether the legend is true or not, the records tell us Eleanor was taken out of the room 'weeping and wailing' and Edward's putrefying flesh was probably cut away by a surgeon.

Though Edward survived, he was forced to abandon further campaigning. In September 1272, he and Eleanor left Palestine for Sicily. While recuperating, they received devastating news: Edward's father, King Henry III, had died. The return home, through Italy, Gascony and Paris, was quite different to the outbound journey. No longer prince and princess, they now travelled as king and queen. Perhaps a parallel can be drawn with the experience of the young Queen Elizabeth II, who learned of the unexpected death of her father, King George VI, on 6 February 1952, while staying at the Treetops Hotel in Kenya during a Commonwealth tour.

Unbeknown to Edward and Eleanor, this was to be the very last of the Crusades, brought to a close by the fall of Acre in 1291. As they arrived on the shores of England in 1274 and prepared for their summer coronation in Westminster Abbey, they also marked the end of an era: 178 years of crusading missions to the Holy Land.

With all this crusading experience, it's no surprise that Eleanor, when she was back in England, stayed at Temple Bruer, first in March 1276 and again in 1283. Mum and I sat on the step of the tower, thinking of her here as she caught up on the updates from the Holy Land or discussed the latest political movements with her knights.

Today, with the forlorn tower, the site evokes a sense of the forgotten fairy-tale castle, a relic from days of brave knights and enchanted forests. But this is no children's story. In 1833, the vaults were excavated by the Revd Dr George Oliver, who painted a sinister picture of what he found:

In one of them a niche or cell was discovered that had been neatly walled up; and within it the skeleton of a man, who appears to have died in a sitting posture, for his head and arms were found hanging between his legs and the back bowed forward.

What heinous acts had taken place here? Had live entombment been used as a punishment? Were people here really bricked up and left to die? Though historians today are sceptical of George Oliver's reports, considering them wildly exaggerated, similar stories emerge from Temple Church in London, where it is said that a knight called Walter Bachelor was left to starve in the penitential cell.

Soon after reading the account, we left the tower with a newfound feeling of unease. Like in fairy tales, we had been lured in with beauty, only for the truth of a cursed reality to make itself known. We'd been given a juicy red apple, only to realise it was poisoned.

We marched on, but couldn't escape the markers of death. As streams of sunlight grew stronger, bursting through the winter mists, the landscape changed once more. Through hedges and brambles, we saw strange concrete blocks in the distance. Underfoot, muddy pathways changed to hard concrete, with weeds crawling from the cracks.

We were walking through the remains of RAF Wellingore. During the Second World War, this peaceful countryside was interrupted by whirring sirens and the cries of fighter units of young men (some in their teens) sprinting to their planes – Bristol Blenheims, Hawker Hurricanes and Supermarine Spitfires – and launching them into the air. From here, they flew to Lincoln or Sheffield and fought off German Heinkels and Messerschmitts in a desperate effort to stop them dropping bombs on the vital industrial sites below.

And then, after a night in the skies, they returned – only to hear news that family or friends were victims of a bombing raid.

Or that fellow pilots had been shot down in the night and were never to return.

That morning, we'd passed the Jew's House in Lincoln, Temple Bruer, and now these Second World War pillboxes. Already, it was becoming clear: if you simply take the time to look, our landscape is dotted with these forgotten memorials to the endeavours and sufferings of generations past.

A straight track stretched ahead, ready for the taking. This was Ermine Street, a major Roman road that runs from London (Londinium was the Roman name) to Lincoln (Lindum Colonia) and York (Eboracum). After Emperor Claudius successfully invaded Britain with around 40,000 soldiers in AD 43, the troops were put to work building a network of new roads, so troops, officials and messengers could move to every outpost in the new province of Britannia.

Ermine Street stretched out before us.

Most Roman roads were created by digging two shallow U-shaped ditches. The excavated earth was piled into the middle, to create a raised bank called an agger. If the land was soft or marshy, the road might be built over timber piles and layers of brushwood. Above the agger, a layer of larger stones was added, with smaller stones and gravel to form a hard, durable, even surface.

Coming across a comfortable-looking tuft of grass, we stopped for a break. After retying our laces, we unscrewed the coffee flask and unwrapped Mum's homemade 'medieval biscuits', containing caraway seeds, crushed nuts and ginger. We thought of the medieval cortège, clattering along the track. Was there a mother and daughter duo in Eleanor's household – like us? Did they pause here, on this little mound, readjusting their footwear, snapping seeded biscuits and talking of the late Queen?

Of course, Eleanor was well acquainted with Roman roads such as these. She was a hardy traveller. Throughout her life she lived in Castile, Gascony, England, Wales, Sicily and the Holy Land, and visited Scotland, Aragon, France, Italy and Tunisia. Her schedule was never-ending. When in England, she was darting between royal estates and hunting lodges, then making visits to shrines and monasteries to make offerings to saints and give alms to the poor. Like the Romans, she was used to covering 20 miles, day after day.

Perhaps the most extraordinary part is that she was often pregnant while doing so. Indeed, despite being pregnant for over a decade in the course of her life, this never stopped her. For example, in late November 1273, she gave birth to her ninth child, Alphonso, in Gascony, in the south-west of France. By April the following year, she had travelled some 500 miles north on horseback. By the summer of 1274, she arrived in Calais, in the north-east, and was pregnant again, at the end of her first trimester. She then crossed the Channel and rode to Canterbury.

When it came to giving birth – as was the custom for royal women – Eleanor was closed off from the world for several weeks. For the process known as 'lying in', her rooms were transformed into a kind of 'second womb': fires were lit, windows were shut up and light – which was thought to harm an expectant mother's eyes – was dimmed. In the summertime, it must have been roasting.

Eleanor might also have been given a sacred birth girdle – perhaps the girdle of the Virgin, held at St Peter's Westminster, or the girdle of St Ailred at Rievaulx Abbey. To the medieval mind, these weren't just good-luck charms, but relics of real power. After all, these objects had been touched by a saint and so forevermore exuded holy radioactivity. 'We've run out of painkillers,' the midwife might have cried. 'Fetch the girdle!'

If the child was safely delivered, the baby went to the care of the wet nurse, then to the royal nursery, then in a household of their own. With Eleanor constantly on the go, many of the royal children grew up close to their grandparents. Princess Eleanor's young life was spent with her grandmother, Eleanor of Provence, at Guildford Castle, where she and her brother, Henry, were indulged with pomegranate, quince and almonds.

Princess Joan was brought up in France with Eleanor's mother, Jeanne, Countess of Ponthieu. Here she was educated in the arts expected of a thirteenth-century princess: reading, embroidery, music, riding, falconry and chess. When she returned to her parents – who were little more than strangers – she 'stood in awe' of them both. Eleanor, too, was concerned to find her daughter had been 'thoroughly spoiled by an indulgent grandmother'.

This might seem cruel or uncaring today, to be so estranged from your children, but this set-up was de rigueur for royal children. And when you consider the manic schedules of Edward and Eleanor, it was probably safer for their health (child mortality was a constant risk) and better for their education. Edward and Eleanor were distant but loving parents, constantly writing letters to check up on the children. We can think of it as a bit like sending a child to boarding school today.

Perhaps – from the children's point of view – it was a relief not to have their parents around. They didn't have to be on best behaviour all the time and were free to enjoy the luxuries of life as a minor royal, in their own households. The household accounts of Princess Margaret – an enthusiastic crafter – are full of purchases for embroidery materials: spindles, gold thread and all kinds of silks in different colours and thicknesses.

Besides, there were plenty of people who looked after them, who became a sort of second family. Within Princess Joan's household was Robert the private tailor, Robert the personal cook, Reginald the keeper of bed and table linens, and James the carter, who transported her personal possessions.

As the children grew older, they spent more time with their parents, travelling with the royal court or making offerings at sacred shrines. When Queen Eleanor died in Harby, it's thought that the eldest daughters, Eleanor and Margaret, were present and subsequently part of the cortège. How strange – how sad – it must have been for those young women, to travel this stretch of Ermine Street, following behind a cart that carried their mother's body.

This brings us to another important point. How did they transport Eleanor's body all that way? Was she carried on a bier, at shoulder height? Or pulled on a cart? There is no record of this, so we have to make our best guest. Rodney the funeral director seemed to think carrying the body the full 200 miles was pretty unlikely: 'If you carry a body out a church, across a churchyard to the grave, you know you've carried them – even if it's just five minutes.'

It was Rodney's instinct that Eleanor's body was transported on some kind of wheeled cart, drawn by horses, but she may have been carried at important moments – crossing rivers or processing into cities and churches. So, along this bit of Ermine Street, Eleanor's body was probably transported on wheels, surrounded by guards.

And what of the body itself? Was Eleanor's face exposed? 'You really think,' Rodney said, 'if it was raining – which it must have done – they wouldn't cover her up? That they'd let the Queen's face be splattered with mud?' When he put it like that, it seems obvious. Eleanor was probably transported within a wooden coffin, the lid of which would be carefully removed once safely in the confines of the church or abbey.

Misty woodland paths near Ancaster.

PERSEVERANTIA VINCIT

The cortège passed through the village of Ancaster – where we arrived at midday. We knew that Ancaster was a Roman town, just by looking at the name. The term for a fortified military encampment was 'castrum' and this evolved into suffixes such as '-chester', '-cester' and '-caster', referring to cities with links to the Roman military.

Past Ancaster and back into open fields, the landscape changed once more. Now, field boundaries were marked with drainage ditches crossed by tiny bridges. We were skirting the edge of fenland country – a low-lying area covering about 1,500 square miles of Lincolnshire, Cambridgeshire and Norfolk. In the medieval period, this was used for summer pasture and year-round foraging, though it was where the dreaded marsh agues were prevelant. Today – now it has been drained with a network of dykes and automated pumping stations, once powered by horses or windmills – it is arable.

After a whopping 22 miles of walking and thoroughly exhausted, our enthusiasm was waning. The light began to fade – and still, there were 6 miles to cover. My lower back had a jabbing ache. Mum's shoes were rubbing. I tried making conversation with an escaped chicken: delirium was setting in.

But worst of all, a terrible reality made itself known via the toes on my left foot. What was that strange warm sensation? Was it . . . no it couldn't be . . . no it can't be! But the truth will always out. I couldn't deny it: my toes were damp. 'Mum', I murmured, 'I don't think these boots are waterproof.'

We had no choice but to press on. As we staggered towards Grantham, I was nearing the end of my tether. Fields of crops changed to tidy estate villages, then manicured parkland. This was the estate land of Belton House, a picture-perfect country house, completed in 1688 and surrounded by a vast deer park. But I was in no mood to glance at fine facades or admire sash windows.

We passed a little courtyard, where visitors milled around the National Trust gift shop. We gazed at those Christmas shoppers begrudgingly. Already, their lives seemed so detached from ours, as if they were in a parallel existence. Had we not taken on this mad challenge, that would have been us, spending the afternoon perusing pastel candlesticks and tartan rugs.

I could feel Mum veering left, drawn in like a magnet to the plants on sale, and I grabbed her waterproof, pulling her back on course. 'We haven't got time, Mum, and besides, you can't start carrying plant pots!'

As the darkness fell, a sense of urgency set in. We realised with alarm that the gates closed at dusk and we were at risk of being trapped in Belton Park for the night. There was no room for error now. Dragging our heavy legs, staggering like zombies, we stumbled through wild, rugged land, over gnarly roots and past marshy ponds.

Delirium sets in.

Those final couple of hours were a hazy blur. As we eventually reached the housing estates on the outskirts of Grantham, our fervour was confirmed. We were greeted by 'Grantham's oldest resident': a magnificent oak with a girth of 7 metres, some 500 years old and now set in a crescent of houses. I gave it a hug for good measure: we needed all the help we could get.

As we sleep-walked through Wyndham Park, Grantham was abuzz with life: school children were everywhere, skipping, cycling, running home. Though medieval Grantham was also a busy town, usually full of wealthy wool merchants, market stalls and carts bashing up and down the high street, when the cortège arrived in 1290, it stilled to silence.

When King Edward arrived on that dark December eve, high on his horse, the people of Grantham lined the streets, desperate to catch a glimpse of him in the flesh. And then, a hushed silence fell as their eyes darted to a cart some metres behind, carrying the body of the late Queen. Did the people throw herbs on the ground or offer up their prayers? Did the bells of St Wulfram's Church toll as Eleanor's body was carried into the nave and a candlelit vigil commenced, which lasted throughout the night?

The cortège may have stayed at The Angel, an inn belonging to the Knights Templar. The original building no longer survives, though a hotel has stood on the current site since 1350. Since then, many kings – the likes of Edward IV, Richard III and Charles I – have rested their weary heads under these beams. To capitalise on this, in 1866, after a visit from Edward VII, it was renamed the Angel and Royal.

To this esteemed list of past guests was added two exhausted, shivering women, splattered with mud. Using the two remaining brain cells still functioning, I checked us in for the night.

It was a heroic moment. I wept with the relief. What elation, to arrive in a cosy hotel with a roaring fire. How heavenly to untie those boots and flex our toes. I peeled off the sodden sock from my left foot, which seemed reluctant to be removed, requiring Mum to give it a final yank to set me free.

As we crawled upstairs to our room, we peeped into a large space on the first floor – the Chambre du Roi – with carved stone ceilings, oriel windows and an enormous fireplace. It was full of partygoers, wearing Christmas hats and pulling crackers and bursting with festive cheer. Perfect for parties – and parliamentary business, too. An enthusiastic waiter informed us that it was here that King Richard III held court on 19 October 1483. How strange it was, to think of Richard in this space – the actual Richard III! – surrounded by great lords of the land.

With this in mind, I was alarmed to be staying in a room directly next door, numbered Room 101. Was this the very room Richard stayed in? Was it here – behind closed doors – he practised speeches in the mirror, pulled on his hose and shaped that princely bob?

Room 101 was, indeed, fit for a king. We stretched and settled into a gripping episode of *Midsomer Murders* ('The Sting of Death', about a deadly hive of bees). The beds proved to be immensely comfortable, and the cup of tea – untainted by the metallic flavourings of a flask – was one of the greatest I had ever known.

What a day! Nine hours and thirty-six minutes of walking, 27.84 miles covered, 57,764 steps, four medieval biscuits and seven cups of tea. But there were pressing questions as I clambered into bed that night.

First, the disaster of the sodden boots was resolved by Mum's careful planning: she had brought a spare pair, which were brand new. But wasn't it a cardinal rambling sin to set off in not-yet-worn-in boots? Was I now vulnerable to an onslaught of dilapidating blisters?

Second, we were only one day in. Could I manage another 22 miles the following morning, and 20 more the next?

Such doubts were put away as I flicked through the local magazine, which informed me of the Lincolnshire County Council motto. *Perseverantia vincit*, it read: 'Perseverance succeeds'.

5. BREAKDOWN ON THE B1176

'Love is the longing for the half of ourselves we have lost.'
Milan Kundera

THE FOLLOWING MORNING BROUGHT AN unexpected challenge. We had transformed overnight into two automatons, only able to move in mechanical jolts. Every inch of our beings seemed to contort with aches and pains, making it impossible to complete the most basic task. All usual sense of weight, of balance, was gone. With shaking fingers, I reached down to tie my laces on the brand-new boots, only to stagger forward and bump my head on the desk in our room. At 5.55 a.m., we hobbled downstairs, taking each step one at a time, checked out and set off. The destination was Stamford, some 23 miles to the south. I opened the OS Maps app and we shuffled out into the sharp December air.

Towering over the town is a huge spire, belonging to St Wulfram's Church, where Eleanor's body most likely stayed the night. Remarkably, some elements of that original church survive – Saxon herringbone masonry and four piers of the Norman nave. Though much changed today, it is one of the largest and most impressive churches in the country, built of creamy Lincolnshire limestone. Simon Jenkins championed it as 'the finest steeple in England' at 84 metres – making it the sixth tallest in the country (cathedrals inclusive) and a celebrity among English churches. The artist J. M. W. Turner might well have agreed, given he painted St Wulfram's in watercolour in 1797. Did Mr Turner himself, as he paced up the nave and sat sketching in the churchyard, ever consider that Eleanor's funerary procession passed through this very spot?

St Wulfram's Church in Grantham.

The Eleanor Cross in Grantham is an elusive one, I'm afraid. After standing tall for more than 300 years, it was destroyed in the Civil War, in the 1640s. We don't even know where it stood. Some suppose on St Peter's Hill or in the current market square, where a new later cross stands and is said to contain some stones from the original.

But there was one small clue to Eleanor's presence here, so we set off down the high street in search of it. Along the way, we bumped into a few famous figures of Grantham's past. First, Sir Isaac Newton, immortalised in a fine bronze statue created in 1858. Newton – one of the most influential scientists of all time – lived in a countryside house nearby, Woolsthorpe Manor. It's well worth a visit – still there is an apple tree, a scion from the original, which was said to have inspired Newton's theories of gravity.

Metres away from Newton's statue is another esteemed Granthamite: Margaret Thatcher. It was here in Grantham that Margaret Roberts (as she was then known) spent her childhood. Her father, Alfred, owned a tobacconist's and grocery shop and, during her childhood, she briefly lived with a companion: in 1938, the Roberts family gave sanctuary to a teenage Jewish girl who had escaped Nazi Germany.

I wondered what Eleanor would have thought of this statue. Would she be heartened to see a woman taking the position of prime minister – the first with a science degree, and the longest serving of the twentieth century at that? They would have respected one another, I think, Eleanor and Margaret: both tough, determined women, equally unafraid to assert themselves in a man's world. No doubt Eleanor would wield a handbag with equal aplomb.

The nod to Eleanor's story is rather less grand. On the walls of Grantham Guildhall is a plaque, installed in 2015, with Eleanor and Edward's heads carved in stone. But on that December morning, it was barely visible. The Guildhall was covered in scaffolding, with several layers of fencing to keep the distance. 'That's it, over there, can you see?' I pointed. We were so far back, Mum had to put her glasses on to even locate it.

Still, it was good to see Eleanor again. This little clue was a friendly wave of encouragement, a cry of 'Well done! Keep going!' from others before us who had also made pains to commemorate Eleanor in years gone by.

The Eleanor plaque at Grantham Guildhall. Not a great view.

Still dark, we breakfasted at one of Grantham's finest early morning offerings, McDonald's. Alongside construction workers and lorry drivers, I chomped through three rashers of crispy bacon in a soft white roll and stirred my tea with a flimsy wooden stick. It was in the glow of the giant 'M' that I re-read St Thomas of Aquinas's prayer. 'Give me, O Lord, a steadfast heart' seemed more urgent than the previous morning. With 20-plus more miles to cover, the polite request was becoming a pressing demand.

For the medieval cortège, the route from Grantham to Stamford was an easy one. They travelled along the Great North Road. Today, this is the A1, which links Edinburgh to London. Here arises a problem for the modern pilgrim seeking to follow in the footsteps of our ancestors' past. When I planned the journey, I had hoped to follow the route of the cortège as closely as possible. This, however, was not always possible.

To follow the medieval route from Grantham to Stamford, you must walk along a dual carriageway. With the risk assessed – that risk being a high chance of being squashed by an HGV – we took a parallel route, adding on about 5 miles, through the villages of Burton-Le-Coggles, Swayfield, Creeton, Little Bytham, Careby and Ryhall.

Long shadows on the walk to Stamford.

Our shadows were long in the morning sun. We crossed mile after mile of cold, hard land, marked by dainty tracks of birds, hoofprints of early morning hackers and remnants of crops – carrots and parsnips, now the home of worms and maggots.

As you walk for hour after hour, your mind begins to wander in all sorts of strange ways. My stream of consciousness was off on a path of its own – thoughts ping-ponging from place to place like a constant refresh of What Three Words. I thought of a trip to Rome in 2013 . . . a scene from an episode of *The Vicar of Dibley* where Geraldine jumps in a puddle . . . an upcoming dentist appointment . . . should I get the oranges out of my backpack? . . . plans for the year ahead . . . whether those medieval travellers went through the same random stream of consciousness.

Among this, I constantly landed back at Eleanor. How mistaken it is, I thought, that the Eleanor Crosses – these memorials to her funerary procession, to her death – are how people tend to think of her. If anything, Eleanor was a woman of action, full of life.

So, while dipping my hand into a large bag of Tangfastics – a fizzy variety of the Haribo family – I considered this. If Eleanor were living and breathing, as you and I are now, and if she joined Mum and me on the walk, what would she be like?

First up, Mum and I would struggle to understand her, because Eleanor couldn't speak English. Her native language was Castilian Spanish (known as 'Castellano'). As Queen of England, she would have also spoken in Anglo-Norman French, which – since the Norman Conquest – was the dominant language of the English court. But please, suspend your disbelief for a moment – not that I am chatting with a medieval queen, but something far more astonishing: that I have finally mastered conversational French.

As Eleanor spent much of her life on the road, travelling about Europe on horseback, she'd have a good sense of direction and little patience for dawdlers. Wearing a simple belted gown and hooded cape, she'd immediately take control, setting a rapid pace: 'Keep up, Alice, and tell your Lady Mother the same!'

As we walked and birds soared high above and hares bounded across the fields, perhaps Eleanor would tell me of her love of falconry. This was a prestigious medieval sport, where trained birds of prey were used to the hunt wild animals. Though Eleanor would have found the landscape unfamiliar (in medieval times, it was far more open), she would have no doubt been delighted by the hedgerows we walked alongside, with their crimson hawthorn berries and rambling tendrils of ivy.

For one of Eleanor's true passions – the subject she could host a multi-episode podcast on – was gardening. This was a woman who would be a religious attendee of the Chelsea Flower Show. She'd visit on the members day and make assiduous notes about drainage systems and repotting techniques, leaving with a handbag full of David Austin catalogues.

You can get a good sense of the kind of gardens Eleanor developed at 'Queen Eleanor's Garden' at Winchester Great Hall. A re-creation of a medieval garden, it features a fountain adorned with bronze leopard heads and a falcon, a camomile lawn, a tunnel arbour, stone seats and bay hedges. It is a peaceful, tranquil spot – easy to imagine Eleanor's velvet robes sweeping past the herbs.

Perhaps, as we climbed over stiles and I offered Eleanor a Tangfastic ('Pray, what is this tart fruit?'), she would tell me about her latest projects. 'Lots going on at the moment. At Kings Langley in Hertfordshire, I've got some gardeners from Aragon – they're digging wells, planting apple trees; there are water gardens, cloisters, a summerhouse, you name it . . .'

Then there were the gardens at the Palace of Westminster. 'You two will have to come and see it,' she might have insisted, 'there's a lead-lined pond with running water, filled by pipes from the river.' As well as introducing the delights of water features and Arabic-style courtyards, Eleanor is thought to have introduced several new plant varieties: cooking pears, sweet rocket, wallflower and lavender.

Thinking of Eleanor in her later life, you get the sense she wasn't dissimilar to our current Queen Camilla. A lover of horses and country sports, always in riding gear and passionate about the outdoors. She was a tomboy at heart – hands rugged and rough from years outside and in the saddle; hair always a little out of place; cheeks pink, having been buffeted by the elements.

When meeting Eleanor, I expect I'd find her intimidating, oozing power and confidence. Everything she said would be effort-lessly cool: 'These old boots? I got these when I was in Acre, on Crusade,' or: 'Sorry I can't come to the girls' get-together, I'm reburying the bones of King Arthur that night.'

The history books tend to remember Eleanor in her role as Queen – her professional she-wolf persona. But peel this away and we see a different woman. For those who worked in her household, she was thoughtful and kind. There are examples of her paying for medical treatment for staff, giving leave if family members were ill and attending servants' weddings as a great mark of respect. A touching insight comes when her laundress, Alice Wisman, was so moved by Eleanor's death that she directly petitioned Edward to make arrangements for a chaplain to chant for Eleanor's soul.

By all accounts, Eleanor was also a good laugh. She employed two fools, Robert and Thomas, who were kind of in-house stand-up comics, and rewarded them handsomely, once gifting Thomas a horse and Robert's wife a pricey fur robe. The house-hold was not a particularly pious, serious space and the seasons were marked by great tournaments, weddings and parties. On one occasion, in Wales, the royal court were dancing so vigorously the floor gave way – a dedication to the party I can only aspire to.

Though Eleanor spent most of her life in practical clothes, there were moments of glamour. Take, for example, her coronation, when she was thirty-three years old. On 18 August 1274, not long after returning from Crusade, Edward and Eleanor made a triumphal entry into London along a 3-mile procession route via Cheapside, St Paul's and the Strand, ending at Westminster Abbey – the same route that Eleanor's funeral cortège would pass along sixteen years later. The streets were lined with swags of luxurious fabrics and the conduits (essentially a kind of drinking fountain) flowed with free wine.

The following day – Coronation Day – was one of shimmering spectacle. Arriving at the newly built Westminster Abbey, Edward and Eleanor dazzled in flowing robes and processed under a silk canopy held up with silver lances. A huge stage was built in the centre of the abbey, large enough to ride under on horseback. Here, Edward made his due promises – to protect the Church, uphold justice and suppress evil. They were anointed with holy oil and crowned – golden lilies for Eleanor and the crown of Edward the Confessor for her husband.

It was the kind of event that would send today's royal correspondents into a frenzy of speculation. Eleanor and Edward were the golden couple of Europe. Now in their early thirties, having overcome the disruption of the Second Barons' War and with a crusading trip under their belt, their reign represented a new chapter of peace and prosperity. Their young children, little Henry and Eleanor, were also present, dressed in new robes for the occasion.

The coronation service was followed by an enormous feast, for thousands. The preparations had begun the previous winter and new kitchens built for the purpose. More than 20,000 capons and hens, 500 oxen and 500 sheep and swine were acquired. Instructions went out across the land, to bishops, abbots and priors, to catch as many peacocks, rabbits and swans as they could. Salmon, eels and pike were also served.

During the feast, the King of Scotland and six leading English earls presented themselves to Edward on horseback, each with perhaps 100 knights, before dismounting and setting their horses free – prizes to whomever could catch them.

And what of her darling beau, Prince – then King – Edward? For many people today, Edward I conjures up an image of the one-dimensional Hollywood villain. The cold-hearted, ruthless, warmongering tyrant depicted with chilling wickedness by Patrick McGoohan in *Braveheart*.

Surprise, surprise, the film is more fiction than fact. When we consider Edward – as is the case with any figure from history – it is imperative to measure him by the expectations and standards of the time, as any of us would expect to be judged by the values of 2025, not those of 2725, whatever they may be.

When contemporary expectations of kingship are properly considered, Edward was an exceptional, heroic warrior king. Soon after his death, he was hailed by an English chronicler as 'the worthiest knight of all the world in his time' – and many subjects would have heartily agreed. To the medieval mind, one of his crowning achievements was in 1296–97 and 1304–06, when he ruled over the entire British Isles. It was a feat no monarch had achieved, except the legendary King Arthur, and a command none enjoyed again until the seventeenth century.

Today, historians consider Edward to be a canny, reforming

politician who provided stability after the chaotic civil wars of his father's reign. He introduced new coinage to restore confidence in English traders. He tackled corruption. He reshaped England's legal system, earning the nickname of 'The English Justinian'.

Perhaps his greatest legacy was the foundations of parliamentary governance – the origins of Britain's modern democracy. On the basis of Magna Carta, if the King wanted to raise money through taxation, he needed Parliament's permission. But Parliament in the reign of Edward's father was still a small group of favoured barons and bishops – many of them French – who met for informal discussions (the word comes from the French *parlement*, meaning 'parley' or 'conversation'). Many English nobles – not included in this chummy inner circle – still felt ignored (cue the Barons' Wars).

So as soon as Edward came to power, he grasped the parliamentary nettle. He addressed the imbalance and diluted the power of the barons by making Parliament more representative of the country. Echoing the principle of Roman law, that 'what touches all should be approved by all', Parliament was opened up to include – alongside bishops and barons – the riff-raff: town burgesses, knights and clergy from every cathedral and diocese in the country.

An historic moment! The first parliament was summoned in April 1275, just eight months after Edward's coronation, and regular sessions were held, twice a year, in spring and autumn. In these great gatherings, new laws and taxes were discussed, while Edward heard local grievances and petitions. It became accepted that the representatives of those most affected by taxation – the ordinary people who had to cough up – had to give their consent to it in Parliament. As such, here lay the early foundations for political accountability.

Though this might all seem like a bit of a history lesson, it was ideas such as these – re-writing the principles of Parliament, royal prerogative – that Edward would have discussed with Eleanor, for hour after hour, year on year, in the privacy of their own rooms: 'Darling, do you think I'm being too heavy-handed with this new wool tax? The parliament was pretty unhappy about it all today . . .' It was in these moments of conversation – perhaps lying together in bed – that Eleanor acted as Edward's confidante and advisor and formed the rock upon which his reign was built.

But there are two sides to every coin. Edward may have been a reforming hero to some, but today's historians also recognise that he ruled with ruthlessness, expelling the Jewish people and brutally crushing the Welsh and Scots. For those he suppressed, their animosity is unsurprising and valid. For the Scots, he 'troubled the whole world by his wickedness and roused it by his cruelty'. Even within England, he was by no means perfect. For one, he left his son facing crippling debts. He could also be hot-headed and arrogant.

'Edward has sometimes been characterised by historians as an autocrat,' writes Dr Andy King in his short guide to Edward I, but 'a degree of autocracy is inherent in the very nature of medieval kingship'. When looking at England's story across the Middle Ages, Edward I comes closest to the medieval ideal of a monarch.

It's important to remember that Edward's story didn't end at Eleanor's death. She was only present in the first half of his reign. Edward ruled for seventeen more years, during which came the wars in Scotland and the uprising led by William Wallace. Plus, in 1299, Edward married once more, to Margaret of France, a political arrangement as part of the deal for peace. But Queen

Eleanor still had a presence: one of Margaret's daughters was named Eleanor, in honour of the late Queen.

Physically, Edward's defining feature was being very tall. In the 1200s, the average height of men in Europe was 5 feet 7 inches (170 cm) – but Edward's stature, at 6 feet 2 inches (188 cm), earned him the sobriquet 'Edward Longshanks', meaning 'Long Legs' – a nickname used in his lifetime. Incidentally, if he were alive today, Edward would stand precisely eye to eye with Henry Cavill, the hunky British actor known for playing Superman.

A kind of Superman is a good way to think of Edward, for contemporary chroniclers described him as a man 'of elegant form and commanding stature, standing head and shoulders above the common people'. He was built to be a brilliant fighter: 'no one was more apt to the use of the sword, which he wielded with wiry vigour', and 'the length of his legs kept him from being unseated by the jumping and galloping of the most spirited horses'. He had a wide brow and – like his father – one drooping eye. He also spoke with a lisp.

Edward's fighting skills were put to heroic use during the Second Barons' War – the civil war that unfolded in Edward and Eleanor's early marriage – and Prince Edward became a hero, saving his father's crown by fighting against treasonous rebels.

So, as a young man, he was the ultimate catch. He was hot. He was valiant. He was everything a prince should be. Jilly Cooper would have had a field day. You can picture the steamy scenes after a tournament . . . Prince Edward jumping down from his stallion, face ruddy, flinging his breastplate aside . . . *cue 'Careless Whisper'* . . . Perhaps it's no surprise Eleanor was pregnant at least sixteen times, often with only a couple of months between each. Things were clearly going well in the bedroom department.

Yet all of this makes it even more striking – more sad – to

consider Edward in December 1290. The lonely, fifty-one-year-old man, struggling with the shock of his wife's death as he travelled alongside her body in a box. And, though King Edward was well trained at putting on a brave face and no stranger to seeing death first hand, inside he was in shock, tormented with grief.

In the century before Eleanor died, the Benedictine monk William of Malmesbury wrote about grief. He acknowledged some basic characteristics: 'it knows no limit' and 'is ignorant of a steady course'. He wrote about the turbulence within the mind: 'For just as a grieving spirit thinks on many things, so speech – the mind's interpreter – keeps turning through many things.' But he also personified grief as an active, living force, with no limit, no order, in fact, no quantifiable aspect at all – so we shouldn't be surprised to not make sense of it.

I'm sure Edward and his daughters, and many people today, would relate to what William of Malmesbury described. As Edward travelled from Lincoln to London, carried by his horse, he must have faced a tsunami of emotions: unpredictable and powerful bouts of sadness, anger, loneliness, confusion, numbness. Sometimes grief would lie low, but other times it would rear its head – and at the most unexpected moments. All of this would continue in the months and years ahead. It was a burden he would only escape in death itself.

Ten miles down and we were staggering. It seemed a never-ending landscape of ploughed fields as we stamped off huge clods of heavy clay mud, only to collect more in the next field. We clambered through gates, skidded over slippy wooden footbridges and extracted ourselves from brambles. We couldn't stop – even for a minute – or our muscles would seize up once more and make it even harder to continue.

Very muddy.

In and out of railway bridges we weaved, under huge brick arches. All the while, we could hear and see the trains whizzing back and forth to London. What torment it was! To think of our fellow travellers in the comfort of a LNER carriage, sipping on tea and eating shortbread biscuits. How warm and cosy they seemed – and covering the miles in a matter of minutes.

As well as my mum, there was another hero without whom I would be lost: the Ordnance Survey map. Most people know them as physical paper maps, which fold out like a newspaper. I can remember drawing the symbols in a geography lesson. Green dash line for a footpath, pink line for an A road and blue line for a motorway. A square with a cross indicates a church with a tower. A circle represents one with a spire.

But as a modern, Gen-Z hiker, embracing the digital age, I had converted to the app format on my phone – which is rather less unwieldy in high winds. Most helpfully, it shows your live location, which is an immense help when standing in the corner of a strangely shaped field zig-zagged with footpaths.

Ordnance Survey maps – better known as OS maps – have long been a staple of the British countryside, stashed away in glove pockets and boot rooms in preparation for muddy days out. Their origins, however, are far more secretive. They were originally created as an arm of military strategy, mapping the Scottish Highlands following the Jacobite rebellion in 1745. Later, as French Revolution and then the Napoleonic Wars kicked off and France threatened invasion, the government ordered its defence ministry of the time – the Board of Ordnance – to begin a survey of England's vulnerable southern coasts. If invasion took place, Britain would be far better prepared for moving troops and planning campaigns.

The first Ordnance Survey map was published in 1801. It depicted Kent, which was most vulnerable to French invasion. The maps were engraved 'in reverse' on copper plate and then printed. In these early maps, even place names were a point of contention and locals would dispute which name was correct. A Name Book system was introduced: every variant name for rivers, hills, villages and towns was recorded in a series of books. From this selection, one was chosen, which became the official name.

It was during the twentieth century that these map-making skills were put to greater use. During the First World War, staff from Ordnance Survey were posted overseas, plotting the lines of trenches. By the end of the war, Ordnance Survey had completed 20 million maps for the war effort. By 1945, at the close of the Second World War, 342 million maps had been produced. Today, all 243,241 square kilometres of Great Britain are surveyed, with up to 20,000 changes to the maps made daily.

But what about in the medieval period? Were our medieval ancestors on horseback, wrestling with a fold-out map, which blew about their faces as they galloped along Ermine Street? The few maps that survive were created for academic study and reference, not as pocket maps to be flipped open, on location, by wandering travellers.

One of these, which Eleanor might have been aware of, was created by Matthew Paris, the Benedictine monk based at St Albans. The map is an addition to his writing, 'A Brief Abridgement of the Chronicles of England', and dates from the 1250s.

Here, Britain is reduced to a strange blob with wobbly edges, resembling something like a jellied monster. Within it are 250 place names – including eighty cathedrals and monasteries, forty-one castles and at least thirty ports, as well as major mountains and rivers. Paris included depictions of both Hadrian's Wall ('the wall once separating the English and the Picts') and the Antonine Wall further north ('the wall once dividing the Scots and the Picts'). Lincoln, Grantham and Stamford feature – though, surprisingly, these are located close to Salisbury.

Towards the end of the fourteenth century, the Gough Map was created, which is perhaps the closest we get to a medieval A–Z road atlas. Its origins, including the cartographer who made it, are unknown, but it is named after an early owner, Richard Gough, who bequeathed the map to the Bodleian Library in Oxford in 1809. It shows Britain with a web of connected towns, to be read in a similar way to the London Underground map. To get to Edinburgh, say, you might take the road to Lincoln, then take the road to York.

Travelling in the medieval period was not for the introvert. It required a lot of asking directions, following the guidelines of roads, paths, rivers and valleys, or paying for a local guide to take you to the next town. Though some stretches of the roads might be empty for miles, there were all kinds of people you might bump into: messengers, pilgrims, merchants, beggars, preachers, soldiers, women and children walking to work. You might use the sun and stars as a compass. You might follow a road until a certain land-mark: 'Turn left at the great oak, then cross the ford and follow the valley.'

Travellers of the thirteenth century faced all kinds of road conditions. There were about 10,000 miles of roads in the network in England. After the departure of the Romans around AD 410, few major roads were built until the 1700s, when private compa-nies called turnpike trusts were authorised by Acts of Parliament to build, maintain and operate toll roads, largely driven by indus-trial growth.

As they were used by the King, the major roads were often well maintained. But they could still fall into disuse. Some stretches were deeply rutted from wheels. Sometimes routes were totally unmarked, save the occasional stone pointer. To reduce the chances of attacks from outlaws, all highways were supposed to be cleared on both sides of trees and undergrowth for a distance of 200 feet. The exception to this was the large oaks, as these were valuable for buildings and ships.

Not all major towns had Roman origins and, as such, weren't connected to a major road – such as Oxford, Coventry, Plymouth and the whole of Cornwall (Exeter was the furthest west the Romans settled). So travellers to these towns would come off the medieval motorway and join local networks.

There were all kinds of roads you might pass through. Drovers' roads, for droving livestock to market or moving them between summer and winter pasture, were wide, unsurfaced tracks, fenced, hedged or walled on both sides. There were also portways (linking towns to ports), cartways (used by carts) and packhorse routes, while monastic roads connected monasteries to their estates.

Corpse roads or lychways were paths used to carry the dead to a church for burial, where the bodies would wait in the lychgate (the 'lych' comes from Old English and means 'body'). These were usually found in remote areas like the Lake District, with low population density, and yet this route of Eleanor's cortège is, I suppose, a very long lychway.

You can often trace historic tracks by the names of the towns and villages that connect them. Placenames with 'way', 'drove', 'gate' (meaning road), 'stretton' (meaning street), 'bridge' or 'ford' indicate there was already a route established when the town developed.

But it was crossing rivers and streams that proved to be the main obstacle for a medieval traveller. In prosperous market towns, you might expect stone bridges, able to bear the weight of the thousands of carts crossing them every year. Old London Bridge was completed in 1209 (lasting until 1831), Old Exe Bridge in Exeter in 1214. These towns had tolls, too: as a traveller, you might have to pay pontage (to cross a bridge), murage (to keep up the town walls) or pavage (to pave the street).

Outside such metropolises, most bridges in the medieval period were simple wooden structures, lasting only a generation or so before they collapsed. The responsibility for their building and upkeep lay with the lord of the manor – the likes of Richard de Weston. Sometimes there was no bridge at all and travellers would find the road disappear into the river. If they were lucky, stepping stones or a rudimentary clapper bridge (formed from a succession of flat stone slabs, placed on piles of stones) might help them over. Fun for today's walkers to prance across in sunny weather, but precariously slippery for the medieval traveller wearing leather sandals in wet weather.

Though we didn't face the difficulties of a medieval traveller, there was a toll of a different kind. Morale was at an all-time low. My body ached. My resolution was waning, my enthusiasm curbing. This was no longer a pleasant stroll. This was hour after hour of long, hard trudging that never seemed to end.

As I climbed one particularly boggy slope, there were distinct overtones of *Lord of the Rings*. I – with the Edward I penny swinging around my neck – played the part of feverish Frodo, burdened with the One Ring. Mum – as she heroically offered the last drops of water – was Sam. On and on we went, this never-ending traipse through Mordor. Perhaps Mum would soon be carrying me and throwing out lines like: 'It's all wrong! By rights we shouldn't even be here, but we are!'

After eight hours of walking, there was still (still!) some seven miles to cover. We stopped at the side of a road. 'You can get a taxi, if you like, I won't mind,' I said to Mum – which she firmly declined.

Was this a fool's errand? To come out here and walk 200 miles in December weather, with no training? Was all of this madness? In the days leading up to the walk, several people had queried whether I would make it. I had shrugged off their doubts. And those doubts had been meaningless, until now – this moment of weakness, at 3.32 p.m., as I stood in the rain on the side of the B1176, chewing a Percy Pig. I began to wonder if they had been right.

Would we make it to Stamford? And would I be able to keep this going for the next ten days? I thought of St Thomas of Aquinas's words – 'give me an unconquered heart, which no tribulation can wear out'. Was this a tribulation too far?

But it wasn't just the walking. I felt a pang of guilt that I had dragged Mum all this way, promising the wonders of a medieval pilgrimage. And yet all we'd looked at so far was a plaque that she was too short to see.

'Come on, we better get going,' Mum said. My mood was low – very low – as we continued onwards, but there was nothing for it but to press on. As the night drew in, the rain fell hard and heavy and our faces were battered by whistling winds. I took comfort in the thought that Edward would have probably endured such weather, wrapping a thick cloak tight, head down, pushing his horse forward.

I cowered over my phone to read the map and we plodded through ever boggier fields. At one point I looked back – Mum was some distance away, her torchlight barely visible in the sideways rain. 'Keep going, Mum!' I yelled, unsure if she could hear me.

Despite all this, I began to settle into the simplicity of walking. There was no real technique, no game plan. I went into a zombie-like state, the physical equivalent of spending days in the library before university finals. All that's required is to keep going. Place one foot in front of the other. Again and again. However bad the weather was or however rough the terrain. Just. Keep. Going. I wondered if the travellers of Eleanor's cortège gave each other this advice: 'That's it, dear, one step after another, not long now.'

Do this simple action some 50,000 times and the cumulative result is immense. After ten hours of miserable, grinding slog, it was hard to believe we had arrived. Finally, I could enjoy the view I had been dreaming of: to look down at my feet and see my muddy boots firmly on the ground of . . . oh joy! . . . a Stamford pavement!

In that moment, standing in the dark streets, I felt I shared a moment with the medieval walker, with those people who walked in Eleanor's cortège. Across the ages we stood shoulder to sodden shoulder. Together, we breathed a sigh of relief and patted each other on the back, saying, 'Well done, old (very old) friend!'

The endeavour was worth it, for Stamford is one of the loveliest towns in England, steeped in history. It sits on the banks of the River Welland, with lanes of honey-coloured stone. In 1290, it was one of the ten largest towns in England, home to a castle, fourteen churches and four friaries. The wealth came from wool, England's most important trade. Stamford was particularly famous for haberget, a woven cloth known for a 'broken diamond' or 'broken lozenge' twill. As Eleanor's cortège arrived in Stamford, they might well have seen the merchants at work, organising cartloads of wool to be transported along the Great North Road or taken away by water on the Welland.

Later in 1333, a disgruntled bunch of Oxford students arrived in Stamford. Fed up with the 'many controversies, contests and fights' of their colleges, they attempted to set up a rival university: the University of Stamford. Horrified at this fracture, Oxford University began to petition King Edward III, describing the 'evil, which we think every way hurtful and pestilential, namely, the new assembly of scholars at the town of Stamford for university instructions', and appealing that 'what was begun by improvident rashness may be quickly put an end to by the royal wisdom, and be a warning to future evil-doers'.

After two years, the unruly scholars were ordered to return to Oxford. Because of this, for 500 years – until 1827 – students at Oxford were required to swear by the Stamford Oath: 'You shall also swear that you will not read lectures, or hear them read, at Stamford, as in a University study or college general'.

It was also in Stamford that King Charles I stayed in the troublesome Civil War year of 1646. Disguised as a servant, he was hidden in a house in Stamford town, then left to join up with the Scottish army – only to be betrayed and handed over to the Parliamentarians. It was at Stamford, therefore, that King Charles spent his last night as a free man. He was executed three years later, in 1649.

Without a doubt, however, the greatest name connected to Stamford – by all metrics – is Daniel Lambert, who found fame exhibiting himself as the heaviest man in England. Despite having a normal diet, Lambert was enormous, weighing a colossal 52 stone 11 lbs (or 335 kg). Though born in Leicester, he was visiting Stamford races when he suddenly died on 21 June 1809 and was buried in nearby St Martin's Church.

This was no small operation. Lambert died in an inn and, to remove his body, a window and part of a wall had to be dismantled. The coffin – made of more than 100 square feet of wood – had wheels fitted and required 'upwards of twenty men' to lower it down a sloping ramp into the grave. Even Eleanor of Castile didn't have that honour.

Lambert's tombstone – which can be found in St Martin's Church, in Stamford – reads as follows:

> *In Remembrance of that PRODIGY in NATURE*
> *DANIEL LAMBERT a Native of Leicester:*
> *who was possessed of an exalted and convivial Mind,*
> *and in personal Greatness had no COMPETITOR:*
> *He measured three Feet one Inch round the LEG,*
> *nine Feet four Inches round the BODY,*
> *and weighed FIFTY TWO STONE ELEVEN POUNDS.*
> *He departed this Life*
> *on the 21st of June 1809:*
> *Aged 39 years*

The Crown Hotel was our lodgings for the night, located a stone's throw from the market square and opposite All Saints' Church. What a blessed relief it was to sit on the front step and – with shaking hands – untie our sodden laces and remove damp socks.

We hobbled to the desk in giddy happiness, passing guests sipping on cocktails in sparkling dresses and fur coats, then spent an hour stretching, bathing and enjoying the complimentary biscuits. Downstairs, we joined the Christmas throng and carb-loaded on a delicious mac and cheese. Revived by such luxuries, I spent the evening tucking into some local reading material: *Stamford Living*.

Stamford, it turns out, is a *scene*. The major feature for December 2024 was a piece on bell-ringing and I read all about the cheerful bell-ringers of St Mary's Church – the 'Greetham Clangers' – who were preparing for the Christmas season.

Of course, bell-ringing is another way of keeping history alive. The peal of bells have long sounded across the English countryside, dating from a period when people didn't have clocks or watches – before we used the phrase 'o'clock'. The toll of a bell might mark moments in the calendar (such as harvest) as well as the day – signalling the time to start and finish work, as well as the break for lunchtime.

'It's not an easy task and it takes time,' Alan Ellis, campanology (the technical name for bell-ringing) teacher, explained in the article. Apparently, the trick to it is not about strength, but learning to keep the bell balanced. There are six bells for the Greetham team to ring, each to remember the six villagers who died in the First World War. The practice sessions are often followed up by tea, cake or a trip to the pub – and romance, it seems: 'You'd be surprised how many married couples are together through bell-ringing,' Alan notes.

Next in *Stamford Living* was a piece on a local gin company: 'Multum Gin Parvo' – a clever pun on the Rutland county motto, *Multum In Parvo*, meaning 'Much in Little' (Rutland is England's smallest county). There was a piece about Peterborough School, which showcased some fine green and red blazers, then some recommendations for local traditions to embrace, including the Hallaton Bottle Kicking and Hare Pie Scrambling, survivors of the ancient football games of England.

The final page was an amusing interview with 'Uppingham's Mr Music', a retired superstar music teacher, Dick Smart, also an ex-RAF pilot, competent apart from one flaw: 'he could never land the damn planes'. Smart was a fine cricketer, too: 'On one occasion he took six wickets for only twelve runs against a clergy team, including a hat-trick where all three of his victims were bishops!'

Heartened by reading about the good folk of Stamford, I concluded this would be a very nice place to live. I could see my life stretching out ahead – house on the high street in Stamford, a bell-ringing husband, evenings drinking Multum Gin Parvo . . . perhaps I was becoming delirious.

Our step count that day had been immense, after all: a whopping 54,179 steps. In the end, factoring in a couple of re-routes, we'd covered 25.85 miles, walking for ten hours and fifteen minutes at an average speed of 2.6 mph. Tomorrow would bring much of the same: another 20 miles to cover, to a little village called Geddington.

But hopes were up, for Geddington held something thrilling to look forward to. Waiting for me there was an original, beautifully preserved Eleanor Cross.

6. A GEDDINGTONIAN
WELCOME

'Our respect for the dead, when they are just dead,
is something wonderful, and the way we show
it more wonderful still.'
John Ruskin

WHEN I STEPPED OUT INTO the darkness on the morning of
Friday 6 December, I ventured out alone. As planned, Mum wasn't
joining me on the third day, so I left her snoozing in the Crown
Hotel. She had earned it, that's for sure.

It was 6 a.m. and, at this early hour, the people of Stamford
were asleep, their curtains drawn. The silent streets were only
disturbed by the soft tread of my footsteps and an unearthly gust
of gentle wind. Perhaps this was what Percy Bysshe Shelley meant
when he wrote about the 'chilling sound' of moonlit winter nights:
'From caves of ice and fields of snow/The breath of night like
death did flow'. Or perhaps – as we learned earlier – it was because
his heart was made of actual stone.

The Eleanor Cross in Stamford was located outside the town, on
the Casterton Road. Before the cross was destroyed during the tumult
of the Civil War, it stood for 350 years. Captain Richard Symonds

of the Royalist army, who travelled through the town on 23 August 1645, recorded it in his diary: 'On the hill before you come into the towne stands a lofty large crosse' – though his understanding of history was confused – 'built by Edward III, in memory of Elianor his queene, whose corps were here, coming from the north.'

The following year it crops up again, in the survey of Stamford of 1646, written by Richard Butcher, the town clerk. Butcher recorded 'an ancient crosse of free stone'. By this time, the cross was in a ruinous state: 'envious time hath so defaced' the cross, he wrote, 'that only the ruins appeare to my eye and therefore not to be described by my pen'.

A century later, in January 1746, William Stukeley wrote to a friend, lamenting the cross was one of many pulled down by the 'reforming rabble' of the Civil War years: 'Their wretched folly robbed the nation of these beautiful monuments.' But all was not lost, as Stukeley reported with excitement: 'On the Saturday before Christmas, one surveyor of the turnpike road opened a tumulus half a mile north of Stamford, on the brow of a hill by the road-side, and there, to our great pleasure, we discovered the foundation of Queen's cross.'

An excavation began and the site revealed a hexagonal base – 'the measure of each side 13 foot – and a beautiful fragment: 'a carved stone belonging to the pinnacle-work at the top, adorned with roses'. This rose feature, now in Stamford Museum, formed the inspiration for a modern revival.

The damage of the Civil War was undone as a new – albeit rather more modern – Eleanor Cross was erected in Sheepmarket, a small triangular clearing. Designed by the fabulously named artist Wolfgang Buttress, who specialises in outdoor sculpture and installations, and made of local Ketton stone, this enormous needle is carved with a repeating spiral pattern of roses (echoing the original fragment) and tapers into an extremely pointy bronze spike. A no-go zone for hot-air balloons.

It was on that eerie morning that I visited this enormous needle. I put my hand to the cold, rough surface and looked up at the beautiful carpet of roses, the flowers Eleanor so loved. What would Edward think to know that, more than 700 years after Eleanor's death, new monuments were being built in her memory? In that moment, connected to this waypoint of love – and reminded of all the people who remembered Eleanor over the centuries – I didn't feel quite so alone.

The new Eleanor Cross in Sheepmarket, Stamford.

Then it was down a steep hill, skirting stone walls, passing a small jumble of houses, and minutes later I was into the wild town meadows. This is a magical land. Here, in springtime, the sweet-scented white flowers of elder fill the hedgerows, transforming to blue-black berries in the autumn. Here, metallic green damselflies dart, with their fluttering pale green wings. The eagle-eyed among us might spot the five-toed footprints of otters or a flash of colour as a kingfisher dives for a fish.

But in the ghostly December dark, such delights were only imaginings. Guided by the yellow spotlight of my headtorch and gripping the fencing tight, I followed the route of the millstream – a flow of water that was mentioned in the Domesday Book of 1086.

This was perilous. The paths were slippery; one wrong foot would see me flying into the black water below, with no one around to hear the splash. I would be found in the morning as a Banksy-style Ophelia: hair tangled among the reeds, fingers trapped in ice, headtorch flickering sadly.

Then came the forbidding underpass of the A1. After scanning it with my headtorch, I stepped into the dank darkness. A walk soon quickened to a scamper, then a half-run, which continued until I was a good deal clear. Next, I came to a railway track and a big sign that insisted I 'Stop Look Listen'. After diligently stopping, looking left and right and standing still to listen, I carefully walked across. I then continued along the route of the Jurassic Way, a long-distance footpath that follows an ancient ridgeway.

I passed All Saints' Church at Easton on the Hill, then Collyweston. At 7.30 a.m., the sun's long rays stretched across the misty skies and I turned the torch off. Day was with me once more. How pretty the cream-coloured cottages looked, with their Collyweston slate roofs, in the soft morning light. There were endless curiosities: a fifteenth-century priest house, leafless trees with tiny apples clinging on, a wide valley that was once the site of an Augustinian priory. I was reminded once again that the remnants of our ancestors' lives are all around – if you only take time to look.

Friday 6 December was the most beautiful of all the days I walked. The sky was blue and clear, the air cold and crisp. An extra blessing came in the form of a friend, Laura, who joined me on the saunter. An ex-army officer now confined to a London desk, she was thrilled to escape to the countryside. The last time I'd seen her was an interrailing adventure the previous year, sharing a bunk bed in a selection of Europe's cheapest hostels – a great test of friendship, if ever there was one.

Laura is an enthusiast, always eager to learn. As it transpired, there was rather a lot to learn. 'So tell me about this Eleanor,' she chirped, as we climbed over a gatepost, 'Princess of Aquitaine.' This prompted my sharp retort of 'Castile! Eleanor of Castile!'

Once we established which Eleanor we were on about, I gave Laura a run-down of her life. 'So, by my age, twenty-nine years old,' she chimed in, 'Eleanor was married, had children, survived a civil war and was about to go on Crusades? And I still can't decide on a career!'

A couple of miles into the jaunt, Laura's tactical training from army days came into play as we were confronted by an alarming adversary: a large herd of cows, bearing enormous, pointed horns. These were the English Longhorn and they were unnervingly interested in us as we peered back at them across the gate.

Laura and I considered the magnificent beasts that stood in our way. Should we cross the field or take another route? Was this herd a serious threat or did we have lily-livered resolve? With military logic, Laura began weighing up the potential outcome of contact with one of those pointed horns – would it merely pierce your body or spear you all the way through?

This mind-mapping immediately clarified my thinking. Calculating that I was probably the weaker of the two, I preferred not to put Darwin's theories of natural selection to the test. A diversion was required. We bade good day to the Longhorns and walked away along the lane, re-joining another cow-free field half a mile later.

At 10 a.m., we crossed a beautiful stone bridge – Blatherwycke Bridge. On that fine December day, the world felt an oasis of calm. Any aches and pains seemed less of a burden, being uplifted by the natural beauty that stretched out before us. The water shimmered in the low sun. Hundreds of geese flew up from the reeds, their flapping wings echoing far across the valley.

The bridge was built of limestone and has two cutwaters – triangular sections that protrude towards the stream, gently directing the water between the piers and giving pedestrians a refuge from oncoming traffic. As we stood in one of these cutwaters, gazing down into the trickling waters below, Laura whipped out a small rectangular package. I knew exactly what it was the instant I saw the flash of bright purple. 'Fruit and Nut?' she asked, breaking a chunk from the Dairy Milk bar.

The delights of Bulwick Village Shop. Heaven!

Not long after the chocolate stop, there were more confectionery delights. We came upon Bulwick Village Shop, an emporium of cakes, chutneys, sweets and – it seemed – pretty much anything you wanted. Paralysed by choice, we had the lot. Hot chocolate with cream. A bacon roll each. A mince pie to share. A bag of fudge for the road.

The obelisk at Deene Park.

The village was also home to an unusual circular stone building tucked in the side of the road. It had a conical roof with a ball finial, a large oak door and no windows. To our delight, this Round House was built in the eighteenth century to temporarily detain drunks overnight. Laura and I enjoyed imagining various friends waking up here. Or the early morning phone call: 'Mum, I'm really sorry, I'm in the Round House again, please can you come and pick me up?'

The route took us along the undulating Willow Brook valley, its ridges framed by wooded hills. We wound through parkland and stumbled upon a strange stone obelisk, topped with what appeared to be a genie's lamp. On closer inspection, we found an inscription: 'HOC MONUMENTUM PARENTUM SUORUM MEMORIAE SACRUM POSUERUNT ANNO MM EB & MB'.

We were in the estate of Deene Park, a medieval manor that has developed over the centuries to become a fine stately home, with 100 rooms. It's been the home of the Brudenell family since 1514. Most famous of the ancestors was James Brudenell, the 7th Earl of Cardigan, who led the Charge of the Light Brigade at the Battle of Balaclava in 1854, during the Crimean War.

One recent owner was Edmund Brudenell. This man was quite a character. True to his British roots, Edmund was obsessed with tea. When travelling, he carried a small leather case, embossed with an earl's coronet and 'C' for Cardigan. Inside were his essential items – not documents or medical supplies, but a teapot and thermos, to provide a cup of tea at any given moment.

At Deene Park, which he spent a lifetime restoring, the dedication continued: topiary teapots ornamented the gardens, and the obelisk, it turned out, was topped with not the usual orb, nor a genie's lamp, as Laura and I had supposed, but a teapot.

As an avid tea drinker, I found this wholly commendable, and Laura and I poured a cup from the flask in solidarity.

The inscription on the obelisk translates to: 'THEY ESTABLISHED THIS MONUMENT SACRED TO THE MEMORY OF THEIR PARENTS IN THE YEAR 2000 EB & MB'. It was built to commemorate the millennium and another great stretch of time: the fifty-nine-year marriage of Edmund and Marian Brudenell, who died in 2013 and 2014.

I was struck, that – just a few miles from the Eleanor Cross – here was another tribute to love. Another marriage commemorated in stone. When building this obelisk, did the Brudenell family have the local Eleanor Cross in mind? Was this another flowering of Eleanor's legacy?

Four miles later, Laura and I found a perch in the form of a woodland log. Laura had brought a spectacular picnic lunch of which the Famous Five would heartily approve. Paper packages of ham sandwiches with thick bread, slices of Camembert and (a genius, but risky touch) a thick spread of Marmite. Luckily, I'm a lover, not a hater. Next, homemade flapjacks, the final chunks of the Dairy Milk and, of course, more tea.

But this sip of tea was a final moment of peace and tranquillity. No more were we bumbling through chocolate-box villages and sprawling parkland. We were on the outskirts of Corby, on kerbs and pavements of A roads, skirting around roundabouts and tracing the boundaries of vast building sites. It was, to put it frankly, less of a vibe.

The first thing to say about Corby is that it is nothing to do with the Corby trouser press (named after the man who invented it). But it still has a remarkable story. In 1931, Corby was a small village with around 1,500 inhabitants. Within a decade, it rapidly grew into an important industrial town, when the Glasgow-based steel firm Stewarts & Lloyds built a large ironstone and steel works. The first steel was produced in October 1935 and, by 1939, the population had boomed to 12,000.

Many were from Scotland, seeking employment after the decline of Clyde Valley's steel industry and, by 1961, a third of Corby's population had been born north of the border. As such, the town is sometimes referred to as 'little Scotland'.

Today, shops stock Scottish staples – square sausages, Bells Scotch Pies, Tennent's Lager, Buckfast (a fortified tonic wine that even the most formidable crusading king would struggle with). There are several highland dancing schools, and football fans support Rangers and Celtic.

'The pub doesn't do Sunday roasts,' one Scottish-born Corby resident explained in an interview in 2014, adding: 'The chip shop up the road will batter absolutely anything – Snickers, Mars Bars, pizzas, Creme Eggs, Chewits.' Presumably Edward Longshanks, too, if he had ever passed the threshold.

But it's Corby's consumption of Irn-Bru that is perhaps most striking – Asda Corby, for example, sells seventeen times more of Scotland's favourite fizzy orange drink than any other store in England. The *Northamptonshire Telegraph* reported in 2009: 'It's one of the stereotypes of Corby – an empty can of Irn-Bru rolling around on the street.'

After skirting around the roads of Corby (no empty cans in sight) and two more miles traversing the countryside, we descended through a large woodland area, which had a clearing to form a fine vista, complete with tall church spire. Suddenly, realising what lay ahead, I felt a pang of fluttering excitement.

After days of disappointment – staring into tarmac or squinting at a plaque through Heras fencing – I was finally on the approach to the real deal. With every step, I got closer to Eleanor. It was like she had been waiting for us for 700 years, and now – finally – the moment of reconciliation was imminent.

We were soon swallowed up between neat garden hedges and, before I knew it, the earthen path became concrete. There was an early clue in the housing estate: a signpost reading 'Queen Eleanor's Road'. Rounding a corner, we came upon an idyllic village scene. Sweet rows of cottages, a village pub and a medieval bridge crossing the stream.

And there it was: right in the heart of it all, soaring high into the sky, like a rocket about to shoot into space. An original Eleanor Cross, in all its glory. And perched halfway up, in a gabled niche, was a statue looking out towards me: I came face to face with Eleanor herself.

We were in the heart of Geddington village. It was mid-afternoon and flooded with young children skipping home after a day at the village school. Cries of 'See you tomorrow' were thrown across the square. These youngsters were full of beans: jumping, hopping and running across the steps. The Eleanor Cross was their playground. One boy stood at the highest step, hand in the air: 'I'm the statue of New York!' he proclaimed.

At the bottom is a set of seven steps that rise more than a metre up from the road surface. Not only does this give the cross great height, but it also provides an excellent spot to sit and watch the world go by.

Next is a triangular shaft, decorated with an intricate leaf-like pattern – perhaps a nod to Eleanor's love of gardens. This soaring tower is adorned with six shields – a pair on each of the three faces – which were originally coloured. Here, for centuries, the people of Geddington glanced up to see blue and gold diagonal stripes of Ponthieu, black lions of León, gold castles of Castile and red lions of England.

Above this are three sculptures of Eleanor, standing in gabled canopies. It is striking that each of the statues sits within a triangular niche, placing them behind a slender column. It means that Eleanor is partially disguised, forcing us to walk slowly around the monument to glimpse her face, her veil and coronet, the folds of her dress, which spill over her shoes. It is like a kaleidoscope – everywhere, Eleanor is watching from this triangular shape. Yet you only ever get a fleeting glimpse before she is obscured once more.

To top it all off are several metres of pinnacles and canopies, crushed together and soaring high. In total, it is 13.2 metres (43 feet) of beautiful stonework. The only part missing is the cross that once surmounted it, which has probably fallen off. This was probably about 3 metres in height, making the whole monument about 16 metres (52 feet) high.

As Laura and I sat on the steps of the Eleanor Cross, observing village life unfold, two young girls approached us. They were sisters, aged seven and five, waiting for their father to buy a hot chocolate from the pub. They were shy at first, then curiosity got the better of them. We were bombarded with questions. 'What's your name? Can you guess my name? Why are you wearing boots? Did you walk here? What's that? Why?'

I pulled out the OS Maps app and showed them the route, which took up 5 cm on my screen. 'When it's little on your phone,' the older girl observed, 'it doesn't look that long, but when you walk it's long.' Having just marched the 20 miles from Stamford, I confirmed that she was absolutely right.

Extraordinarily – in a twist I can hardly believe – the elder sister was called Reina, meaning 'queen' in Spanish. How curious that we should meet here, on the steps of Queen Eleanor's memorial, all these years later. I looked up to see Eleanor's face, carved in a statue – was this a sign, a message from Eleanor herself?

Like the cutwaters of the Blatherwycke Bridge, was she gently guiding me on my way?

Enjoying a drink on the steps of the Geddington Eleanor Cross!

Though Geddington is a small village today, this was once the site of a major royal hunting lodge, favoured by Plantagenet kings who enjoyed the sport of nearby Rockingham Forest, which, in medieval terms, was an area of woodland or open land with particular hunting rights.

Initially, the house – which was located just behind the church – was a large timber-framed building. Over the centuries, stone buildings were added – private chambers for the King and Queen, knights' lodgings, stables, mews and kennels.

It was a complex extensive enough to host the Great Council of the King, which gathered here first in 1177, and then – in the aftermath of the news that Jerusalem had fallen – in 1188, to levy a tax for another Crusade (which never took place). In 1194, Richard the Lionheart met William, King of Scotland here. It's quite something to walk around the little village today, to think of 'all the chief persons of the whole of England' – bishops, crusading knights, princes and a king – arriving in their finery to discuss affairs of state.

The importance of Geddington was reflected in the privileges granted. In the medieval period, holding markets required permission from the local lord or sometimes even the King, granted through a royal charter. On 28 November 1248, King Henry III decreed that 'at his manor at Geytinton, a market shall be held every Wednesday'. It was around this time the beautiful village bridge was constructed – a bridge with cutwaters that Eleanor would have crossed – which still stands strong all these years later.

Edward and Eleanor were familiar with Geddington and stopped off here many times. Perhaps this is unsurprising, for Eleanor and her family adored hunting. Some of her hunting lodges were vast – at Odiham in Hampshire, they had stabling for more than 200 horses. Here at Geddington were extensive kennels for the royal greyhounds and a mews for the royal falcons.

By all accounts, the rooms at Geddington manor were lavish. Great halls with stained glass, rooms painted green and spangled with gold and decorated with gilt shields. When it came to Eleanor's interior design tastes, she preferred a maximalist style. Her favourite colour scheme was red and green – whether for decorating rooms or adorning herself (she went for rubies and emeralds). Her private chambers were filled with bowls from Andalusia, cloth from Tripoli, vases from Venice, tapestries from Cologne and enamel caskets from Limoges. She ate with knives made of jasper and forks of ebony and ivory.

This brings us to another of Eleanor's great legacies. She was a cutlery pioneer, being the first person in England to be recorded using a fork. This was highly unusual for the day and didn't catch on. For centuries, rich and poor continued with good old English ways – picking up food with fingers or spearing it with a knife.

It wasn't until 1611 that the fork was first referenced in English literature and, even then, with great suspicion. The travel writer Thomas Coryat mentioned it in his wonderfully named travelogue *Coryat's Crudities: Hastily Gobled up in Five Moneth's Travels*, which describes how 'the Italian do always at their meals use a little fork when they cut the meat'.

Still, fork-use was met with scorn, and the habit considered effeminate and un-English. It wasn't until the late seventeenth century – 500 years after Eleanor's pioneering habits – that it finally caught on. Thus began another great romance of British history – a romance to rival Arthur and Guinevere or Edward and Eleanor. It was the most perfect pairing of all: the knife and fork.

While staying at Geddington, Edward and Eleanor worshipped

in the nearby Church of St Mary Magdalene, which still stands. How remarkable to think that every English king from Henry I to Edward I, along with queens and other magnates of the realm, entered this church decked in their fine robes, processing for mass.

When Eleanor's funeral cortège passed through Geddington on 6 December 1290, her body lay in the parish church – the church that still stands today. It is a curious thing that, after passing through with Eleanor's body in December 1290, King Edward's visits became more and more infrequent and, over the years, Geddington fell out of prominence. Though the church survives to this day, by 1324 the manor was 'wasted for lack of good keeping'. By 1374, the village's weekly market was worthless because 'nobody comes there'. And so it has remained the size of the small village we see today.

As dusk fell, we sat on those stone steps of the Eleanor Cross and considered all this – how memories can be so embedded with places. Perhaps that's why you find benches left in memory of a loved one, marking the spot where they sat to enjoy the view. These were places where, even in death, their shadow was heavy. Was there something about Geddington – a place of happy memories with Eleanor – that Edward found simply too painful to revisit?

7. THE TREE OF HAPPY THINGS

'And it is characteristic of grief that it knows no limit and is ignorant of a steady course.'
William of Malmesbury

WHEN WE LOOK AT HISTORIC family trees – those neat little diagrams that help us make sense of succession – the name of Eleanor of Castile sprouts six lines, for six children. But this would have immediately struck a jarring chord for Eleanor – perhaps a feeling of anger. Because these simplified graphics overwrite decades of trauma and suffering.

This was a woman crushed, at least ten times, by the emotional turbulence of miscarriage, stillbirth, neonatal death and child loss. I often wonder: were her professional interests – where she played the assertive CEO – a coping mechanism in this private life of personal tragedy?

Though familial relationships – especially between parents and children – were quite different in the medieval period, and death was a familiar feature of the medieval day-to-day, this commonality didn't diminish its impact. After his wife died, the fifteenth-century Valencian poet Ausiàs March addressed this directly:

*Why does an event so common as Death seem so severe to whom-
ever it wounds? Why at times does man's reason hide itself away
and passion assembles all its strength?*

In the fourteenth century, Christine de Pizan, Europe's first professional female writer, was tormented with grief after the loss of
her husband, battling thoughts of self-destruction:

*I can never forget this great, incomparable suffering, which brings
my heart to such torment, which puts into my head such grievous
despair, which counsels me to kill myself and break my heart.*

When fourteen-year-old Princess Joan perished in the Black
Death, her father, Edward III, wrote a grief-stricken letter to
Alfonso of Castile, whose son, Pedro, Joan was betrothed to marry:

*But see (with what intense bitterness of heart we have to tell you
this) destructive Death (who seizes young and old alike, sparing
no one and reducing rich and poor to the same level) has lamen-
tably snatched from both of us our dearest daughter (whom we
loved best of all, as her virtues demanded). No fellow human being
could be surprised if we were inwardly desolated by the sting of
this bitter grief, for we are humans too.*

We are indeed. Such emotions are the great leveller throughout
society and across time, where we stand hand in hand with our
ancestors' past. Though we must be very wary of applying modern
psychology to medieval lives, it's interesting to consider, for a
moment, the modern experience.

When people talk about grief today – though it varies massively
from person to person – there are marked traits that differ between

men and women. According to the bereavement support charity Sue Ryder, 80 per cent of men admitted to feeling alone in their grief, while 52 per cent confessed to bottling up feelings from their loved ones, wanting to appear 'strong'. Such patterns of behaviour play into traditional gender and cultural stereotypes, where male sadness or crying is perceived as weak.

It's not hard to believe that King Edward would have bottled up his emotions, keen to appear a tough leader in this moment of upheaval – though behind closed doors, things might have been very different.

In the weeks following Eleanor's death, we have a glimpse of that. He retreated from public life and wrote those immortal words of Eleanor in a letter to the Abbot of Cluny: 'who in life we dearly cherished and who in death we cannot cease to love'. In these words, we see a flicker of something incredibly intimate: the private sorrow that was hidden from public view, the grief that plagued his most private thoughts.

There is another pattern to consider. Modern men tend to be 'action-focused grievers' or 'instrumental grievers'. While bottling up emotions, they distract themselves with practical matters, busying themselves with funeral preparations or funnelling their energy into new projects.

Traditional Catholic practice – with the spiritual framework of purgatory – provided a good outlet for 'action-focused grieving'. There were all sorts of after-death rituals. The poor might pay a priest to do a commemorative funeral service thirty days after a death. Wealthy members of society might build a new chapel and pay for a priest to say masses and commemorative funeral services every day, for ever.

If history could show us any 'action-focused griever', King Edward I certainly ticks the box. At some point in the spring of 1291 – just months after Eleanor's death – the finest masons in the land were summoned. Take a moment to imagine the scene . . .

A group of men stand in a line in Westminster Hall. Their skin is rugged and their hands are coarse. But they are finely dressed, as these are the greatest artists and craftsmen of their age: the master masons – superstars of the day. Among the group is Michael of Canterbury, John of Battle and the brothers Richard and Roger of Crundale.

Their work steers the course of architectural history, and each man has a combination of extraordinary skills – the precision of Gustav Fabergé, the artistic dynamism of Pablo Picasso, the mathematical brain of Ada Lovelace, the engineering expertise of Isambard Kingdom Brunel.

These men are pioneers of design, who push the boundaries of what is possible, building immense windows of stained glass or stonework hundreds of metres high or stone carvings of aston- ishing intricacy. All to create sublime spaces to the glory of God – and the men and women who pay for them.

They wait in silent anticipation. As the great doors of the hall open, they quickly drop to a knee and make a deep bow, listening to the heavy thud of footsteps. A thunderous voice instructs them to rise, and only then, they look up to see an enormous man. This is Edward Longshanks, their anointed King.

'Gentlemen,' he booms, 'I have summoned you here to announce a new project. A building scheme unlike anything ever attempted in this country, and I doubt any you'll ever work on again.'

The King pauses, closes his eyes, takes a deep breath. When he looks out again, his expression is kinder, softer than usual: 'Think of the most beautiful things of God's creation – the early morning light shining through the mists, the cool rush of river water, the sweet scent of a perfect rose, the sound of waves upon the shore.'

The masons glance at one another, fascinated at what this warrior king – usually so brash, who talked of Crusades and campaigns – was suggesting.

'This divine beauty, you must capture forever, in stone. In every town and place where Eleanor's body rested, you must build a cross of cunning workmanship. There will be twelve crosses in total – the most magnificent you can create – to honour my Eleanor. They will show sculptures of Eleanor and bear her coat of arms – England, Ponthieu and Castile. And I want them taller, grander and more beautiful than the crosses built for the French king, Louis. Aside from that, choose your own design.'

The King turns, sweeps his cloak and marches out. As the great doors crash closed behind him, there is a moment of silence, then the masons erupt into chatter, astonished and excited at the task ahead, their brains whirring with the possibilities.

Equipped with that instruction, between 1291 and 1295, the masons were sent to each town the cortège passed through. Here they led teams to create extraordinary monuments, each at least 13 metres tall. They were marvels of design: an explosion of complex geometry, painted inscriptions, heraldic devices and exquisite full-size sculptures of Eleanor where stone was transformed into flowing drapery. Each one was like an enormous multi-layered wedding cake, all of which was topped with a Christian cross.

Building a stone memorial was nothing new. The first stone

crosses in Britain and Ireland were set up as memorials to powerful men, particularly in the Celtic regions of Ireland, Scotland and Wales. A little later, the English and the invading Vikings followed suit. The crosses were explicitly Christian, representing the execution of Jesus, but these early crosses often blended Christian and pagan imagery, a mix of old Norse gods, biblical scenes and ornamental knotwork.

By the medieval period, there were plenty more crosses around. Some were simple and rustic stone blocks, others intricately carved with steps. They could be found in churchyards, where they were used for processions, preaching and marking rights of sanctuary. Sometimes crosses marked boundaries between parishes or settlements. In marketplaces, crosses might be used to preach or validate transactions. Some commemorated the site of a battle or were linked to particular saints.

By the 1500s, the end of the medieval period, there were probably 12,000 crosses in England, though many were damaged or destroyed in the Reformation. Today, some 2,000 medieval standing crosses are thought to exist.

So why was this set of Eleanor Crosses so extraordinary? What was totally unprecedented in Britain was to build not just one, but a series of *twelve* crosses, of immense size and grandeur, spread across 200 miles. The scheme was inspired by the French *montjoies*, which were a similar set of crosses erected to mark the course of King Louis IX's funeral procession of 1270–71, just two decades before (the same King Louis who had died on the Eighth Crusade).

From Lincoln to London, the Eleanor Crosses became greater in height and complexity. In these designs, the boundaries of English Gothic design were expanded. Was this architecture? Was this sculpture? Was this art? For the first time, no one knew. It was unlike anything they'd seen before. The project was charting new architectural waters, exploring new creative territory. Of all the crosses built, only three survive today, and Geddington is the most complete.

All of this – this explosion of creative flair – was a reflection of Edward's deep love for Eleanor. A love forged over a thirty-six-year marriage – one of horses, hunting, chivalry, chess, building projects and politics. But most importantly, through thick and thin, they were a team, together, utterly devoted to and considerate of the other.

One of the reasons for this – I think – was that though they had different roles and responsibilities, there was no 'Team Eleanor' or 'Team Edward'. Perhaps it was Eleanor's independence – built up by her property empire – which enabled their relationship to be one of co-operation over one-sided reliance. There are endless occasions when they helped each other out: sometimes Eleanor lent Edward money when he was short of cash; other times Edward helped Eleanor fund her property projects.

And, behind their hard-nosed public personas, they were surprisingly sentimental. When Eleanor was ill, away or about to give birth, Edward sent gifts of food – venison when she was 'lying in'. Eleanor once gifted Edward a beautiful hunting bird for his birthday, and Edward, in turn, commissioned fine books to satisfy her reading.

In the depths of his grief, I expect Edward found building the crosses – or at least commissioning them – cathartic.

When I visited Rodney, he told me of a rising trend today for pure cremation or direct cremation, which became normalised by the limitations of pandemic lockdowns. This is where there is no funeral and no ceremony. The body is taken to the crematorium and the ashes returned. It is seen as a 'no-fuss' approach, costing more than £2,000 less than a ceremony or funeral.

But, Rodney explained, it can have an adverse effect. Months or years later, people often come to him saying things like, 'You know, we never said a proper goodbye to Mum.' They struggle to cope emotionally, having been unable to quite draw the chapter to a close.

So, whether Edward realised it or not, I suspect the crosses helped him move forward. Though he would never 'cease to love' Eleanor, this act of remembrance probably gave him distance from the loss and some degree of closure.

For reasons unknown, the cortège took a day off at this point – perhaps staying an extra night in Geddington. So, following the original journey, for the next couple of days I did the same, in the spell of the Eleanor Cross.

The Eleanor Cross at Geddington, the best surviving of all the crosses.

The Friday night was spent at the Star Inn. I bought a round of 'that one please', pointing at a tap badge featuring a countryside gate, labelled 'Fool's Nook'. It turned out to be a good choice: a golden ale with a fruity touch.

The locals of Geddington were happy to chat and proved to be a valuable fount of local history. Laura and I settled into the window seat, joined by a cheery fellow with a mop of blond hair. This was Adam, a roofer by trade. By good chance, he was a history enthusiast and something of an expert on one important local, Sir Thomas Tresham, who lived during the reign of Queen Elizabeth I. Tresham was a dedicated Catholic, determined to practise his faith, despite risking being imprisoned for fifteen years for refusing to convert. He was also the father of Francis Tresham, one of the notorious Gunpowder Plotters.

'My favourite place around here,' Adam the Roofer enthused, 'is that house without the roof.' Not far from Geddington is Lyveden, the house that Tresham was building on his estate at the time of his death. It was never completed and it remains virtually unaltered since work stopped around 1605. Another important historical building – and a famous one in the world of follies – is located just 4 miles from Geddington. It is a peculiar triangular tower, Rushton Triangular Lodge, which was also built – and completed this time – by Tresham, between 1593 and 1597.

The entire thing is a subtle nod to Tresham's Catholic faith. The number three, symbolising the Holy Trinity, is evident everywhere. There are three floors, trefoil windows and three triangular gables on each side. The facade bears the inscription '*Tres Testimonium Dant*' ('There are three that give witness'), which is a quote from St John's Gospel, referring to the Holy Trinity. It is also a pun on Tresham's name, for his wife called him 'Good Tres' in her letters.

As we chatted with Adam and I considered this triangular lodge, built 4 miles away, this all seemed to ring a bell . . . A tall stone tower . . . in the shape of a triangle . . . Hadn't I heard of one of those before? Sitting in the corner of the Star Inn, I gazed out the window . . . then the lightbulb moment arrived, made more profound by several pints of Fool's Nook. I connected the dots for the first time.

When Tresham was building his famous triangular tower, he was certainly aware of the Eleanor Cross nearby. How could he not have been? We know Tresham passed through the village, and there are Treshams buried in Geddington's churchyard. So, being a local lad, like Adam, the Eleanor Cross was well on Tresham's radar.

Cheered by this unexpected revelation, I bought another round. The hubbub in the pub began to rise with chit-chat and laughter and the merriment of a Friday night in the lead-up to Christmas. In a dining room was a private party. There sat some twenty women – colleagues, it seemed – all different ages, who were full of cheer. Prizes were given out: for being the 'Excel Expert', one for being 'Calm, Cool, Collected', another 'Always On the Go' (Eleanor would certainly win that one). There were also 'Can't Say No' and 'Slightly Losing It' awards, each announce-ment followed by gleeful whoops. Then came karaoke, performed with the utmost gusto. As the group began to filter out around 10 p.m., it emerged they were the local nursery teachers, cele-brating the year passed.

The following day we spent recuperating. The only place to stay in Geddington is an Airbnb, the home of an elderly woman called Margaret. As an ex-B&B hostess extraordinaire, she was brilliant at putting out a sumptuous breakfast. Toast in a rack, with jams and marmalades to spare. Cereals, orange juice. Teas, coffees. The works. On Saturday morning, we helped her pull the ladder from the loft and Laura retrieved the Christmas tree. (That military training put to good use once again.)

For a day we wandered around Geddington, walking the little lanes back and forth, trying to retrace the steps of the cortège. We gazed upon an empty patch of land where the grand manor house once stood and imagined Eleanor gliding through the space in furs and silks. We sat on the churchyard wall, watching village life unfold around the cross. The postman doing the rounds. Friends stopping to chat. Little children wrapped in scarfs and hats, whizzing about on bikes and scooters.

There was something remarkable about the cross, a magnet around which everything else revolved, like the sun in our solar system – both emitting energy, yet too distant to ever reach. If this was an episode of *Doctor Who*, the Eleanor Cross would be a time portal, transporting a young girl – perhaps called Reina – back to 1290 to save the medieval villagers from an alien invasion (and I don't mean the Scots).

We pushed open the door of St Mary's Church and found – to our surprise – a small forest inside. On display was the 'Festival of Light', an array of Christmas trees decorated in different styles by various villagers. One was adorned in Quality Street chocolates, each branch holding a different sweet. Another – with toothpaste and toothbrushes – was a tribute to oral hygiene.

But the best was surely Entry 17, the 'Tree of Happy Things'. Here, villagers of Geddington had been invited to contribute a thought, idea or experience that made them happy. They had written it down with a Sharpie on a thin sheet of bauble-shaped wood, which was hung on the branches with string.

It was an eclectic, delightful mix – darting all over the place, like the lyrics of 'My Favourite Things' in *The Sound of Music*. There were no rules. For some, it was the company of loved ones:

141

'Spending time with grandchildren', 'A good moan with friends', 'My Cockapoo Beau', 'The love of my life at the weekends', 'Paula and Richard', 'Two family babies arrived for Christmas', 'Going to the park with my bff', 'My cat, Petal'.

One child had drawn twenty stick figures, some circled 'friends' and the rest labelled 'family'. There was 'G.C.C.' – a loyal member of Geddington Cricket Club, with a fine drawing of bat and ball. Nearby was 'Dementia Choir. Giving back to others who are less fortunate than me'.

For some, it was activities that made them happy: 'The pub + grub', 'Having a roast dinner', 'Cheese!', 'Having a nice cup of TEA'. From one of Geddington's crafters, 'Making things', along with a drawing of scissors and a ball of string. Another was labelled 'Getting air!', accompanied by a figure on a bike, flying high in the sky. Music was on the list for some: 'Listening to La Bamba makes me HAPPY'.

What would Eleanor's contribution be? 'Playing chess with Edward' or 'Seeing the first fruit on a new apple tree'? What would mine be? And what about yours?

On the Saturday night, at the recommendation of Reina – who I increasingly thought of as a kind of guiding light in this quest for Eleanor's legacy – we headed to the church. She was starring as an angel in the panto-tivity, a forty-minute nativity with some eccentric pantomimic elements: angels dressed as TikTok goths, a pantomime horse, references to the film *Elf*, jokes about Taylor Swift. It was a charming – albeit wacky – *Vicar of Dibley*-esque performance.

This was full Bring-Your-Own-Costume-and-Props – wise men holding *A Guide to the Night Sky*, for example. Listening to all this talk of long journeys – of the long journey to Bethlehem – I thought of Edward and the royal party, all those years before.

Surely, as they walked, they thought of the journeys of Mary and Joseph, of the shepherds and wise men? Did Edward compare himself to Joseph, who led a donkey, and Mary, who carried the Son of God? How different Edward's situation was, as Eleanor's cold body was transported in a coffin, and Edward, on the horse, carried the great weight of grief.

Early Sunday morning, Laura returned to London and I went back to the church. There were seven people in the congregation, plus the organist and the vicar. We gathered for the annual 'Requiem Mass for Queen Eleanor of Castile', marking her body lying in this space, exactly 734 years before. As the service began, we shared this moment with those medieval mourners, bound across time by prayers to 'remember in love Queen Eleanor of Castile and those whom we have placed in your hands'.

The Church of St Mary Magdalene, in Geddington.

143

We exchanged the sign of peace – a moment of goodwill, of shaking hands with strangers – and considered the remarkable history that brought us together.

Afterwards, curiosity got the better of the little congregation. I was clearly no Geddingtonian and my strange apparel of anorak, high-vis and walking boots gave me away as either incredibly cautious in wet weather or a traveller. I shared the details of my journey, which they listened to with great enthusiasm, and thrust a cup of tea in my hand.

At nine o'clock, I stepped out of the church, leaving the team to prepare for the morning service. In the churchyard, after zipping up my waterproofs and setting the OS Maps app running, I noticed – for the first time – a rough block of stone with a metal plaque, in the shadow of the Eleanor Cross. It read: 'CELEBRATING THE PLATINUM JUBILEE OF QUEEN ELIZABETH II 2022. GEDDINGTON, NEWTON & LITTLE OAKLEY PARISH COUNCIL'. Here they were, two queens commemorated in such different ways – though Eleanor got rather the better deal, in this instance.

Crossing the ancient stone bridge, with muddy waters rushing by, I thought of the medieval travellers carrying Eleanor's body – on this very same bridge – as they continued their journey south. Did the children – little girls like Reina – run out across the road, as they had during my time in Geddington? Did they wait in the cutwaters and offer posies of winter snowdrops to the royal princesses, wrapped in thick furs?

How strange for the village of Geddington to say their final farewell to the Queen, who had been a regular visitor and worshipper. And what of King Edward? Would he take comfort in the knowledge that this was a place where villagers would – more than 700 years later – continue to say prayers in her memory?

THE TREE OF HAPPY THINGS

As I left Geddington that Sunday morning, it was horribly windy and wet – 'dreich', the Scots would say. Weather warnings for 'Storm Daragh' had been issued. But I left with my heart held high. Geddington had been a village of such life, full of characters. This was a village with spirit. And at the heart of it all – the magnet around which this village life revolved – was the Eleanor Cross. As I stood on that ancient bridge and looked back at the cross through the rain, I had no doubt: here in Geddington, Eleanor's legacy was very much alive.

8. THE QUEEN ELEANOR
INTERCHANGE

'Is it nothing to you, all you who pass by? Behold
and see if there is any sorrow like my sorrow.'
Lamentations 1:12

STORM DARRAGH PROVED TO BE a difficult walking companion. He was out in full force, a powerful extratropical cyclone from the Atlantic that battered British shores. This was weather that filled the newspapers with reports of power cuts, uprooted trees and cancelled Christmas markets.

Luckily, where I was, any cyclonic strength had mellowed to a bluster. But the wind still whipped my hair, the air was filled with the ominous rustle of trees and I kept my wits about me for any sight of fallen branches. Each time a car passed, I braced, fearful of being drenched with puddle water, à la Bridget Jones. Lucky I was wearing trousers!

There is something confusing about high winds. All sense of rootedness, of calm, of order, is torn up. Whenever the winds pick up, I think of how Dorothy Wordsworth mulled over the chaos in verse: 'What way does the wind come?' she writes. 'What way does he go?' The answer remains futile: 'There's never a scholar in England knows.' The wind rides 'over the water, and over the snow,/Through wood, and through vale; and o'er rocky height,/ Which the goat cannot climb.'

There were no goats to be seen that morning, but there were some fine houses (as Gen Z would say, GOATs in their own way). I was in Northamptonshire now, the county of 'squires and spires', known as such because it's dotted with stately homes – more than any other county – and fine churches.

While walking along the main road from Geddington, I could see Boughton House, built by Ralph Montagu, later 1st Duke of Montagu. As an English ambassador to France and an enthusiast for French fashions, he expanded his family seat with a little architectural *je ne sais quoi*. The resulting masterpiece is often referred to as 'the English Versailles'.

Like Mr Montagu, Eleanor was well versed in managing and developing big estates. Property was her 'thing', if you will. Her life was summed up by one annalist as 'A Spaniard by birth, who obtained many fine manors.' Why was Eleanor so focused on building this portfolio?

In the thirteenth century, English queens were in a pickle, because they were almost totally financially dependent on their husbands (who were themselves often short of money). Their income came from the 'Queen's gold' – an additional 10 per cent charge on fines or taxes owed to the King – or, sometimes, debts or fines that were owed to the King were diverted to the Queen instead.

All these payments were erratic and unreliable, therefore, and never came close to the amounts required to support a royal household. It made things pretty unrelaxing: queens were required to uphold an appearance of grandeur, while constantly unsure whether they could pay the next bill.

Some queens had tried to overcome this limbo – Eleanor's mother-in-law, Eleanor of Provence, pushed the limits of Queen's gold, but became unpopular by doing so. Keen to avoid similar bad press, Eleanor of Castile sought to find a permanent solution. As such, she assembled a property portfolio that would guarantee a regular, significant income.

Eleanor proved to be a savvy operator. By the time of her death, she had acquired more than 200 properties – manors, farms, priories and ports. These yielded around £2,500 a year (around £2.8 million today), the equivalent income of any great lord of the realm. After Eleanor's death, it formed the backbone of English queens' dower assignment for the next century (a dower assignment being the provision accorded to a wife should she become widowed).

Did you ever play Monopoly as a child? I did and I have vivid memories of tensions running high, as well as emotional rollercoasters – immense satisfaction, then frustrated tears. There was always one player who was ruthless – buying full sets, smothering them in hotels and creating danger zones. Every roll of the dice was a potential death knell.

The other players – facing the miserable reality of bankruptcy – were forced to exchange their modest assets for some humiliation – Water Works or a measly Get Out of Jail Free card – when, with the dangers lurking, you'd much rather be stuck in jail, thank you very much! In moments of final desperation, there were accusations of fraud – especially when the winning player was also, conveniently, the banker. Remember that person? That Monopoly demon? That was Eleanor.

From a base of properties in Derbyshire, Nottingham and Essex, Eleanor acquired more lands to form her own estate, picking properties that were close to each other to benefit from economies of scale.

As Queen, Eleanor had plenty on her plate, so the details of property management could have easily been delegated, as earlier queens had done. But our Eleanor was a details woman, dotting each 'i' and crossing each 't'. She was the kind of woman who would return a document covered with red pen with comments like 'Are you sure this number is correct?' or 'CHECK AGAIN PLEASE', underlined twice.

Consider that Eleanor had some 200 properties to oversee – while also managing her children, pregnancies, rebellions, King Edward or lying on her actual deathbed – and you get the sense that she was a pretty efficient woman.

There was a team to help with his mega-operation, of course. Eleanor's lands were divided up geographically and each area appointed with a bailiff. The bailiffs would oversee a small army of administrators, who proved to be super-efficient. Once a grant was made to Eleanor, administrators put plans into action within twenty-four hours, so there was no time wasted.

Eleanor's letters were delivered by a team of at least eight messengers. About half were given the formal title 'nuntius' (Latin for 'envoy'), while the remainder were only entitled 'cursor' (Latin for 'runner'). They galloped at full speed, with wind in their hair, delivering messages to bailiffs, stewards, seneschals, treasurers and sheriffs. To give you a sense of just how rapid they were, one messenger managed three visits to France in six weeks.

Even though Eleanor only acquired property to match the incomes of the great lords of the day, she was conscious it might appear avaricious and make her unpopular – as it had for Eleanor of Provence. A letter from 1265 ends with a plea to 'deal with this matter in a way which ensures that they shall not set it down to covetousness' – aka, making sure it didn't make her appear greedy.

Whether her reputation survived is up for debate. When contemporary chroniclers wrote of Eleanor, it wasn't beauty or piety that sprung to mind, but hard-nosed business: 'The King would like to get our gold,' one rhyme went. 'The Queen our manors fair to hold.' There was some bad practice: sometimes land was purchased, forcibly taken or seized from those unable to pay their debts.

Eleanor's 'bad practice' as a businesswoman was subject to wider scrutiny, as the idea that the Queen benefited from the sin of usury ruffled feathers in church circles. In 1283, the Archbishop of Canterbury, Archbishop Peckham, wrote a letter to the Queen: 'For God's sake, my lady, when you receive land or manor acquired by usury of the Jews, take heed that it is a mortal sin.' Three years later, in 1286, he penned another letter, concerning the Queen's reputation: 'There is gossip and debate about this in every part of England.'

The archbishop's letters are the major piece of evidence used to discredit Eleanor, but evidence from other annalists tends to cast doubt on the dramatic assertion that England was abuzz with gossip at Eleanor's expense. Can we wholly trust the letters? How could the archbishop possibly have an honest report of the chit-chat from 'every part of England'? Is there a chance the archbishop was exaggerating for his own interests? Would you think it reasonable if your own reputation was judged – by historians 700 years to come – on a couple of emails sent by a colleague, who didn't like your work?

Or here's another way to think of it. Imagine it's Storm Daragh in full force. Blustery winds, sideways rain. Imagine the full set of documents relating to Eleanor's life are out on a library table. Piles and piles of letters, household accounts, leases. A comprehensive supply to make a decent, evidence-based judgement, where Eleanor's voice shines through.

But suddenly – just as you turn to pick up your cup of tea – the window swings open! In swoops Storm Daragh and, in an enormous force of suction, all the documents fly out the window, up, up and away, never to be seen again. All that's left are a few pages, trapped in the window hinge. And it is from these few pages that an entire judgement of Eleanor's life is to be made. Many of the sources relating to Eleanor's life are similarly lost to the mists – or winds – of time, so you'll see why we must be sceptical about two letters, from one archbishop, to draw a conclusion.

Another event that has tainted Eleanor's reputation took place after her death, namely an inquest into her property affairs – carried out on Eleanor's instructions – during which all sorts of complaints emerged.

Of all the contemporary records that survive from Eleanor's life, this is the largest volume and the most cohesive, which, really, is terrible luck when you consider the countless other documents and (perhaps complimentary) letters that haven't survived. What's more, many complaints were quickly dismissed (some didn't even relate to people in Eleanor's service), some were withdrawn and others abandoned.

Some complaints were certainly justified. There are some accounts – moments that would make newspaper headlines today – of the viciousness of administrators acting under Eleanor's name. Sometimes bailiffs bullied tenants to pay increased rents or rent was demanded even though a rent-free period had been agreed. One house was improperly seized from its owners, whose baby was dumped in a cradle in the middle of the road. On another occasion, a family was ejected from their home so the local bailiff could use it to entertain a prostitute.

So was Eleanor complicit? She couldn't have been aware of the full extent of what was going on, everywhere, though perhaps she turned a blind eye for convenience's sake? On her deathbed in Harby, she was insistent that her estates' affairs be investigated – so was she aware that injustices had been done under her name?

What can be said is that when she was made aware of injustice, she made pains to right a wrong. If lands were wrongly seized,

Eleanor restored them to their rightful owner. If she heard about property being wrongly damaged, she made sure to pay the repairs. The problem was, for mistreated tenants, it was virtually impossible to reach her – like calling up a customer service number, to spend hours listening to hold music with the occasional interruption: 'Please hold. Thank you for your patience.'

Eleanor was no doubt an impressive businesswoman. She was rigorous, hard-working and bullish – but we should be able to respect this as efficient professionalism, rather than seeing her as a monster. Certainly, while playing hard, she could overstep the mark. But she also achieved something quite extraordinary: financial independence, not just for her, but for generations of English queens to come. That alone should put Eleanor down as a heroic medieval woman.

But back to the blustery roundabouts of Northamptonshire. After a couple of miles walking, I found myself in Kettering. Once a bustling haven for cloth, silk and leatherworking, today it's a small market town. Shivering under a bus shelter, I met up with my next hiking companion: Jamie, a ruddy-faced, football-loving accountant with an encyclopaedic knowledge of medieval warfare.

As we battled the sideways wind, shouting from our anoraked hoods, I updated Jamie on the progress. Only in this moment did I realise quite how much had unfolded. Was it only four days since I'd been in Lincoln? Had I really covered 70 miles? I told Jamie everything in an enthusiastic blur: the bakery with iced buns, coffee breaks on Ermine Street, Longhorn cows, the water meadows of Stamford, the thrill of seeing the first Eleanor Cross, the roofer in the Geddington pub, the jokes from the panto-tivity, the marmalade put out at Margaret's breakfast.

As we crossed a bridge over the A14, we swapped roles. Jamie had just come out of London, which was in full Christmas party season swing. I heard about the drinks party in Oval that was deemed a 'flop', the carol service that ran out of mulled wine (this was, Jamie confessed, the main reason he had attended) and a party in Tooting where my friend Isobel fell down the stairs (a victim of satin jumpsuits, apparently). All this modern stuff seemed rather a world away from my *Olde Medieavale Walke*, with 5.30 a.m. alarms and evenings reading *Stamford Living*.

The route through Kettering took us past pleasant rows of houses, then industrial estates. Then, through a small passage, we emerged – so suddenly it surprised us – into a vast field. This is the funny thing with walking – the variety is immense. In one moment, you're trotting along tarmac pavements, sheltered by cul-de-sacs. A minute later, you're ankle-deep in mud, fighting the bracing wind.

Serious mud!

Splashing through puddles, we passed through Pytchley village, Orlingbury, Hardwick and Mears Ashby. We took shelter at W. H. Thomas farm shop, where locals were picking up their Christmas sausages and we both bought a sausage roll topped with apricot jam. After tucking them firmly within the waterproof lining of our rucksacks (triple wrapped in plastic coating) and zipping up every pocket, we stepped, once more, outside.

The countryside was battered by the weather. The heavens had opened overnight, the land was boggy and mud heavy underfoot. The grass paths were saturated with great pools of water, the churned-up fields forming strange, galactic surfaces. If we weren't careful, a boot would be left behind, claimed hostage by the suction.

The lanes had streams running either side and drains clogged up with twigs. Jamie the Accountant was wearing totally inappropriate footwear (sports trainers, forsooth!), which were soon soaked through.

But as we squelched and skidded, we pondered how our medieval ancestors would have fared. Did they have waterproof clothing? Or did they just hope for the best, with trench foot being an occupational hazard for the thirteenth-century rambler?

It turns out, the natural world has some pretty brilliant solutions for almost everything, so they made the best of the materials available, covering cloth in fish oil, animal fats, whale blubber, resin or hot wax to create a waterproof layer. Some of the cortège would wrap themselves in furs – the wealthy in ermine, sable and marten, the wealthier in squirrel and fox, while the less well-off donned lambskin, rabbit, goat or cat.

Others might have worn woollen cloaks, which were naturally water-repellent thanks to the waxy substance, lanolin, which is secreted from the sheep's fleece. Yet wool is not fully waterproof:

in a heavy shower, water would soak through. For this, however, there was a solution: fulling. This involves cleaning and shrinking woven cloth to create a thicker, smoother and more water-resistant fabric.

First, the wool was cleansed with stale urine (which contained ammonium salts) or fuller's earth (a soft, clay-like material) to remove the oils and dirt. Different breeds have different levels of grease in their wool, but most British breeds have around 15 per cent. Historically, flocks would be driven through a river to wash them prior to shearing. There is a village in Devon called Sheepwash, which was first documented in 1166, because sheep passed through for this purpose.

Once sheared, the wool was processed. During the medieval period, much of this was done in a fulling mill, also known as a walk mill or a tuck mill. In Wales, it was known as a pandy. The felted cloth was beaten with fulling hammers, then stretched on great frames known as tenters, attached with tenterhooks. This gives us the origins of the phrase 'on tenterhooks', meaning, to be in a state of nervous anticipation or suspense.

In Scotland, this process was known as waulking, and manual methods remained in place until the 1700s. In Scottish Gaelic tradition, women sang waulking songs to set the pace, and each of the stages gave rise to common surnames: Fuller, Tucker and Walker.

These methods were well known to the people of Northampton – the town that Jamie and I descended upon. In the medieval period, this was the most important town in the Midlands. Kings kept court at Northampton Castle and the streets were thronged with cloth merchants, travellers and royal messengers.

It was a place Edward was very familiar with. Not only did he regularly stay in Northampton Castle, but sixteen years before, he played his part in the 1264 Battle of Northampton, a decisive moment in the Second Barons' War. Here, twenty-five-year-old Prince Edward – alongside his father – led a large army to take the castle. They advanced over the water meadows, attacking the main gate with ladders and breaching walls. The royal party won the day, pillaging the town, taking prisoners and capturing Simon de Montfort the Younger.

How things had changed, Edward must have thought, as he strolled freely into the city in 1290. No baronial force this time, but no Eleanor either.

I'd never walked through Northampton before, only travelling by train or driving on the main roads. In my mind it was urban and industrial, a place of metal and concrete. But our arrival could not have proved me more wrong. Passing by a twelfth-century church, we were guided into the city with the welcoming arms of a line of trees, gently sloping into the town. This was Britain's answer to LA's Palm Tree Avenue.

Scarlet berries and smooth, silvery bark identified them as rowan trees. This is a native breed with deep mythology – its old Celtic name means 'wizards' tree'. The avenue had a sense of grandeur, as if these were a row of guards, awaiting a ghostly procession. It would have been suitable for the cortège no doubt, with this solemn cast of witnesses observing in silence.

Indeed, it emerged that this was an avenue of memorial trees, named 'Celebration Avenue'. Here, the trees were championed as 'long-standing hearts of nature' and 'absorbers of human strife'. Each one had a small rectangular plaque, written by people of the parish to remember their loved ones.

We zig-zagged down the avenue, taking care to read each message. 'In Loving Memory of Josephine Rolfe', one read. The dates of Josephine's life were included – '03/04/1961–10/12/2016' – along with a sentiment: 'We will always love and miss you. Fly high flower. Too well-loved to ever be forgotten xxxx'. There was Peter Cole, a 'beloved Husband, Father, Grandfather and Friend', remembered as 'A TRUE SAINT'. Next, 'Wendy Devine, a Loving Wife, Mother & Sister, In our hearts forever'.

Celebration Avenue on the outskirts of Northampton.

What would Edward have made of this processionary route, filled with these tall, silent memorials – tributes to loved ones passed? He would likely have taken comfort in the words on the plaque dedicated to Barbara Morton: 'Weep if you must, parting is hell. But life goes on, so sing as well.' Would the memorial to Betty Legg – 'Treasured Mum & Nan/You are missed every day/Night Night. God Bless xxx' – have been fitting to Eleanor? Edward's own words were hardly different.

It's not difficult to imagine reading on Celebration Avenue: 'Eleanor, who in life we dearly cherished and who in death we cannot cease to love'.

It is a wonderful thing, to remember a loved one with a tree, because it continues to grow, keeping their spirit alive. But in a strange way, this was the same with the crosses, because their presence inspired people to offer prayers for Eleanor's soul. If the initial act of building the crosses was planting the seed, the prayers offered were the tree that sprouted and, as more admired and continue to admire the crosses' beauty, the branches of her memorial never cease to blossom.

I later discovered the land for Celebration Avenue had been owned by W. Pearce and Company, a major leather manufacturer (the same trade that held Northampton in good esteem during Queen Eleanor's day). The factory was opened nearby in 1939, in a wonderful art deco style, with plenty of simple, geometric shapes, giving it a streamlined, modern, manufactured look. It's derelict today and this land was donated to the parish council. What a wonderful gift it was, to bequeath this green space, for this avenue of trees to be planted.

For the final mile, we pushed on along a raised footpath. Jamie's trainers squelched with every step, which was liberating – he began jumping into deep puddles with gay abandon. On one side was the roaring A45. On the other, great, green swamps – the kind within which I'd imagine alligators might lurk. We passed stretches of land so flooded that ducks paddled about.

It was strangely exhausting walking beside the roar of traffic, like being in a room with loud air con – you only realise how noisy it is when it's suddenly gone. So it was a relief to step into the tranquillity of Delapré Park. Here, on the outskirts of Northampton, are 500 acres of woodland, lakes and greenery.

Next to a golf course, we perched on a damp bench and – finally – munched happily on sausage rolls.

As we shivered in the drizzle, I gazed out at this expansive sloping ground. Had we been sitting here in December 1290, we might have seen groups of women in long black habits and white hoods, collecting firewood or pulling up traps from the water to collect fish.

For this was the site of the Abbey of St Mary de la Pré. The name meant 'in the meadow' and was shortened to Delapré Abbey. It was established around 1145, endowed with 3,060 acres of land, and an abbess – a woman named Azelina – appointed.

Have you ever considered life as a medieval nun? Not in a career sense, I mean, just out of curiosity? Perhaps you're imagining a meagre, tedious life marked by promenading through cloisters in silence. Or perhaps you're visualising a thrilling life of debauchery and drunkenness, where religious houses descended into a den of iniquity.

In reality, it was neither such extreme – comparable to living in a girls-only boarding school, where you were stuck for life. There were cons – a vow of celibacy, a uniform, daily schedules – but the pros were immense: no arranged marriage, no fatal risks of giving birth, reasonable food, potential for intellectual, spiritual and creative fulfilment, as well as a position of importance in society, with power and responsibility. And an extra plus: there was the potential for it to be quite good fun.

In 1285, one of Eleanor's daughters began a life in this world. At six years old, Mary was sent to Amesbury Priory in Wiltshire, where she lived alongside her grandmother, Eleanor of Provence. She was educated alongside thirteen noble girls and formally veiled as a Benedictine nun in December 1291, at the age of twelve.

It was a comfortable set-up. Mary was granted £100 per year

for life (around £120,000 today). What's more, she had an annual provision of Bordeaux wine and forty oaks from the royal forests each year to provide wood to keep her chambers warm.

Apart from such luxuries, Mary's day-to-day was mostly reading, praying and contemplating. Each day was scheduled according to eight services of the Divine Office, beginning with Matins around 3 a.m. (though they could go back to bed after) and ending with Compline, long after the last meal.

Between the rigorous schedule of services, nuns had time to become accomplished artists and scribes – a kind of worship in itself. The Benedictine monastic motto was *Ora et Labora* ('Pray and Work') and there are some beautiful objects that are testament to this. In the collection of the Victoria & Albert Museum, for example, is a fourteenth-century frontal band – probably a piece of material used to adorn an altar. The red linen it is made from has been stitched with silver-gilt thread and coloured silks and was created by an English nun, Johanna of Beverley. On the reverse, she threaded her name: *Domna Iohanna beverlai monaca me fecit* ('Sister Johanna of Beverley made me'), which makes it the only surviving signed piece of English medieval embroidery.

In charge of abbeys were abbesses and at priories were prioresses, who played a role somewhere between headmistress and CEO. The daily running of a religious house was a big job: incomes, expenses, taxes, legal cases, VIP visits and ecclesiastical disputes all had to be managed.

At Delapré Abbey, it seems there was another challenge for the abbess: discipline. In 1300, three nuns, Isabella Clouvil, Matilda de Thychemers and Ermentrude de Newark, were publicly expelled for 'throwing their modesty to the winds' and having 'abandoned themselves to the hateful lusts of the flesh, and of their own accord given up their innocence.'

What on earth did Isabella, Matilda and Ermentrude do to warrant this expulsion? A wild night with the soldiers of Northampton Castle, perhaps? Sneaking out to the nearby monastery? Or was this loss of innocence something more sinister?

When the cortège arrived at Northampton on the evening of 8 December 1290, it seems likely Eleanor's body was left in the care of the nuns of Delapré Abbey. You can imagine a huddle of women, dressed in robes, gathered outside the gates. Here, King Edward would have given them his blessing. 'Take good care of her, sister,' he might have whispered as he left for his lodgings in the castle.

That night, 8 December 1290, has forever been commemorated for the people of Northampton. Just outside the site of Delapré Park, raised up on the kerb of the A508, Jamie and I arrived at something quite thrilling: the second surviving Eleanor Cross.

We bounded up to it as soon as we saw it, leaping up the steps two at a time, tracing our hands over the wet stones, taking time to decode the historic graffiti. We put our faces to the surface, to feel the dank cold, before walking around it in the rain, anti-clockwise first, then clockwise. We considered it from every angle and, even though it was drizzling, we sat on the steps to consider the nearby setting, too – the woodland, the bus stop, the road.

Each of the crosses, I've realised, has a different personality. The Northampton cross is quite different from the delicate design at Geddington, which has an ethereal, ballerina-esque elegance. In Northampton, the cross is chunky and strong; it has attitude. Gen Z would call it 'thicc'.

While the Geddington cross has a triangular design, the Northampton one is octagonal. From a base of steps rises a broad shaft decorated with heraldic shields and open books, which might have contained prayers to be said for Eleanor's soul. Above this, another stage has four niches containing statues of Eleanor. At the top, the cross itself would have emerged, though it was broken off in the seventeenth century.

When the cross was originally built, this was in a village of Hardingstone, located outside the city walls. Today, it is now amalgamated into Northampton. Over the years, the cross has seen its fair share of drama. In 1460, during the Wars of the Roses, it was a viewing platform for the second Battle of Northampton, which took place in the parkland of Delapré Abbey. Nine years later, in 1469, it was the site of several executions.

Being located in such a prominent position, the cross pops up in a few historic travel writings, too. In the 1540s, the antiquary John Leland recorded passing 'a right goodly cross, called, as I remember, the Queen's Cross'. Daniel Defoe also mentioned it in his *Tour Thro' the Whole Island of Great Britain*, when he wrote of the Great Fire of Northampton in 1675. He described the 'Queen's Cross upon a hill, on the south side of the town, about two miles off'.

In 1697, a woman trotted by on horseback. This was Celia Fiennes, the travel writer, who travelled the length and breadth of the country to record the sights and 'regain [her] health by variety and change of air and exercise'. Had Celia been alive today, she would be making history videos on Instagram, showing her followers churches, cathedrals, monastery ruins . . . Which sounds rather familiar . . .

The Northampton Cross, feat. Jamie's thumb.

Her travelogue, *Through England on a Side Saddle*, described the Eleanor Cross outside Northampton. It was 'a mile off the town' and was known as 'High-Cross'. She described the features: '12 steps . . . stone carved finely . . . 4 large niches . . . the statue of some queen' – clearly, Eleanor of Castile's links were unknown to Celia. She described the top of the cross with splendid detail: 'and so it rises less and less to the top like a tower or Piramidy'.

As dusk fell, I bade goodbye to a rain-sodden Jamie. After navigating the maze of paths to cross the enormous roundabout, the Queen Eleanor Interchange, I arrived at my lodgings for the night: Premier Inn. Once clean and dry, I settled in for a hearty meal at the pub next door, the Queen Eleanor. Only then I looked at my stats to realise we'd walked more than 21 miles. That made almost 100 miles in all so far. Maybe I was getting used to this hiking malarkey.

As I untucked the crisp sheets and climbed into bed that evening, I thought of Eleanor's body lying in a small stone chapel all those years earlier, safe in the feminine care of the nuns of Delapré Abbey. Automatically, I visualised the scene. The flickering candlelight softly illuminating Eleanor's pallid cheeks, dancing across her wrinkled eyelids. Around her, several women standing, cloaked in black robes. Some silent. Others singing laments, their breath visible in the cold air.

It was, no doubt, the same visions that came to Edward that night, as he lay in bed in Northampton Castle. As I switched off the light, an unsettling realisation came to me. By retracing Edward's footsteps and recreating his physical journey, I was also beginning to inhabit the most private of things: the shadows of his mind.

9. A FIVE-LEGGED TANSY BEETLE

*'There is nothing like employment, active indispensable
employment, for relieving sorrow. Employment, even
melancholy, may dispel melancholy.'*

Jane Austen

WHEN YOU THINK ABOUT IT, there were all sorts of ways in
which Edward could have commemorated Eleanor. A long poem,
created by her secretarial team. A fairy-tale garden, with fruits
and flowers from Castile. A tournament, to honour her memory
with acts of heroism and knights picking up ladies' handkerchiefs
with a lance.

In the end, the answer was obvious. An architectural legacy
was the only fitting tribute. Not only did Eleanor spend years
acquiring estates and land, but she developed and improved them.
One of the greatest was Leeds Castle, which is located near the
village of Leeds, in . . . er . . . Kent. The name derives from the
Old English word *Esledes*, meaning 'slope' or 'hillside', and causes
much confusion – as well as, potentially, a 240-mile detour.

When Leeds Castle came into Eleanor's hands, it was a dilapi-
dated defensive castle, built on an island on the River Len. Under
Eleanor's watch, it was transformed into a luxurious palace, with

a gloriette at its heart (from the Spanish term for a pavilion at the intersection of pathways in a garden).

Soon, it boasted all the mod-cons: a tiled pool room – a kind of private spa – known as the 'King's bath house'; a central court-yard, with piped water to create a fountain, in the Castilian fashion; an enlarged moat, to create the impression of a castle floating on a lake. There were also substantial security measures: a curtain wall around the larger island, a barbican bridge connecting the two islands, and a gatehouse.

Eleanor's property know-how was put to good use in Edward's building schemes – and because of politics of the day, there were plenty of them. When Edward and Eleanor were crowned in 1274, the memory of the Second Barons' War was still fresh in their minds. It was a turbulent, dangerous time, when King Henry III and the royal family were captured and imprisoned. The ultimate humiliation – failure, even – for a medieval king.

Leeds Castle in Kent. On the left is the gloriette, which Eleanor developed.

Keen to avoid similar shame and eager to reassert the strength and authority of the English crown, Edward had no time for defiance. Early on in his reign, however, he was tested by the repeated refusal of Llywelyn ap Gruffydd, Prince of Wales, to pay him due homage. Losing patience, Edward took radical action and invaded Wales in 1277, starting a vicious war that lasted until 1283.

For the Welsh, this was a battle for national identity, the right to traditional Welsh law and for their leaders to claim the title of 'Prince of Wales'. For Edward, it was about bringing the kingdoms and princedoms of the British Isles under English control. He set out to 'put an end finally to the matter . . . of suppressing the malice of the Welsh', and native Welsh princes were suppressed under the crown of England and forced to submit to English laws and administration.

Thus, the Principality of Wales was annexed and incorporated into the Kingdom of England. Edward and Eleanor's son, Prince Edward, was crowned 'Prince of Wales' – a title that continues to be held by the heir apparent to the British throne to this day.

It is for this reason that the Welsh dragon is nowhere to be seen on the Union Jack, which contains only the red cross of St George (representing the Kingdom of England, within which is the Principality of Wales), the white saltire of St Andrew (the Kingdom of Scotland) and the red saltire of St Patrick (representing Ireland – though only Northern Ireland is now part of the United Kingdom).

It's the same with the Royal Standard. There are four quarterings – England (three lions passant) in the first and fourth quarters, Scotland (a lion rampant) in the second quarter, and Ireland (a harp) in the third quarter. But – despite four perfectly even boxes – the Welsh dragon is nowhere to be seen, having been rampantly gobbled up by England's lions in the 1280s.

What all this meant was a huge surge of building works. As

Edward took control of Wales, he cemented his position by building a ring of blockbuster castles – Caernarfon, Harlech and Conwy, to name a few. The cost of these castles was colossal – some 90 per cent of his nation's annual income.

No expense was spared: Caernarfon's building works were overseen by Jacques de Saint-Georges, the master military architect in Europe. The result was immense: colossally thick walls with octagonal towers, decorated with bands of coloured limestone and sandstone. It was as the building works were in progress, when Eleanor stayed in makeshift accommodation within the walls, that she gave birth to Prince Edward in April 1284, known thenceforth as 'Edward of Caernarfon'.

Even after giving birth, it's not hard to believe that Eleanor was heavily involved with the building works. 'Are you sure about those foundations, dear?' she might have prodded while walking the site with Edward.

Certainly, her influence can be seen in the finished structure. Inside, Caernarfon was decorated to Eleanor's taste: magnificent murals, glass in the windows, running water. The Eagle Tower (though completed later) has three tall turrets – an exact echo of the castle depicted on the arms of Castile. At the top of the tower was an eyrie of birds – high nests, where three eagles were kept. This symbolism – signifying the power and military might of Ancient Rome – was not lost to Edward's subjects at the time.

But the design also played into a Welsh legend. In the quasi-historical folk tale, 'The Dream of Macsen Wledig', Magnus Maximus (or Macsen Wledig) dreams of travelling to a Welsh castle with coloured walls, turrets and a throne decorated with three eagles – which bears a striking resemblance to Caernarfon. Not only was Edward subduing the Welsh with military might, he was also embedding himself in Welsh folklore.

Either way, with all these building schemes, Eleanor was well acquainted with the medieval equivalent of high-vis and a hard hat. Some kind of architectural monument was the perfect way to remember her. And there was no better time than the 1290s to embark on such a project, for architectural design was flourishing in England.

There were a few long-term factors for this. After the invasion of 1066, the Norman newcomers hurried to make their mark, building castles, monasteries and great churches wherever they could confiscate a plot of land. As such, the demand for capable craftsmen shot through the roof. Skills were developed, expertise refined and infrastructure ingrained into English daily life. Stone was shipped from Normandy and quarries established on English soil.

A new class of English masons and carpenters emerged, whose work became more ornate and intricate with every passing generation. So by the time of Edward I's reign, skills were perfectly primed for any daring architectural project – say, a series of twelve crosses – to flourish.

This was also an important moment of stylistic change. For centuries, the rounded arch had been de rigueur. In the ancient world, Romans built their aqueducts, arenas and imperial gates with the semi-circular arch. The Normans – who championed the Romanesque style – favoured thick stone walls and arcades of rounded arches. But in the thirteenth century – during the lifetime of Eleanor – a new shape came to prominence. This was the hot new thing of interior design: the pointed arch.

This shape probably came from the Islamic world, the knowledge of which spread across Europe via crusading knights, travelling diplomats and stonemasons (who would often work abroad, learning and bringing home the new techniques), wandering pilgrims or Muslim conquerors. Or – as was the case with Eleanor – through royal princesses bringing their childhood customs across the seas, when they married a foreign prince.

The impact of the pointed arch was immense. By transferring more of the forces downwards (rather than outwards), pointed arches allow for taller buildings, thinner walls and – best of all – lots more windows. Thick walls were replaced with sheets of jewel-like stained glass, flooding the interior with coloured light. This new feature became the building block of a new style: the Gothic.

One of the Gothic marvels of the age was Sainte-Chapelle, the royal chapel on the Île de la Cité in central Paris. The Sainte-Chapelle was consecrated in 1248 – when Eleanor was seven years old. King Henry III paid a visit to the new chapel in 1254 and was so inspired by the beauty, he opted to rebuild Westminster Abbey with similar features. So, by the time the Eleanor Crosses were commissioned in the 1290s, the Gothic style was only forty years old – the newest trend, still on the rise.

It's worth remembering that throughout the medieval period, the term 'Gothic' as we know it didn't yet exist. In fact, it was first used retrospectively as an insult. In his book *Lives of the Artists* (1550), the Italian architect and historian Giorgio Vasari described the 'barbarous German style' of the medieval world, which he linked to the Goths, a Germanic tribe that had sacked Rome and, in Vasari's view, contributed to the decline of Roman civilisation.

While we're on the subject of etymological factoids you can impress your friends with . . . have you ever wondered where the word 'medieval' comes from? It originates from the Latin phrase *medium aevum*, where *medium* means 'middle' and *aevum* means 'age' – literally, the Latin translation of 'the Middle Ages' – a period in European history from about AD 500–1500, roughly between the fall of the Western Roman Empire and the Renaissance.

According to the *Oxford English Dictionary*, the earliest use of 'medieval' was 1817, in the writings of the English clergyman and antiquary, the Revd Thomas Dudley Fosbroke. Incidentally, 1817 was the debut for several other words, including 'unalike', 'worrying', 'realism', 'pianist', 'nicotine', 'entitled', 'frump', 'svelte' and 'acidimeter'.

But off the acidimeter and back to crosses. Time for the stone-masons to have their moment in the spotlight. It's only by going through their processes step by step that you begin to understand the time and labour required to build each cross and appreciate the scale of what Edward was commissioning – which, in turn, is an immense reflection of Eleanor herself.

Don't forget, today, memorials and public statues are two-a-penny. But in the medieval period, something as large and ornate as an Eleanor Cross was a real rarity. If you think it's Instagrammable now, it was a hundred times more so in the past – not only because it was beautiful, but because everyone knew the expense and skill behind it.

For architectural projects of the medieval period, such as the Eleanor Crosses, the job was overseen by a master mason – an artist, architect, craftsman, engineer and manager all rolled into one. He discussed the brief, ordered the stone, hired and paid workmen, oversaw work, signed off on the completed project and answered to a king or queen if things were delayed. He would have dressed grandly, roaming the site in robes trimmed with squirrel fur, purse hanging from a studded belt. One famous mason in Calais, Simon of Ardes, was so experienced he was able to take measurements 'not so much with his measuring-rod as with the yardstick of his eyes'.

The first team on site would be the carpenters, who would clear the area, order trees from the royal woods and build a lodge for tools to be stored in and masons to work. For a large project – say a cathedral or church – the lodge would be more extensive. There might also be a lime plaster tracing floor, where master masons could draw out plans to scale.

With the lodge in place, the masons arrived. They had a practical uniform: an overcoat of thick wool, known as a garnache, a studded leather belt, bindings on the legs and working gloves on the hands. In the lodge, detailed drawings were created on parchment or vellum. These designs, made with a pointed metal stylus, could be rubbed off afterwards and were then transferred onto wood or canvas and cut out, creating a pattern for the masons to cut in stone.

Once the stone was acquired from the quarry, it was roughly hewn or 'scappled', which involved splitting it by driving iron wedges called plugs and feathers along marked lines, then prising it apart with a heavy crowbar. Another way to split the stone was to drive in wedges of dry oak, then soak them with water. As the oak swelled, the stone would break apart.

Once a rough block was obtained, it was squared off using a pick or hammer axe – to get it to the approximate size of the pattern. Like wood, stone has its own grain, so it might be best cut on the freeway or crossway. If you misjudged this, you were in danger of 'plucking' – accidently picking out more stone than you wanted. Sometimes this job took place at the site of the quarry, to reduce the weight of stone to be transported.

Parts of the crosses of Geddington and Hardingstone were made of local Weldon stone, a medium-grained, hard, oolitic limestone, which had a pale brown-buff colour. The quarry is located just outside Corby. Over the centuries, this stone was used for some important projects, including Rockingham Castle, some Oxbridge colleges (including the resplendent King's College, Cambridge), Kirby Hall and Old St Paul's Cathedral, which was destroyed in the Great Fire of 1666.

In preparation for the walk, I sought to get a better sense of Eleanor's architectural legacy. It's one thing reading about these historic processes in books, but to really have a deep understanding of how it works, you need to get hands on.

So, with that in mind, I headed to the charming market town of Driffield, some 30 miles east of York. Here is the studio of Alan and Tracey Micklethwaite. They have spent a lifetime working with stone: Alan a mason, Tracey a sculptor. For many years, Alan was the head carver at Lincoln Cathedral and was also part of the conservation team that worked on the Northampton Eleanor Cross in 2019, up on the scaffolding, replacing unstable blocks.

I had signed up to one of Alan's day courses and was guided by his expertise for eight hours. First hand, I saw the skills he'd perfected over a lifetime, the techniques that had been passed across the centuries. How would Alan compare to the stonemasons of 1290, I asked, if he was sent back to work on the original Eleanor Crosses team? 'The basic techniques haven't changed much,' he told me. 'Despite seven hundred years between us, I'd probably be OK to slot in – if they'd have me.'

Alan and Tracey's studio is a light and airy space, with walls adorned with photos of past projects, including grimacing gargoyles for Ripon Cathedral and Selby Abbey. There were three of us on the course. The other two were a couple in their twenties who lived in York (making me rather a third wheel). This stone-carving course was a surprise date – love flowering once more, through the stones!

We spent a day working on a single piece of Ancaster stone – a creamy-coloured limestone quarried in Lincolnshire, near to Ancaster, the Roman town Mum and I passed through on the way to Grantham. Ella – a Belgian medical researcher – worked on a Celtic knot design. Oliver – an engineer – carved a tansy beetle, a beautiful, jewel-like creature that, although once wide-spread in the UK (and a familiar creature to Eleanor and Edward), is now only found on the River Ouse in York.

For me, Alan provided a detail from the Northampton Eleanor Cross – a section he had replaced, as it had become unstable. It was a leaf detail that formed part of the gablet (a small ornamental triangular gable), which sits above one of the Eleanor statues. How thrilling it was, to be working on a part of the Northampton Eleanor Cross, using the tools and techniques of the original medieval masons!

Our blocks of stone rested on tall, sturdy wooden tables, covered with old bits of carpet to stop them slipping around. First, I traced the medieval leaf motif using carbon paper. When you reverse this, place it on the stone and push down hard, the design is transferred. Then, I used a pointed utensil – a scriber – to make a shallow scratch on the lines. This made it easier to precisely cut into the stone, to have some grip, without slipping and sliding.

Throughout the day, I chipped away at this little block, just like those medieval masons did in the 1290s, sitting in a wooden lodge, in places like Geddington. For this detailed, decorative work, I used two main tools: first, a sturdy dummy hammer, with a wooden handle and a polished steel block at the end; the second, a steel chisel with a modern addition, a tungsten carbide tip (which remains sharp for much longer than a standard steel blade).

By tapping the end of the chisel and directing the other end on the stone, incisions can be made in the block. Slowly but surely,

I marked out the edges, until shallow scratches became deep grooves. *Tap. Tap. Tap.* Blow away the dust. Reposition the block. Stand back and squint. *Tap. Tap. Tap.* Realise you've gone wrong. Repeat. Alan made it all look so easy. After this, I used a claw-ended chisel to scoop out chunks of unwanted stone and a bull-nosed chisel to create concave shapes.

My workstation – in need of a tidy-up!

In terms of creating the gentle foliate shape, the most difficult part was achieving a naturalistic curve. Much of the afternoon was spent perfecting this. The tiniest *tap-tap-tap* would reduce a potentially beautiful leaf shape into a sluggish blob – the most nerve-wracking thing being, of course, that once you go wrong, you can't go back. Oliver the Engineer discovered this the hard way when, in one tap, his six-legged tansy beetle became a rare, five-legged variety.

A wonderful day with Alan at his stone-carving course.

Nonetheless, all of this was an immensely satisfying process and I felt a great sense of achievement as I jumped on the train at York station with a stone block in my handbag. It had been enlightening, too, and I learned a couple of lessons from the experience.

Firstly, we don't tend to appreciate the details of cathedrals from all the way down on the ground, but a day as a stonemason's student gave me an immense appreciation for the time, patience and skill required, even in the finest details. Each flower or leaf formed from stone is a remarkable work of art in its own right. They are swirling rhythms of sinuous curves, flowing lines, wavy forms. It gives Art Nouveau a run for its money.

The other thing that became evident was the vast amount of dust. It was everywhere – on the tabletop, on the window glass. It was a Hoover's dream. We wore safety goggles to protect our eyes and used large paint brushes to sweep the dust away, but by the afternoon, my clothes were shrouded in fine powder. My hair – alarmingly – turned from brown to Einstein grey, with strands flying outwards.

When you think about those medieval masons, working like this every day – years of the sound of metal meeting stone, of dust flying through the air and lumbering heavy materials – it must have taken a significant toll. Silicosis was the stonemason's occupational hazard, a chronic lung disease caused by inhaling silica dust.

In a project like the Eleanor Crosses, there were two main types of mason. First, the hewer mason, who prepared the stone, like I had. These were sometimes known as banker masons – referring to the 'bankers' they worked on – heavy working benches of blocks of wood or stone, which brought the stone up to a suitable working height.

It was these hewer or banker masons who left personalised 'mason's marks' on the reverse of each block, a kind of signature by which they would be paid. Some masons were paid by block. Journeymen – from *la journée*, the French word for day – were paid by the day.

The other type were fixer or setter masons, who laid the stones in position. On a big project, the stone blocks might be delivered by barrowmen, who carried them using a wheelbarrow or a beading barrow – a wooden platform carried by two men, similar to a modern medical stretcher. It was hefty, back-breaking work.

The individual blocks were bonded into a wall or decorative feature by a mortar made from a precise mixture of lime (processed chalk), sand and water. Creating the lime was an important job and one that required attention day and night. First, chalk was burned in a kiln or pit, producing a fine white dust. This was mixed with sand and passed through a large sieve to remove any lumps, after which water was added to create the wet mortar mix.

As it set very quickly, the mortar needed to be used that day, which is why it was made onsite, then heaped onto a tray called a hawk board, which the mason would hold in one hand, scraping off the mortar with a trowel and placing it on the stone – the same method bricklayers use today.

The stones were laid in layers or courses. Built over foundations of rough stone, the bottom layer was known as the ground table, earth table or water table. It was important to build each course slowly, to allow each one to settle into position, otherwise structures might begin to lean (as was the case with Temple Church in Bristol, which goes by 'the Leaning Tower of Bristol'). All of this was constantly measured and checked using rods, T-squares and Euclidean geometry.

To lift the heavy blocks of stone into position, the team had a few different methods. Sometimes, wooden rollers came into play; at others, counterweights were used – perhaps a basket full of stones. Blocks could also be raised with a rudimentary crane, pulley block and winch – either powered by hand or by a tread-mill. This movement required the blocks of stone to be drilled with holes, which allowed an iron lifting device to grasp hold of the block and lift it into position.

If everything went to plan, the blocks slotted together to form a perfectly smooth surface. William of Malmesbury described the work at Salisbury Cathedral as 'so correctly laid that the joint deceives the eye and leads it to believe that the whole wall is composed of a single block'. Sometimes, if the local building stone didn't cut very square, such as in East Anglia, inner walls were plastered and outer walls rendered, to neaten it up.

As the courses rose higher, scaffolding was required – again, built by the carpenters on site. The uprights of wood were criss-crossed with horizonal poles, known as liggers, or putlogs (which is why castles now often have horizontal lines of 'putlog holes' on the outside, where the scaffolding timbers were once encased in the wall). The joints were tied with supple lengths of willow or strips of leather. There was also the job to create the steps and ladders, to reach the scaffolding itself.

So carpenters were an essential part of the project, on site from start to finish. As well as building the lodge, scaffolding and machines to hoist the stones in position, they crafted stakes to mark out foundations and barrows for carrying stone. To create the stone arches that would encase Eleanor's statues, the carpenters made 'falsework', an arch shape of wood around which the stone was placed. Once one arch was complete, the wooden false-work was removed, placed in the next position, and another arch built around it.

Once several courses had been built up, the final touch for the Eleanor Cross was a stone cross, placed on an iron dowelling pin and secured with mortar. Then, intricate detailing was carved, mismatched joints rubbed down and statues of Eleanor brought to life with vivid colour. If any surface needed to be smoothed down finely, they used the medieval equivalent of sandpaper: the rough skin of a dogfish.

In the summer, the masons worked through the daylight hours, from dawn to dusk. It was a twelve-hour day, with a midday nap. It's likely that the crosses were completed in a few months, across one summer season, but had there been a delay then work would have been paused during the winter months and the cross covered in straw to protect it. In this time, some masons might have worked on blocks within the lodge or found work at a quarry, where the frost and rain helped split the stone.

All this labour was worth it, however, for the result was spectacular. When the crosses were finished, they were some of the first and finest expressions of the new Gothic style, pioneering the 'ogee' shape – a strange new S-shaped curve.

You can imagine the scene as ladders were removed and the team of masons stepped back to wipe their brow and admire the last two or three months of work. Only, no doubt, to overhear the villagers muttering: 'Thank goodness it's finished, we can finally get the cart through the marketplace again without being covered in dust.' For some, perhaps, the design would have been too radical: 'It's nice, I suppose, but there's something about those pointed arches that feels a bit *continental*. A bit *nouveau*.'

It always made sense to me that some kind of architectural monument was the fitting tribute to Eleanor, who spent her life overseeing construction at the forefront of design. But after completing a day in the life of a stonemason – which I'd recommend to anyone interested – and having a greater understanding of what it all takes, my inklings were confirmed. Not because this reflected Edward and Eleanor's interests, but, rather, their dedication to one another.

In a strange way, the process of stone carving is a little like true, romantic love. Both require years of patience and devotion and neither can be rushed. I'm reminded of a quote by the author bell hooks*: 'The word "love" is most often defined as a noun', she writes, yet 'we would all love better if we used it as a verb'.

Couples might feel an initial burst of attraction – or perhaps lust – at first. But to form a deep love, action is required – an endless tap-tap-tapping and blowing away the dust. Love demands intention. It is ever-changing and requires sacrifice. Like a stonemason must work around the natural course of the stone, so too couples must work hard to carve their path.

It's striking to think that the marriage of Eleanor and Edward was an arranged one, a product of politics. Yet some research suggests that such marriages have a longevity because couples are more proactive in making it work. Edward and Eleanor spent thirty-six years together, only apart by absolute necessity and battling some of the most difficult challenges – the crown's heavy burden, constant travel, endless pregnancies and child loss. Perhaps it was in these dark, difficult moments that their love was forged.

Like the stonemason who spends decades chipping away stone, Edward and Eleanor's marriage was fortified by almost four decades of small acts of tenderness, commitment and mutual respect. The result – like a soaring cathedral – was a love of immense strength and, even to the smallest detail, a thing of exquisite beauty.

* Yes, she uses all lowercase!

10. TRAPPED 'TWIXT MARSH AND LAKE

'Love is patient, love is kind. It does not envy, it does not boast, it is not proud.'

1 Corinthians 13:4

I AM VERY LUCKY TO be a historian. It is a wonderful job and one that occasionally has moments of glamour – film premieres in Leicester Square, book launches at Hatchard's Piccadilly, drinks parties at St James's Palace. But the morning of Monday 9 December 2024, when I stood in the drizzling rain, in the car park of Northampton South Premier Inn – was not such a moment. With torchlight on, half-asleep and eating a squashed banana, I listened to the din of the four-laned A45 on the other side of the hedge.

My spirits were soon lifted, however, as three fellow ramblers arrived on the scene. My mum was back, joined by Rory, a friend who worked in antiques, and my sister. At 6 a.m., I assembled this motley crew outside the Queen Eleanor pub. It felt good to be outnumbered. I was no longer a solo walking aficionado, but a team leader, from whom my anorak-clad disciples sought wisdom and advice. 'Don't wear a snood, you'll overheat,' I warned. 'You'll need a high-vis on that backpack,' I instructed. I threw out

185

words of encouragement, too: 'Those shoes are definitely not suitable, Rory, but it's a bit late now.'

After a very quick headcount, we set off into the darkness. Once more unto the breach, dear friends, once more! The destination was Stony Stratford, 13 miles away. I guided the troops through suburban housing estates, passing only cats on their night-time wanderings and a lonesome fox. We crossed the M1, gazing down from the bridge through a wire mesh, at a never-ending stream of cars and lorries. They would be in London within the hour – a journey that would still take me a week to complete.

Words I never thought I'd say: 'I wish I was driving along the M1.'

We trampled through vast muddy fields of enormous wind turbines, past thatched cottages in the village of Hartwell and across tarmac paths of new housing estates in Hanslope.

This landscape would have been totally alien to Eleanor. In the thirteenth century, the countryside was formed of enormous fields, hundreds of acres in size. These were shaped by the political system of the day, which was based on the idea that the King was the country's chief landlord. The King leased land to nobility – clergy, lords and barons – in return for military service and loyalty, and the nobility, in turn, granted their lands to knights (like Sir Richard de Weston, from Harby).

At the very bottom of this triangle were peasants who lived and worked on the land, under the protection of the lord. This peasant class had few rights and little power on their own – though occasionally, as a collective group, they were a force to be reckoned with, as evident in the Peasants' Revolt in 1381.

Within this feudal system, the primary source of wealth and power was land ownership, the basic unit of which was the manor. Through the manorial rights, Richard de Weston lived in a manor house and enjoyed the demesne land (pronounced *dem-ain*), which was his personal domain. He also enjoyed seignory, the right to benefit from the estate and collect payments from peasants who toiled the fields.

The peasants also had traditional rights, which varied from manor to manor. There were also areas of land that were used in common with others, and those who used these were known as 'commoners'. There were different types of 'common land'. Pasture was where horses, cattle, sheep or swine could be kept, and pannage was woodland where pigs could be taken to sniff around for acorns and nuts. Commoners might also be granted 'estovers', which meant the right to take wood – most likely gorse or fallen branches.

As we rambled, sharing Sesame Snaps and Tangfastics, my sister – the most beady-eyed of the group – noticed some remnants of this lost medieval landscape. Here were strange lumps, rising and falling across the fields. It was as if a giant had been pulling an enormous rake across the land, leaving deep ridges as they went.

So what were these peculiar features? In the medieval period, most of southern and central England was covered in massive, irregularly shaped fields, between 700 and 1,200 acres in size, devoid of hedges or fences. Within each of these great fields were long, parallel strips, and these strips (known as lands or selions) were ploughed, planted and harvested by a different family.

The strips were grouped together to form furlongs, referring to the length of the furrow, which would have been equal to the long side of an acre – an acre being the surface area that could be ploughed by a yoke of oxen in a day. Each family would have a bundle of strips scattered across different fields, to ensure the good bits of land were shared equally.

Medieval ploughs were pulled by oxen (castrated male cattle, bred to be strong but docile) and had one blade, which pushed the soil to the right. Each day, a plough team would cover about an acre, which might mean walking 11 miles each day. As the plough crossed the land, soil was pushed aside to create a ridge – a fertile seedbed ready for planting. In between these ridges, the soil level fell lower, creating a furrow.

Medieval ploughs were bulky and awkward, sometimes needing a team of eight oxen to pull them through heavy soils. To minimise turning, the land was ploughed in long strips and sowed with wheat, barley, rye and oats. The strips ran the length of the field like a ribbon, creating a striped pattern.

The result was a 'ridge and furrow' structure and, even though the strips would be ploughed anti-clockwise every third or fourth year and left fallow (to re-level the field and give the soil a chance to recover its nutrients), this surface structure is still visible today, where the fields haven't since been ploughed.

By recognising the ridge and furrow structure in those fields near Northampton, we were getting a glimpse of our ancestors' lives. This was the very land, the very earth, they toiled. I looked down at the path underfoot. Had this mud once been the soil in their fingernails? Had these stones been held by my long-forgotten ancestor, before she cried, 'Geroff me barley!' and flung them in the air to scare the birds?

About 90 per cent of England's medieval population were peasants, so it's likely this is the life I would have known, had I been born in, say, 1253. Along with my mother and sister, I'd have spent the months breaking up the clods (clod hopping), sowing seeds in the fields that had laid fallow the previous season, covering seeds using a horse-drawn harrow, hurling stones to scare off the birds or slaughtering the pigs that had spent the autumn fattening up on acorns.

Would we bicker over who would do the nasty jobs? Would I be the one to cut up the family pig, to pull out the entrails and transform them into black pudding – and, worse, go to bed that evening without a shower?

Traditionally, the winter season was bookended by two dates: Michaelmas, a feast day that marks the end of harvest on 29 September; and Candlemas, the presentation of the infant Jesus at the temple in Jerusalem, which was on 2 February, when it became warm enough to till the land again – though you probably wouldn't do much sowing until Lady Day, on 25 March.

As I walked, I was curious to know: what were these winters really like? When we walked in December 2024, were we facing the same kind of conditions Eleanor would have known in this season? Is a medieval, Tudor or Victorian idea of 'chilly' the same as ours?

Over the past thousand years, Britain's climate has subtly altered, in centuries-long periods of atmospheric ups and downs. In the High Middle Ages (around AD 1000–1300), Western Europe experienced a 'climatic optimum'. It was, in layman's terms, the 'Medieval Warm Period'. Temperatures were up, harvests were earlier, frosts were fewer and, most importantly, monks in England planted vines to produce homemade wine. It was the Age of Al-Fresco.

Then, in the fourteenth century, not long after Eleanor's death, temperatures began to drop. This 'Little Ice Age', as it's now known, stretched to the early nineteenth century, with the coldest temperatures occurring around 1550–1700. There were weather anomalies, too – sudden floods, hail and snowstorms, temperature fluctuations and intense rain.

It's incredible to read about the winter of 1683–84, when London endured the Great Frost. By 5 January 1684, the River Thames had completely frozen over and was covered by a solid sheet of ice. It was so thick that a coach and six horses were driven across it and 'a great street from the Temple to Southwark was built with shops, and all manner of things sold'.

This was partially a result of Baltic temperatures, but also the particular shape of London Bridge. The piers of the bridge were spaced so closely together that sheets of ice would become lodged, slowing the river and making it more likely to freeze. The last London Frost Fair (featuring a parading elephant) took place in January 1814.

Since then, the climate has started to warm once more, back to the temperatures of the early medieval world. So we can be fairly confident that the conditions experienced by the 1290 cortège were similar to those of today. Had Tudor enthusiasts set out to walk from Lincoln to London, however, it might have been a good few degrees colder.

After passing the 10-mile mark, we settled on a bench in the charming village of Castlethorpe. I doled out the lunchtime rations: ham and cheese sandwiches, oranges, a pack of KitKats and two flasks – one tea, one coffee. As I sat in contented silence, I thought of the medieval people of this village.

How long they would have sweated and laboured, to enjoy such a feast as ours. For bread – ploughing fields and harvesting wheat. For ham – rearing and slaughtering pigs. For cheese – milking cows and processing the milk. For chutney – ploughing, sowing and harvesting onions. The rest of our meal would have been unknown to medieval Castlethorpians. Tea, coffee and chocolate didn't arrive in England for another 400 years, in the seventeenth century.

Another feature of the village that would have been mind-blowing to medieval Castlethorpians was a wooden cabinet located in a grassy square. On one side it was beautifully painted with medieval knights and heraldic devices, on the other, it read: 'Books are the quietest and most constant of friends, they are the wisest of counsellors and the most patient of teachers'. I hope, dear reader, this book is no exception.

This little box was Castlethorpe's village library, a selection of thirty-two books, free to whoever required them. For medieval peasants, though they would have seen books in church, a visit to this cabinet, where they were free to pick up and browse a selection of such a large number of books would have been a bucket list highlight. Though they wouldn't be able to read the text (even as late as 1820, England's literacy rate was only 53 per cent), they would still be appreciated as objects of beauty and craftsmanship.

In Queen Eleanor's time, it would have become a shrine for bibliophiles and she would have certainly made a pilgrimage here, for she was the greatest bookaholic of the lot.

Luxury comes in many forms. Paris Hilton had a $325,000 mini mansion for dogs in her home, while Beyoncé installed a two-lane bowling alley. But one might argue that Eleanor of Castile's home had the ultimate extravagance: a scriptorium. Usually found only in monastic spaces, it was the only one documented in any court in Northern Europe at the time.

Had *Architectural Digest* ever explored Eleanor's scriptorium, they'd have found two scribes, Roger and Philip, working away, and a 'pictor' called Godfrey who was responsible for colouring the pages and illuminating the details with gold leaf. They were well equipped with all the materials required: vellum (prepared animal skin), ink, quills, gold leaf, boards for binding books and glue. The inks were made from natural materials, lapis lazuli or indigo, for example, and mixed with a binding solution, such as egg whites.

Once completed, the books were stored in a specifically built chamber, a bit like this little cabinet in Castlethorpe. As well as books about St Thomas Becket, a Roman military handbook and a chess manual (a gift for her brother, King Alfonso X), there were classics, too: old Arthurian tales of Camelot, Sir Gawain and Sir Lancelot.

Had Eleanor peered over my shoulder as my companions and I inspected this little library, she might have appreciated a few titles. The romantasy titles would have certainly satiated her Arthurian interests and I'm sure she'd have been fascinated by *The Complete Gardener: A Practical, Imaginative Guide to Every Aspect of Gardening* by Monty Don. Though I'm not sure Judy Murray's debut fiction tennis thriller would have had the same appeal.

We continued onwards, happy in the knowledge that there was under an hour of walking left. 'Final stretch,' we happily chirruped. The day's endeavour was in the bag. However, as events unfolded, it emerged we were overly confident. Rain had swelled the river and paths were swallowed up by streams. The green dash of a footpath on the map proved rather different in reality. Here were vast flooded plains, where every step threatened to pull off a boot.

Eleanor would have adored Castlethorpe's library.

Staggering through the mud and facing near embogulation, we headed for a small bridge in the corner of the field. Clinging onto flimsy barbed wire, one by one, we took an enormous leap of faith, flying through the air to grasp hold of a rickety gatepost the other side. Relieved to have escaped the swamp, we were horrified to see, on the other side of the bridge, an enormous, deep puddle, 4 metres wide. 'A lake!' Rory cried. 'We're trapped! Marooned!' What to do? Could we skirt around it? Someone suggested building a raft. Or should we retrace our steps, leaping once more, back towards the bog, to find an alternate route?

Rory – whose shoes were already soaked through – volunteered to sacrifice himself and stepped straight into the puddle. It was deeper than we suspected, reaching his knees. Then, one by one – and amid fits of giggles – he hoisted us three damsels in distress in a fireman's lift and carried us through the perilous waters to safety, setting us down carefully on a tuft of grass. He made six trips in the end, wading across the water; back and forth, back and forth, back and forth. This episode will go down in the history books (indeed it is, with these very words!) alongside Sir Walter Raleigh throwing his cloak over a puddle before Queen Elizabeth I. Chivalry, I am pleased to announce, is alive and well.

The final squelch towards Stony Stratford took us along the Grand Union Canal. Linking London to Birmingham, this part of the waterway is 137 miles long, with 166 locks. In this small stretch, we passed a cast-iron aqueduct carrying canal boats, some 11 metres above another body of water, the Great Ouse river. This incredible construction was built in 1811 by canal engineer Benjamin Bevan.

As we stood at the canal towpath, looking apprehensively down to the boglands below, a flowery anorak approached and tapped on my shoulder: 'It's totally flooded down there, by the way. Where is it you're walking to?' My reply of 'London' took the cheerful woman by surprise and she glanced at Rory's sodden trousers. But with the clarification of '. . . but first, Stony Stratford', she offered us a valuable detour along non-flooded pathways.

At 2 p.m. – after 14 miles of walking and 35,000 watery steps – we wandered into Stony Stratford, past terraces of brick houses and family businesses, some five generations old. The name is Anglo-Saxon in origin, meaning 'stony ford on a Roman road'. The Roman road in question is Watling Street, which runs from Wroxeter in Shropshire, through London and down to Dover.

Water, water everywhere.

The town is centred around a long high street, bedecked in twinkling Christmas lights in winter and bunting in summer. When Celia Fiennes trotted through Stony Stratford, she found it a hubbub of industry, recording that the people 'make a great deal of Bonelace . . . they sit and work all along the street as thick as can be'. Bone lace, now known as bobbin lace, was created by braiding and twisting lengths of thread. The weaving was held in place with pins set in a pillow. It was originally known as bone lace, as early bobbins were made of bone or ivory. I'm sure Eleanor's embroidering daughter, Princess Margaret, would have found this thrilling to see.

One of the most fascinating historic buildings of Stony Stratford is a little cottage. It has a front door, four windows and a red circular plaque: 'This house was anciently the Rose & Crown Inn,' it reads, 'and here in 1483 Richard, Duke of Gloucester (Richard III), captured the uncrowned Boy King Edward V who was later murdered in the Tower of London.'

Indeed, following the death of King Edward IV in 1483, his twelve-year-old son and heir, King Edward V, travelled from Ludlow to London for his coronation. On the way south, young Edward stopped off at Stony Stratford, staying at the Rose and Crown Inn (believed to be this cottage).

But while staying at the inn, his uncle Richard, Duke of Gloucester (later Richard III), intercepted the royal party. The events that unfolded piqued the interest of Charles Dickens, who wrote it up in his book, *A Child's History of England*:

> *Just as they were entering Stony Stratford, the Duke of Gloucester, checking his horse, turned suddenly on the two lords, charged them with alienating from him the affections of his sweet nephew, and caused them to be arrested by the three hundred horsemen and taken back.*

The captured lords, Earl Rivers and Sir Richard Grey, were marched away and later executed at Pontefract Castle. Now completely in Uncle Richard's custody, young Edward was taken to London and joined by his younger brother, Richard, in the Tower. In the coming months, the brothers disappeared from public view. They died in 1483 – some say, at the hands of King Richard himself. So – like Charles I's last night as a free man in Stamford – it was in Stony Stratford that Edward V spent his final night free from the claws of Uncle Richard.

Dramatic tales such as these have long thrilled the people of Stony Stratford. This is a hotspot of gossip. Located on a major road, Stony Stratford – or Stony, as the locals say – was a trading town, welcoming every kind of traveller coming and going, recounting news from afar. In these inns and pubs, outlandish stories were retold and reworked, to the delight of captivated audiences.

Had you peeped in the windows, you'd see rooms packed with attentive listeners, whose eyes widened in disbelief, jaws dropping at the punchlines. Two rival inns on the high street, The Cock and The Bull, became famous for this fake news reportage, told with increasing embellishment. These pubs became notorious, giving us the phrase, 'a cock and bull story', used to describe any tale of dubious validity.

But what of Eleanor's tale in Stony? Hers was to be a brilliant subject for storytellers of old, for the records are scarce, with plenty of gaps to fill in and beef up. We aren't sure where Eleanor's body lay and it may even have been kept nearby, in the village of St Mary Haversham, where she owned property, or at Bradwell Priory, 2 miles further on.

But there was a cross here, which was built by John of Battle in 1291–93 and stood at the lower end of the town towards the River Ouse. By 1607, it was described by William Camden as 'none of the fairest', suggesting it was in a state of disrepair. Then, as was the habit, the cross was destroyed in about 1643 by Parliamentarian troops. The only trace of its existence, for visitors today, can be found at 157 High Street. Here is an unassuming suburban brick house and above the driveway is a rectangular plaque that reads:

Near this spot stood the Cross erected by King Edward the I to mark the place in Stony Stratford where the body of Queen Eleanor rested on its way from Harby in Nottinghamshire to Westminster Abbey in 1290

When I marched my troops to this spot and flung my arms out to declare 'Behold! The plaque!', the response was muted. This little panel, which you must squint to see, is a meagre reward for 14 miles of walking and demands rather a lot of imagination. But Stony had more to offer. We traipsed back down the high street and the squadron came to a halt once more. I instructed them to shield their eyes and guided them, hand in hand, over a little lane. I turned them into position, one by one. After a countdown of three, two, one, 'Eyes open!', the view took them by immense surprise.

Here was an enormous vision in glorious technicolour: Eleanor the Giantess. The entire gable-end of a building had been transformed by a 30-foot-high mural. This was Eleanor like never before. Eleanor the rock star, about to play a set at Glastonbury. Eleanor the supermodel, on the cover of *Vogue*. Eleanor the muse, fronting a psychedelic album cover.

The mural was created in 2019 by a local artist, Luke McDonnell. Once a drummer who had toured the world, Luke has thrown himself into an equally rock-and-roll scene: life in lovely Stony Stratford, where he runs galleries and works as a mural artist.

A couple of months after the walk, I returned to Stony Stratford to meet him. We met at The Bull – of 'cock and bull story' fame – and when I arrived, Luke was already chatting away to people in the pub. He seemed to be a well-known face around these parts. We settled down in a corner in the front room and ordered some lunch.

For an hour or so, Luke told me his story and how he joined the queue to commemorate Queen Eleanor. It started with a love of history, inspired by his grandfather. Hearing Eleanor's remarkable story, he set out to put her back on the map – or, indeed, the wall.

With council approval, Luke got to work – and there was no lack of helpers. 'Everyone here is very passionate about the history of Stony Stratford,' he explained. The design was a collaborative effort, with history tips from elderly enthusiasts and abstract design inputs from the very young attendees of a summer holiday club. The model for Eleanor herself was Luke's sister, whom he photographed wrapped in a bedroom sheet.

With a design agreed, next came the challenge of transferring it onto an enormous wall. Projectors were the answer, in the dead of night. 'What I didn't take into account is that the road is really narrow,' he laughed. It took six separate projections to get Eleanor up there, in proportion and in line. After that, Luke spent two weeks buzzing up and down on a scissor lift, covering the wall with every shade of paint. This peculiar spectacle attracted considerable attention. Locals brought coffees and pints of cider. The BBC came for an interview. One lady serenaded him with opera.

But the endeavour was worth it, for the result is magnificent. Here is Eleanor, with arms to her neck, head leant back, gazing wistfully to the sky. It is a masterclass in trompe-l'oeil, for we look up at the underside of her chin. 'This angle gives her a grandeur,' Luke explained, 'because it's as if you're looking up at a statue.'

The gesture – with hands resting gracefully in front of her chest – gives a wonderful flowing quality. It's a pose inspired by the work of the Pre-Raphaelite artist Dante Gabriel Rossetti, whose muses, Jane Morris and Alexa Wilding, were often painted in this manner. Behind Eleanor is a circular halo-like shape, filled with a pattern like that of the Victorian designer William Morris, who was enraptured by the medieval world.

Above Eleanor, in a flowing ribbon, are echoes of those divine words of Edward I: 'whom living we dearly cherished and whom in death we cannot cease to love'. It was this quote that first caught

Luke's imagination: 'A big thing for me is that it's all about love,' he told me. 'Edward's quote is so gorgeous, so beautiful.'

Beside Eleanor are birds from the Great Ouse river: the kingfisher, a symbol of peace and prosperity; and a heron, a symbol of birth and death. There are petunias and geraniums, too, a nod to Eleanor's love of gardening and 'Stony in Bloom' – the dedication of so many to keep the town looking beautiful.

In the background, to the left of Eleanor, is a depiction of the Eleanor Cross, the start of that long history of memorial of which Luke's work is now a part. On the right are a selection of sixteenth-century trading tokens, particular to Stony. There were around fifteen varieties, sold to travellers by innkeepers and tradesmen, and many of these were taken on the travellers' onward journey and never returned – a savvy move on the issuers' part.

Luke beside his wonderful mural.

As plates were cleared and we ordered a coffee, Luke told me that while working on the project, he had gone through a difficult break-up. 'It was brutal,' he remembered. 'Halfway through this painting, my heart had fallen out of my chest.' Yet he continued on. How strange that, from those ashes of romance, he created an ode to love itself, this vision of gentleness and grace.

We stepped into the sunshine to visit the mural. 'It's faded a lot,' Luke said, though I thought it still looked vivid and striking. 'People come from all over the world to see it, to have selfies,' he laughed. Since the mural was completed, Luke has visited local schools to talk about Eleanor. Now, every day – along with the sign for the Queen Eleanor Roundabout – the people of Stony are reminded of Eleanor, of that night long ago when her body passed through their town.

On the night I first arrived in Stony Stratford – alone once more, having bade farewell to the little party of walkers – I slept at the Old George, a sixteenth-century inn on the high street. A former posting house, it sits low beside the pavement, at the original medieval street level.

The Old George is located directly opposite Luke's Eleanor mural. Before I went to bed that evening, I stepped outside, in the moonlight, to catch a glimpse of her once more. I looked at the William Morris detailing and was reminded of his famous quote: 'Have nothing in your house that you do not know to be useful or believe to be beautiful.'

Could Morris's theory be applied to the curious little town of Stony Stratford? The Queen Eleanor Roundabout was eminently useful, of course, but there was no doubt that Luke's mural was a work of ethereal beauty.

11. A PILGRIMAGE TO DUNSTABLE

*'All my life through, the new sights of Nature
made me rejoice like a child.'*

Marie Curie

IT WAS 10 DECEMBER 2024. After breakfast in that creaky, crooked inn, I was zoomed forward in time, spending the day in the company of one of Britain's newest cities. For some 8 miles I rounded the roundabouts and zig-zagged the pavements of Milton Keynes. Built in the 1960s to house a population of 250,000 and to ease the congestion of London, today it boasts more than 20,000 parking spaces and 130 roundabouts.

The layout makes it all feel distinctly un-English, as it's based on a North American-style grid road network. All main roads use an H or V, indicating whether they run horizontally or vertically. There are boulevards, and streets numbered 'Fifth Street' and 'Sixth Street'.

It was an odd thing, to walk through this most modern, most artificial of towns, in search of a long-lost past. I went by the headquarters of Badminton England, with world-class courts and Olympic gym facilities. I sat on a bench in an enormous car park, working through a pack of Jammie Dodgers, as station commuters disappeared into huge glass buildings around me.

Even in modern cities such as these, there's still history all around – it's just not always as obvious and it presents itself in surprising ways. I ducked under dingy concrete underpasses, their names a nod to landscapes of old: 'Winterhill', 'Oldbrook', 'Leadenhall'. There was nature, too – a rat scuttled past.

I walked through Beanhill, an estate of bungalows. There were signs to Bletchley, where Second World War codebreakers cracked the Enigma code. I danced across pavement cracks and manhole covers. On and on, along walkways, through underpasses – and still, I couldn't escape the concrete sprawl. A wooden gate adorned with a ram's head brought some hope of the return of rural life.

Then came the vast Caldecotte Lake, a manmade balancing lake that controls flood water on the River Ouzel, and Monellan Crescent, a strange, semi-circular form, like an ancient amphitheatre filled with water. At Bow Brickhill, I stood in line beside the cars and waited for a train to rush past.

The destination for 10 December was Woburn, a charming trading town. Here were bowed windows, fine front doors with brass knockers and elegant walls of red brickwork. It is a ready-to-go Regency film set. You can almost hear the clopping of horses on the pavement setts and easily imagine a bonnet ribbon fluttering in the wind, disappearing around the corner.

After walking the 13 miles from Stony Stratford and passing the county border from Buckinghamshire to Bedfordshire, I settled into a late lunch. Flootes is the place to go – a charming cafe where I enjoyed a pasty, a piece of carrot cake and a cup of Earl Grey tea.

Though a sweet town, Woburn has had its fair share of drama over the years, facing three terrible fires. In the medieval period, a chimney fire spread through the thatched roofs. Then, during the English Civil War, the Cavaliers gave it another heavy toasting. In 1724, there was another fire, which is why it's dominated by the Georgian style we see today.

During the Victorian period, Woburn became an important stopping point on the London–Northampton turnpike (a toll road). The town had the first twenty-four-hour post office outside London as well as a whopping twenty-seven inns. In the years since, the Grand Union Canal and the West Coast Main Line railway route took away the major part of its footfall. So it remains a pretty town, built up with wonderful historic buildings from its moment of wealth, but no longer encumbered by a major road or busy traffic.

It's a funny thing, these 'desirable' English towns. Many have ended up like this by virtue of economic failure, being preserved through lack of modernisation. Take the case of Lavenham in Suffolk, renowned for its timber-framed buildings: it was a wealthy medieval wool town, but fell on hard times in the sixteenth and seventeenth centuries. Another pretty place is Topsham in Devon, which was a prosperous port until Exeter took over in the nineteenth century. On the other hand, the small market and trading town of Birmingham did so well in the nineteenth century that it grew, modernised and – though has delights of its own – isn't generally sold as a 'charming' place to live.

On the evening of 10 December, I stayed the night at Longs Hotel & Inn. My room was on the third floor, with three sash windows overlooking the high street, a view thousands of travellers had enjoyed for hundreds of years.

Early on 11 December morning, I continued onwards, diligently following the route on the OS Maps app. We'd come a long way together, Oz and I (as I'd begun to refer to him). I was beginning to feel quite fond of the constant companionship, that little red arrow that directed me, like Mary and Joseph guided by the star in the east.

With Oz's direction, I walked through the magnificent parkland of Woburn Abbey, weaving between age-old trees standing tall. It was dawn and the frosted grass crackled underfoot. Deer jumped up as I passed, perplexed at this early morning visitor, and birds fluttered from the trees, soaring high above the lake. The sky warmed to a pinky shade, the sun's rays refracted through the early haze. All was calm.

In the medieval period, this site was the home of a Cistercian abbey – Woburn Abbey. Founded in 1145 by monks from Fountains Abbey in Yorkshire, by the thirteenth century it was one of the richest in the country. So it was likely that this is where the royal party stayed as they passed through, and here Eleanor's body lay.

The Eleanor Cross at Woburn was built, once again, by John of Battle, in 1292–93. It has, I'm afraid, completely disappeared and there is no record of its aspect or location, though some say it stood in an area known as The Pitchings, a now-cobbled area next to the old town hall. The abbey, too, was dissolved in 1538, and Henry VIII gave the property and the surrounding lands to John Russell, the 1st Earl of Bedford, whose descendants have lived there since, rebuilding the abbey as a grand, classically inspired stately home. The Bedfords have been an important family over the centuries, developing many parts of London's Bloomsbury, including Russell Square.

As I passed through the grounds, Woburn Abbey was visible in the distance. One of the treasures of the house is among the most famous images of English queenship: the Armada portrait of Queen Elizabeth I. There are three versions, but this is the best (though don't tell Royal Museums Greenwich I said that).

Created in 1588, the portrait shows Elizabeth triumphant after the defeat of the Spanish Armada. There is no diplomatic subtlety here. With a hand on the globe, she basks in the victory. Behind her are scenes of the Spanish ships facing advancing English fireships, dashed against the rocky coast by a 'Protestant Wind'.

It is a strange twist of history that the body of Eleanor, the Castilian princess, was once venerated on this ground. Then, centuries later, Woburn Abbey continues to care for another English queen – this one triumphing in the face of Spanish despair.

It was one week since I had left Lincoln and I had covered more than 120 miles. Strolling through the parkland, I was no longer new to the walk, but had comfortably settled in. Each day was no longer such a dive into the unknown, but a routine with a familiar rhythm.

Today, research suggests that walking a very long way – exhausting your body – should make it difficult to focus and leads to irritability. But pilgrims past had seen it a different way: by pushing your body to the limit, you can reach a space that dulls your mind and sets it free to think intensely, without distraction.

Take the example of Chaucer's pilgrims, who journeyed to Canterbury. Though they had a purpose – to visit the shrine of St Thomas Becket, where they would pay their respects or seek an urgent cure for injury or make payments to reduce their time in purgatory – there were other perks to the big trip. The thrill of adventure, the chance to *get away from it all*, the social scene of pilgrim routes, the opportunity to explore great cathedrals. They were the interrailers of medieval England and the walk to Canterbury was the Full Moon Party of old.

But what strikes me about *The Canterbury Tales* is that it is not about the destination; what Chaucer writes about is the journey itself. As they walk, each pilgrim passes the time by telling a story,

207

a kind of medieval therapy session. Many modern pilgrims talk of the journey – the oddness, comradeship or discomfort – giving as much purpose as the final destination. Which is an obvious point, really. Otherwise, nowadays, you'd drive to the shrine or hop on the train.

Which of Chaucer's pilgrims was I? Perhaps the infamous Wife of Bath, who had been married five times, travelled on pilgrimages to Jerusalem three times, was deaf in one ear and had a gap between her front teeth? Or was I more the Miller – a drunken, brash and vulgar man who rips doors off hinges and tells blasphemous tales? Perhaps the Friar – the roaming priest who accepts bribes. Or the Clerk, a sincere, devout student at Oxford University who loves learning and spends all his money on books. Was I a wayfarer, traveller, wanderer, devotee, spiritual tourist or curious passer-by?

The answer could be found in the village of Milton Bryan. Here, I waited beside a timber-framed thatched house, which was equipped with every possible village accessory: a post box embedded into the wall, bags of kindling, a stall of homemade jars. There was Christmas village chutney, gooseberry chutney, pickled shallots, pickled onions – all pre-fridge, long-life foods, which may have been familiar to our medieval ancestors. As I admired the goods on sale, a taxi rolled up. Out stepped a tall, dark-haired young man with a winning smile.

This was my next accomplice: Guy, a pilgrim extraordinaire. Alongside performing musical comedy sketches (he is one half of 'Bounder and Cad', though I'm not sure which half), Guy runs the British Pilgrimage Trust, a charity that celebrates the ancient practice of pilgrimage. Like monasteries, abbeys, saints days, confession and mass, pilgrimage was a major part of English medieval life, but all these things were removed in the Reformation.

Pilgrimages were banned by an Act of Parliament shaped by Thomas Cromwell in 1538 and the practice never really picked up again.

It is Guy's mission to revive this lost practice. But what does a pilgrimage look like in the modern world? For Guy, it's a broad term, where pilgrimage is a practice, not a belief system. It can be spiritual or simply an act of walking in the footsteps of our ancestors, visiting sacred locations – cathedrals, ancient trees, river sources, holy wells, standing stones.

'All you need to be a pilgrim is good intentions and a heart open for transformation,' Guy explained as we strolled along the lanes. 'Pilgrimage is not about how far you travel, but about how deeply you travel.' It's different to a walk, because you're opening yourself up to experience the unexpected, heading towards an unknown destination. Tourists come with expectations, but pilgrims are open to what the journey will show and grow in them. Walking is for the body; pilgrimage for the soul.

In medieval times, the destination was even more unknown than now, where our phones show us photos of the destination before we see it in real life. But aside from the physical end point, the true unknown destination is the person we become, transformed by changes within. 'Pilgrimage can be a process of days or months or even years,' Guy told me, 'but you can also make a pilgrimage in a matter of hours.'

My walk, from Lincoln to London, seemed to have all the characteristics of a pilgrimage. Following the footsteps of ancestors. Tick. In memory of a person. Tick. Being open to experiencing the unexpected. Tick. Passing sacred places. Tick. Making friends with deans. Tick. Ending up at a shrine. Tick.

Guy's sense for the divine was obviously pretty powerful, because we came across a sacred space within only a matter of

209

minutes. An innocuous-looking pond, beside which – among long reeds – was a sign. This was the site of 'The Chapel over the Pond', a Methodist chapel that stood, on stilts, raised up above the village pond, from 1861 until 1981. A timber building with a slated roof, it could seat up to fifty people.

'During its life,' I read aloud from the plaque, 'the Chapel was maintained meticulously with loving care by the villagers who ensured that the pews were kept beautifully polished and the wooden floor scrubbed white. Very often, the sound of ducks under the Chapel accompanied any worthy sermons and hymn singing.' There was no explanation of the obvious question: why was the chapel built on stilts, on water, rather than the perfectly good ground nearby? A planning issue? Or an attempt to rival our Venetian friends?

Nonetheless, the plaque continued: 'Many happy memories of this Chapel and the spirit of the departed generations are held by families in the village.' How lovely it was to gaze at the still waters, imagining the years of joyful hymn singing, accompanied by quacking and splashing, which once filled the air. 'You see,' Guy said, 'pilgrimage is full of surprises!'

As we walked, sharing the space with that 'spirit of the departed generations', as the plaque put it, Guy explained another concept. 'Thin spaces' are spots that hold spiritual significance: a parish church, a long barrow, a stone circle. Here, some people believe, the veil between this world and the sacred world is 'thin' – where the walls of the world are weak and there is little barrier between heaven and earth. It's in those places where you feel a spine-shiver of something beyond words – something transcendent or perhaps divine. Perhaps it was the kind of spiritual otherworldliness that Mahatma Gandhi described: the 'indefinable, mysterious power that pervades everything'.

Had there been any moments such as these so far, for me? There was something ethereal about standing alone by that Harby field, thinking of Eleanor taking her final breath, of her soul leaving her body. Or what of the cross at Geddington, with its strange magnetic force that seemed to keep the village in check?

Another important part of pilgrimage, Guy explained, is the act of being physically in a place. Not just reading a book about places or watching a video, but standing with feet on the ground, breathing in the fresh air. To discover the spirit of a place, to get a feel for people – and, in turn, see how you slot into the picture – boots on the ground is of vital importance.

Walking is brilliant for that: hours and hours to take in the landscape, to gaze at the skies. Your mind is free to become bored, to aimlessly wander – to notice tiny, unexpected details that the motorist or cyclist might speed by. It also allows you to travel at a pace that links humankind across time and space – by foot.

As Guy and I talked of pilgrimage, something about the crosses suddenly occurred to me. How did Edward expect the crosses to be received? Were these twelve separate memorials, to be admired by each town, plus whoever happened to pass by? Or was Edward actively marking out a pilgrimage route? Did he expect, or hope, that Eleanor devotees might set out to retrace his steps and use the crosses as waypoints towards Eleanor and the shrine of Edward the Confessor? Was I following in the footsteps of thousands of other pilgrims, walking the medieval equivalent of 'The Eleanor Trail'?

I was reminded of another trail that did just that. On 30 June 2000, the Diana Princess of Wales Memorial Walk was unveiled. It is a 7-mile-long walk laid out around St James's Park, Green Park, Hyde Park and Kensington Gardens – all places associated with Diana's life. The route is charted by ninety plaques on the ground, each marked with a rose motif. It is a design strikingly similar to the rose pattern that survived from the original Stamford Eleanor Cross and inspired Wolfgang Buttress's pointed needle. Did the design committee for Diana's walkway take inspiration from that?

I find it interesting that Diana – and possibly Eleanor – was commemorated by a trail, which is quite different to a set of statues. A trail requires action; it's an invitation. You are required to actively participate. In fact, the memorial isn't complete without your participation, so here we see the journey is embedded in the act of remembrance, as important as the physical monuments or shrines that guide you.

Guy and I took a break in a churchyard. Here – like in so many churchyards – were an abundance of yew trees. We walked among them and lay beneath their branches, to feel – like the yews themselves – rooted to the cold ground.

As I lay on the ground, gazing up at the needles silhouetted against the grey sky, I considered how yews have long been associated with something otherworldly and revered in all kinds of ways over the centuries. Were these trees markers of the thin spaces we had discussed?

According to the Ancient Romans, the yew was a tree of hell and was positioned at the entrance to the underworld. For Christians, yews can represent the blood and body of Christ, as the heartwood of the tree, when freshly cut, is red and sap is white. They are also incredibly hardy, able to survive for centuries on infertile soil, so they have associations with rebirth and resurrection. The Fortingall Yew in Scotland is estimated to be 5,000 years old.

But there are practical benefits to planting yews, too. They are the finest wood for making traditional longbows. In 1307,

Edward I ordered that yew trees be planted in churchyards to protect the buildings from high winds and storms.

What's more, yew trees are highly poisonous to humans and animals. The witches in Shakespeare's *Macbeth* concoct a poisonous brew with 'slips of yew silvered in the moon's eclipse'. So planting yews in the churchyard was a way to stop people grazing their livestock on church land. Today, they are a medicine used to treat cancer: the Pacific yew bark is the source of paclitaxel, a chemotherapy drug. So this is a tree of life and death, on the knife-edge between the two.

By early afternoon, Guy and I strolled into the town of Dunstable. In centuries past, this was an important town, with an enormous priory. It was here, in 1533, that Katherine of Aragon's marriage to Henry VIII was declared null and void – a major triumph for Team Boleyn. Following this, the Augustinian canons no doubt felt they were in King Henry VIII's good books – only to be evicted less than a decade later in 1540, when the priory was catalogued and sold off during the Dissolution of the Monasteries.

It was probably at this same priory that the cortège rested and Eleanor's body stayed in 1290. It was recorded:

> [W]hen the body of Queen Eleanor passed through Dunstable, it was placed in the middle of the marketplace, with a reliquary on top, until the Lord Chancellor and the nobles who had gone there chose an appropriate place where they would later – at the King's expense – erect a cross of admirable size. And our prior sprinkled holy water to bless the chosen place.

This is an important account, for it indicates there were plans to build some sort of monument even as Eleanor's body was passing through the towns. It raises the question about whether Edward had already fully conceived the idea of the crosses in December 1290. Was he giving early instructions for the crosses to be built, as he travelled through each town?

Or, had Edward discussed it with Eleanor when she was alive, knowing that – being constantly on the road – it was likely she might die far from home? What if Edward died first? Would Eleanor have commemorated her husband with the 'Edward Crosses'?

Either way, it was in the autumn of 1291 that the stonemasons arrived in Dunstable to begin work on the cross. It stood tall for three centuries and was recorded by William Camden in his write-up of Dunstable:

> *In the midst of the town is a cross, or column rather, to be seen with the arms of England, Castile and Ponthieu engraven thereon, adorned also with statues and images which King Edward the First erected, as he did some others, in memorial of Eleanor his wife all the way as he conveyed her corpse out of Lincolnshire with funeral pomp to Westminster.*

The cross no longer stands – yet again, it was destroyed during the turmoil of the Civil War – but there are still snippets that emerge in the annals of Dunstable's history.

In 1821, a local history of Dunstable, snappily titled, *Dunno's Originals: Containing a Sort of Real, Traditional and Conjectural History of the Antiquities of Dunstable and Its Vicinity*, was published. In it, the legendary origins of Dunstable were recalled, with the tales of Robert Dunn:

> *You've read the tales of Robin Hood,*
> *That fam'd outlaw and archer good,*

Of Wallace bold, that Scotsman brave;
But not of Dunn, his horse and cave;
Lo here the very tale you have.

Among the book's descriptions of Dunstable's historic past, the Eleanor Cross gets a mention: the 'cross or rather column . . . was adorned with statues and the Arms of England, Castile and Ponthieu'. What's more, around the year 1803, the foundations were discovered on the site of the Rose and Crown pub: 'part of the foundation was discovered enclosed or set round with oak posts, in a circle, at equal distance'.

Today, the site of the cross – a large crossroads with run-down, scruffy buildings – has rather lost its medieval splendour. All that marks this once-monumental architectural triumph is a plaque, bolted onto an abandoned 1980s office block.

The plaque to Dunstable's Eleanor Cross can be seen on the left, above the bin.

Nearby, tucked away from the high street, is the Eleanor's Cross Shopping Precinct. Here is a 1.5-metre-tall bronze statue, almost life-size, of Queen Eleanor. It's a nondescript, in-between spot for a statue – almost car park, almost courtyard.

As Guy and I arrived, a woman was perched on the little wall beside the statue, cigarette in one hand, walking stick in the other. 'Don't trust her! It's an alien!' she chuckled as she noticed us admiring the statue. 'Not from Dunstable, that's for sure.'

The woman's comment took me by surprise, though as we gazed upon this strange turquoise figure, surrounded by an oval arch, some sort of cosmic branding rather made sense. Eleanor seemed to be passing through space, arriving through a time portal.

The sculpture was the work of local artist Dora Barrett, who grew up in nearby Luton and trained at the Westminster School of Fine Art. When Dora was interviewed in the 1980s, she was described as 'a small lady in her early sixties, unpretentious in manner and dress'. The kind of modest person who you would pass in the street 'without realising that here was a highly gifted and determined character'.

Dora sculpted Eleanor in her garage. It was then cast in bronze at the Whitechapel Foundry in London and erected in Dunstable in 1985. From that point on, the shopping precinct was celebrated as an area of 'attractive modern architecture', where shoppers were lured in from the high street with 'a riot of luxury items on display'. The luxury on offer included W. H. Bonham, specialists in ladies' wide-fitting shoes; Eleanor's Gallery, for all your artists' materials and picture-framing needs; and Duet, a wide range of wool and fashion yarns.

Aside from providing the name for the Queen Eleanor Shopping Precinct, the statue had a legacy in ways Dora could never have imagined. On 12 May 1988, it featured in the *Dunstable Gazette*.

Here was a large photograph of a man wearing a white shirt and holding an enormous toothbrush up to the mouth of Queen Eleanor. The caption reads: 'Brush strokes – dentist Mark Elvins gets into the spirit of National Smile Week with some polished work on Dunstable's Queen Eleanor statue.'

Dora Barrett's statue of Eleanor in Dunstable's Eleanor's Cross Shopping Precinct.

The accompanying article (titled 'A bridge, tooth, AARGH!') advertises an open session at the Dunstable dentist. It's a lively write-up. 'According to local dentists,' the piece reports, 'modern dental care is pain-free (well, they would say that, wouldn't they!)' It invites locals to visit the dentist to find out 'everything you ever wanted to know about crowns, bridges, fissures and fluorides'. Demonstrations of modern treatment were also on offer ('no volunteers will be called for!'). There were stickers, balloons, games and videos for children; tea, soft drinks and some nibbles ('sugar-free, of course') for grown-ups.

Perhaps Eleanor would have benefited from this trip to Dunstable's dentist. In the medieval period, dental care was rudimentary. Ordinary people relied on local barber surgeons, their friends or even – for a serious obstacle – the blacksmith. One home solution for toothache was to collect insects – 'those nasty beetles which are found in fens during the summertime' – and reduce them to powder in an iron pot. 'Wet the forefinger of the right hand, insert it in the powder and apply it to the tooth frequently, refraining from spitting it off, when the tooth will fall away without pain.' The instructions end with an ominous line: 'It is proven.'

It was time for lunch. Guy – as mentioned previously, well versed in seeking out the divine – found a gem of a place. We settled into Lombardo's, an Italian deli. This was clearly *the* place to be on a Wednesday lunchtime in Dunstable. Everyone was here, packed into small tables. Guy went for lasagne; I had ciabatta (and a pack of Italian chocolate biscuits for pudding). We left thoroughly replenished, revitalised and apologising profusely for scattering the floor with clods of mud.

As I bade goodbye to Guy at a Dunstable bus stop, I was sad to see him go. Sharing a day together had been uplifting. We'd chatted about all sorts of things – yew trees, thin places, experiences of pilgrims across the world. All of which clarified my understanding of the journey I was on.

As he left, I realised – until that point, I had been unsure of myself, not knowing whether I was a historian, tourist, visitor or rambler. But now, looking at all this through Guy's perspective, I saw it didn't matter. All these aspects came under the pilgrimage umbrella, where the journey itself was just as important as the destination. The important thing was to open yourself up to experience the unexpected, to stay permeable to the world as it unravels before you.

Just as I contemplated the next steps, I was surprised to hear a shout across the road. It was the man from the deli. 'Miss! You forgot this!' he cried in a thick Italian accent. He thrust my phone in my hand, which I must have left at the till while I was paying. I thanked him profusely, knowing I'd have been in a sticky situation without it, navigating to London.

Guy's lessons, it seems, would take me time to fully understand. Though he had told me 'to lose myself in the journey', perhaps I shouldn't have taken it quite so literally. As much as I was ready to embrace my inner pilgrim, it was probably best to keep hold of the map.

12. PURPLE FROGS FOR DINNER

*'Nothing can seem extraordinary until you have
discovered what is ordinary. Belief in miracles, far
from depending on an ignorance of the laws of nature,
is only possible in so far as those laws are known.'*
C. S. Lewis

FOR MOST PEOPLE, THE TOWN of Luton is synonymous with
one thing: cheap Ryanair flights from London Luton airport. I
spent many a painful night here in my teens, lying on a bench,
shivering in beach shorts and T-shirt, to catch an early flight to
southern Europe.

But in the past, this area – Luton, Dunstable and the nearby
villages – were famous for something quite different. This was the
home of straw hats. These villages were the bonnet factory of the
world, with boaters flying off the production line faster than they
could be frisbeed.

The industry took off during the Napoleonic Wars, when trade
from the continent was disrupted and a gap emerged in the market.
Bedfordshire's rich soils produced the perfect plaiting straw, and
local plaiters took the opportunity to learn new techniques from
French prisoners of war.

It was a cottage industry originally. Had you peered into the windows of Dunstable's high street in, say, 1780, you'd have seen a hive of activity. Children surrounded by piles of straw, cleaning it, removing the knots and leaves, cutting it into lengths of 25 cm and sorting it into bundles. Some had a strange scar in the corner of their mouth, caused by moistening each straw between their lips to soften them, which could cause cuts.

To turn a straw plait into a hat – listen in, crafters – it was hand-stitched in a continuous coil, starting at the crown and ending at the brim. Then there was blocking and stiffening (moulding a hat shape), bumping (the final felting of a hood) and crabbing (the final touches, such as brushing).

By the 1800s, there were more than 500 hat manufacturers in Luton. In 1858, the arrival of the railway ensured products could be exported worldwide. Factories were established: machines whirred and throbbed in enormous rooms with saw-tooth roofs and large windows. Many workers – especially women – flocked to the towns where they could earn a good living. In 1878, this was revolutionised by local engineer Edmund Wiseman, with his concealed-stitch sewing machine. By 1930, Luton was producing an astonishing 70 million hats a year, shading foreheads across the world. Though this mega-trade no longer exists, there are a smattering of designers, dyeing works and block makers today who keep the history alive.

It was through this world of bonnets and boaters I walked on 12 December 2024. Eleanor's cortège travelled along Watling Street, which today is the thrumming A5183, so I plotted a route that weaved alongside it, through villages and fields.

As I trampled through the foggy woodlands, I realised I was not alone. Glowing orbs appeared in the undergrowth – the eyes of woodland creatures watching me. For a modern traveller, the presence of a badger, fox or deer is a friendly one, but for a medieval traveller, it might have been alarming – a moment when King Edward would have unsheathed his sword. Here lurked lynx or, even worse, hungry wolves.

Before sunrise on the way to St Albans.

For many centuries, wolves were a common feature of the British landscape. Along with the herds of deer, elk and boar, they travelled to Britain when it was still physically connected to Europe, crossing the land bridge. That's until the Ice Age ended, sea levels rose, the land bridge was flooded to form the English Channel and the animals were stuck here, for good. No return tickets issued.

You can see these creatures creeping into our language. Many Anglo-Saxon names used the word 'wulf', including Wulfnoth, Wulfhere, Ethelwulf and Wulfstan. They were names that represented strength and terror, for the wolf was a dangerous predator.

Wolves terrorised the land, digging up graves and feasting on corpses, attacking travellers, stealing children and devouring herds of cattle. In 1281, King Edward employed a wolf-catcher, Peter Corbet, who was instructed to take and destroy all the wolves he could find. Despite this, wolves caused so much damage to the cattle herds of Sunderland that in 1577 it was made compulsory for local people to hunt wolves three times a year. Villagers took to burying their dead on wolf-free islands. Perhaps stories such as Little Red Riding Hood aren't so fantastical after all.

As well as ferocious beasts, this stretch of Watling Street was notorious for she-wolves of another variety. On the approach to the village of Markyate is a large, rectangular, brick-built house with corner turrets, set in parkland.

In Eleanor's day, this was a priory, founded by an eleventh-century aristocratic woman named Theodora. Disguised in men's clothes, she escaped the clutches of an arranged marriage and set up Markyate Priory, where she rebranded as 'Christina of Markyate' and became prioress of a community of Benedictine nuns.

Many years later, in the seventeenth century, this was the home of another daring, cross-dressing woman: the 'Wicked Lady', Lady Katherine Ferrers, who, during the Civil War years, turned to an alternative career: lady by day, highwaywoman by night. Legend has it, in the dead of night, she dressed in men's clothing, slipped away via a secret staircase, galloped to Watling Street and demanded money from terrified travellers.

Safe from wolves and she-wolves, I strolled, unscathed, into the village of Flamstead. Here were many beautiful historic buildings. Some were built with timber frames, in-filled with brick (called 'brick nogging'), while others had walls with squares of cream stone, intermixed with knapped flint, creating a pattern like a chess board. But it was a row of fairy-tale houses, all with small doors, little windows and picturesque chimney stacks on a red-tile roof, that caught my attention. I half expected a withered old hag to lean out the window: 'Hello, dear. Would you like some ginger-bread, fresh from the oven?' Not falling for that old trick!

After scanning the brickwork, I found the golden clue: an inscription, giving me the date – 1669 – and purpose. These were almshouses.

There is a long history of charitable giving in Britain. In the medieval period, monasteries and priories ran 'bede houses' or hospitals, in the sense of providing hospitality as well as medical care. The Hospital of St Oswald in Worcester was founded around 990, with instructions for the brethren to minister to the sick, bury the dead, relieve the poor and give shelter to travellers. Today – over a thousand years after it was established – it still exists as a foundation to help the elderly. Another is the Hospital of St Cross in Winchester, founded in 1132, where hungry visitors are given a cup of ale and a chunk of bread even to this day.

Our Eleanor was part of this history of charitable giving. Between April 1289 and November 1290, acting with the profits from her property empire, Eleanor provided meals for 9,306 paupers, at a cost of what would be almost £6 million in total today. Aside from general donations to the poor, she also established religious houses that provided vital community support systems for the most vulnerable: infirmaries to care for the elderly and sick, education for poor children, and shelter and food for travellers.

By the end of the medieval period, there were about 800 hospitals across England – nearly all closed during the Dissolution of the Monasteries, in the 1530s and '40s. But the craft guilds – City Livery Companies – continued to build almshouses to provide care for 'elderly decayed' members (I look forward to being described as 'decayed'). Benefactors came from all walks of life: kings and queens, archbishops and clergy, aristocracy, merchants and liverymen.

The almshouses that I gazed upon in Flamstead were built by Thomas Saunders, of nearby Beechwood Park. Saunders made the history books in 1654, when he was one of three who put his name to the famous 'petition of the three colonels' that criticised Oliver Cromwell's regime.

Aside from stirring the pot and causing trouble for the Lord Protector, he left an endowment to build almshouses for the poor. He died in 1688 and the little row of houses were built five years later. Saunders' will read: 'I do give and bequeath unto the Overseers of the Poor of the parish of Flamstead being the place of my nativity and residence', a sum of ten pounds.

This was to fund 'an almshouse for the habitation of four poor persons'. Each house was intended for a poor married couple and, more than 300 years later, the almshouses are still maintained by the charity set up for them. A wonderful legacy, which I'm sure Eleanor would have approved of.

Despite the temptation to explore lovely Flamstead, there was no time for lingering. There were still some 7 miles to cover until I arrived at St Albans. I stood on a bridge that crossed the M1, watching yellow and red lights blurring in the fog, then pressed on through the village of Redbourn, a lovely place with Georgian sash windows a-plenty.

No longer preoccupied with bonnet production, Redbourn seemed to have carved out a new niche: quirky shop names. In this high street, pun-mania abounds. I passed a small wooden board advertising 'The Barefoot Accountant': 'accountancy services for creative types', then saw a tea room whose sign had symbols from *Alice's Adventures in Wonderland* – the Mad Hatter's hat, a pocket watch – and bore the establishment's name: 'The Queen of Herts' – a nod to the county of Hertfordshire.

Next, a hairdresser's, named 'Knock Knock Who's Hair'. Nearby, a dog-grooming spa and boutique named 'Clippin Marvellous' and a fish-and-chip shop, 'Fishy Fryer'. The Salon of Gems advertised its services with the inspirational slogan: 'Life is short. Make every hair flip fabulous!'

Escaping pun-land, the path became wild and rugged – back into the world Eleanor knew. I was in Hertfordshire now, a name that derives from the Old English, 'ford where hart, stag or deer came to drink'. Next came a disused railway, the 'Nickey Line', and a pathway beside the River Ver, where water voles lurked and watercress sprouted. I stooped through corridors of woven branches and sploshed through marshes, with reeds as tall as a man. Then appeared an old mill of brown brick, with a steeply pitched tiled roof, sitting atop the trickling stream. It was the sort of scene Constable might have painted.

Marshy land outside St Albans.

After 14 miles, I neared one of the most historic cities in the country: St Albans. In Roman times, this was known as Verulamium, the second largest town in Roman Britain after Londinium.

Like the cortège, I entered the city through what is now Verulamium Park. As the royal party passed through this land, solemnly processing with Eleanor's body, did they, too, marvel at the Roman walls? On the edge of the park is St Michael's Church, built to receive medieval pilgrims. When the cortège of Eleanor arrived at St Albans, on 12 December 1290, the town gathered at this place of worship in mourning. It must have been a magnificent sight. The abbey's chronicler recorded: 'When her body . . . approached St Albans all the abbey, solemnly dressed in albs and copes, went out to meet it at the church of St Michael on the edge of the town'.

So here, at St Michael's Church, the royal household – chaplains, tailors, messengers, maids and cofferers – were welcomed by the townsfolk of St Albans. The great bishops solemnly bowed their heads as King Edward leaped down from his horse. Little children clung to the sleeves of their parents, wide-eyed as the cart trundled past with a wooden box carrying the late Queen's body.

Tired now, after 12 miles covered, and looking forward to a cathedral cafe lunch, I ambled through charming rows of terraced houses. At each turn, the view of the cathedral came into greater clarity.

St Albans Cathedral is the oldest site of continuous Christian worship in Britain. It was built on the site of St Alban's martyrdom and a church was built around his grave. In 731, the Venerable Bede recorded that 'a beautiful church worthy of his martyrdom was built, where sick folks are healed and miracles regularly take place to this day'.

In 793, a monastery was founded on the site by King Offa of Mercia and this became one of the richest and most powerful

Benedictine monasteries in the country. The building you see today is Norman, built from bricks and tiles saved from the ruins of Roman Verulamium. Discussions that led to Magna Carta took place here in 1213. The chronicler Matthew Paris penned his most famous works here – the *Chronica Majora* and *Historia Anglorum*. So, by the time the cortège arrived in 1290, this was already a place of immense significance.

The great attractions were the two shrines – one of St Alban, the other of St Amphibalus. Pilgrims came in their thousands, providing a handy money spinner for the cathedral. The more relics the merrier. You can imagine the strategy meetings: 'If we want to rebuild the chapter house by 1315, we need to boost pilgrim numbers by at least thirty-five per cent. I want two new relics. And the entrance fee up by ten per cent.'

St Albans Cathedral in the mist.

The wonderful thing about visiting cathedrals today is that they each have their own quirks and traditions, rare survivals of the Catholic medieval world, developed by pilgrims over the centuries. At Canterbury Cathedral, there are the Pilgrims' Steps, with all sorts of strange dips and bulges – the wear of thousands who have crawled on hands and knees to visit the shrine of St Thomas Becket.

At Salisbury Cathedral, the shrine of St Osmund has three 'portholes' on each side, allowing those seeking cures to place the affected limb close to the relics. At Winchester Cathedral there is a small hole cut into the retrochoir. Here pilgrims crawl inside a passage, coming closer to St Swithun's bones.

Imagine, for a moment, you are a medieval peasant, visiting a sacred shrine. Your life has been spent in the fields, defined by regular rhythms of the seasons. You've never left the few miles of your patch – until now. You've travelled hundreds of miles, through towns and cities. You've gawped at vast walls, battled through the hustle and bustle of traders in the marketplace and been left awestruck by the sheer size of great monasteries and churches.

Then, along with thousands of others, you solemnly enter the abbey church – the largest building you've ever been in. You shuffle up weathered steps and wait in line, all the while the exotic smell of incense growing stronger, the divine chanting sounding louder. Finally, you enter a small stone chapel, with brightly painted walls. Here is the shrine, which contains a reliquary, made of brass or gold and adorned with dazzling jewels. This is where the relics of a saint are kept.

For most people, this was the most extraordinary moment of their lives. A day you'd never forget. 'What was the shrine like, Granny? Did you see any miracles?' grandchildren would still be asking, decades later – just like I expect my grandchildren might ask me in years to come – when I am 'decayed' – about queuing to see Queen Elizabeth II.

It's important to remember that medieval people believed these saints' remains had a real, divine power, akin to how we might today recognise electricity, magnetism or radioactivity. So, while some pilgrims lit a candle or left a votive offering, others remained in the space, hoping to be cured of their plight. Those who were ill, injured or disabled stayed in vigil, desperately praying for their crippling pain to disappear.

Eleanor regularly took her family to visit shrines. In 1284 alone, the royal family visited Bury St Edmunds, Canterbury, Walsingham, Bromholm and St Albans, leaving gifts of statuettes and gold cups. The following year, they travelled down the river from Westminster and then on to Chatham, making offerings at the Church of St Mary. Their payment this time came in the form of wax candles of a total length equal to the combined heights of the royal family.

It was also in 1285 that they visited Bury St Edmunds, as reported:

The King of England, with the Queen and his three daughters, in order to fulfil a vow made to God and St Edmund during his Welsh campaign, arrived at Bury St Edmunds on 20 February with deep devotion and reverence.

What did Eleanor pray for? Perhaps the health of her newborn boy, little Prince Edward. 'Please, Lord,' she might have whispered in the candlelit shrine, 'I ask for Your protection over Prince Edward. Keep him safe from illness and injury.' Perhaps she made an offering for the souls of her children, already departed, to speed them through purgatory.

A vibrant insight into the medieval world of pilgrimage can be found at York Minster. Here is a magnificent stained-glass window, recording the dramatic events that unfolded at York's shrine of St William.

One panel shows a royal visit of 1283, when Edward and Eleanor were invited to attend the translation of the new relics. The grand opening, if you will. In another panel, a man kneels at the shrine, offering a large model of his leg as thanks, after recovering from injury. Another shows a freed prisoner, offering his old chains.

Sometimes the holy relics were carried around the city – as shown in a two-part scene. During a procession there is an accident: a woman falls into the River Ouse. In a second panel, the procession comes to a stop, the woman is retrieved from the rushing waters and she kneels beneath the reliquary in thanksgiving.

But the most remarkable miracle of York's windows shows a terrible culinary accident: a woman swallows a frog. In Panel 1, an enormous purple frog lurks on her plate – which she somehow fails to notice. Part 2 shows her visiting the shrine with her husband, to seek help. Luckily, God works his miracles: the purple frog has been vomited up on the floor. The priest looks on with a blank expression, no doubt thinking, *And I thought I'd seen it all* . . . I expect the frog thought the same.

When I stepped inside St Albans Cathedral, it was a hive of activity. There were primary-school children sprinkled everywhere – some sitting on the nave, looking up to the vaulting; some wandering the aisles, perhaps hearing tales of purple frogs. In the nave – the longest in the country – were a team of flower arrangers preparing the cathedral for Advent.

In the south aisle were boxes of flowers piled high with all kinds of labels: 'High altar candle sticks' and 'White poinsettias'. A bucket of carnations was labelled 'Niche 1'. The lilies were for 'Niche 4'. I enjoyed watching a Mothers' Union event, where an enthusiastic clergyman did his best to encourage unruly toddlers to sing 'Away in a Manger'.

Following in the footsteps of millions, I visited the shrine of St Alban, a Roman who lived in Britain in around A D 300. It was during this time that the Emperor Diocletian undertook the final, and perhaps most relentless, Roman campaigns of Christian persecution. But being sympathetic to their plight, Alban sheltered a Christian priest, Amphibalus, from the authorities. Alban then became a Christian himself, swapped places with Amphibalus and was executed for his beliefs, making him Britain's first Christian saint.

The shrine of St Alban at St Albans Cathedral.

There was one other man present, with hands in prayer. I lit a candle and sat for a while thinking of St Alban, buried on this site 1,700 years ago. There is a wooden watching loft above, where hawk-eyed keepers of the shrine were hidden, like a medieval CCTV system. It's a job I'd have enjoyed, shouting, 'Oi! I saw you put that ruby down your hose! Put it back!'

Metres from the shrine is the spot where Eleanor's body was brought, on 12 December 1290. It was recorded as follows: 'her body was taken to the choir of the church, before the high altar. That whole night it was honoured by the entire abbey with great devotion, with services and holy vigils.' There's a chance that the two little children, Elizabeth and Edward, were present, for they were based at King's Langley, just 7 miles from St Albans.

It's heartbreaking to think of Elizabeth, only eight years old, and Edward, just six, visiting their mother's body – holding each other's hand as they rested their chins on the edge of the open coffin, reaching out a hand to stroke Eleanor's face.

As I write this – currently Thursday 24 April 2025 – the medieval vigils that took place at St Albans play out before me. Three days ago, on Easter Monday, Pope Francis died. Yesterday, on Wednesday 23rd, his body was processed from Casa Santa Marta to St Peter's Basilica, carried on a bier at shoulder height by twelve men who wore white gloves and white bow ties. This is similar to how Eleanor's body was carried, in a procession, from St Michael's Church to the high altar of the Abbey Church of St Alban.

Today, open on my laptop, is a BBC livestream from St Peter's itself: 'Crowds File Past Pope Francis' Open Coffin'. In a modern way, I am there in this very moment, watching as mourners file down the nave, beside St Peter's Baldachin – the seventeenth-century Baroque canopy sculpted out of bronze. There I see Pope

Francis' body in an open coffin in front of the altar – exactly how Eleanor's body was, in St Albans, all those years before.

Even on a livestream, the basilica sound is so evocative – the rustle of feet, the echoey murmurings of hushed tones, a baby crying, shoes squeaking on the marble floor, bells chiming, Latin chanting and prayers sounding from services continuing in other chapels. As Eleanor's body lay in St Albans Cathedral, the same vigil was held, the same sounds were heard. This is the soundscape of Eleanor's vigil and, if I close my eyes, it is a vivid evocation of those events of 1290.

Then, I watch the livestream, alongside 3,208 others. It is a never-ending flow of mourners in their thousands. I see a middle-aged Italian businessman, in suit and tie, bow his dead. Now, a nun taking a selfie with the coffin in the background. Next, a Japanese woman on crutches, who sits down. Now I'm watching a young couple – probably tourists – one with cap in hand and sunglasses tucked in his T-shirt neck. They'll probably spend the rest of the day sightseeing and eating carbonara and sending photos to their parents. All of these – local businessmen, nuns, visitors, tourists – are the same cast of characters who would have paid their respects to Eleanor.

For some years, a beautiful painting, titled *The Passing of Queen Eleanor through St Albans*, hung in St Albans Cathedral, which depicted the funerary cortège. It was painted in the early twentieth century, by a young artist called Frank Salisbury, and was a vast piece of art, measuring 17 feet by 5 feet.

Frank Salisbury was a local boy, brought up at nearby Harpenden, the son of a plumber and glazier. He went on to become a great artist – Sir Frank Owen Salisbury, RA – creating portraits of Queen Elizabeth II and, in 1942, iconic images of Churchill during the war: *The Siren Suit* and *Blood, Sweat and Tears*.

Thirty years before all this, he dedicated an enormous canvas to the procession of Queen Eleanor. It was in theatrical medieval style – as if you're looking at a cast on a stage. In the background, Eleanor's body is carried on a golden bier. Beside her are hooded figures in red and golden robes, carrying torches of fire. Her shields – that of England, Castile and Ponthieu – are borne, held up high. To the left of the painting, a pensive King Edward rides on a magnificent black horse, followed by a bevy of knights. He is decked in full armour, with a crown perched upon his head.

It's thought the subject was prompted by a 1907 pageant in St Albans, the participants of which were used as models for the painting – which puts a rather different slant on things when you consider how this sombre painting of a great medieval procession might have been reduced to comments like 'That's not King Edward, that's the butcher!'

The painting was bought by the Mayor of St Albans in 1918, for presentation to St Albans Abbey. The international context is important here. The previous year, in 1917, Jerusalem surrendered to British troops. Was this image of King Edward – the last of the crusading kings, who had fought for the deliverance of Jerusalem – a nod to this, that Edward's unfinished business was finally complete?

The painting was castigated by purists – amazingly confident in their knowledge of the cortège – as 'a grossly inaccurate parody of a medieval scene', but Salisbury defended his position:

In painting an historical scene there are many problems to consider that make absolute accuracy difficult . . . To be correct, the King should have been at the foot of the coffin, but that would have ruined the rhythmic beauty of the procession, so I had the effigy carried with the feet first.

The painting was displayed in the south transept of St Albans Cathedral. Finally! Eleanor's story was given the attention it so deserved, given a space in this great cathedral, where it would hang for centuries!

It would not be for long, however, as, on the night of Saturday 13 October 1973, robbers burst into the cathedral and ransacked its treasures. As Monday morning's front page of the *Birmingham Post* recounts:

> *Thieves broke into the twelfth-century St Albans Abbey at the weekend and stole articles worth, according to church authorities, about £5,000. They cut a large oil painting by Frank O. Salisbury,* The Passing of Queen Eleanor through St Albans, *from its frame and also took the silver gilt top of a processional cross, a pair of silver vases and three pairs of silver candlesticks.*

What a violent gesture it was, to cut out a painting from a silent cathedral, in the dead of night. Yet again, Eleanor's story was ripped from our memory, as so many of her memorial crosses had been violently pulled to the ground.

A quick flick through Facebook and it seems many remember this terrible day. 'I too loved the painting,' one woman wrote. 'It was a rare reminder that St Albans was a place where Queen Eleanor's body rested on the procession back to London.' Another commented, 'I remember when this happened. I always loved that painting as there was so much going on in it and the colours were amazing.' One woman – whose father must have been part of the clergy – wrote: 'Dad says . . . later pieces of it turned up in Italy. He also says it was very heavy to carry when he was serving.' The mystery remains unsolved – and one for a budding art detective to investigate.

My trot around St Albans Cathedral was followed by late lunch at the cafe (jacket potato with cheese and beans – a winning combination), then a potter about the shop. Here were all sorts of intriguing cathedral-themed products, including candles that make your home smell like a chapter house and earrings inspired by fourteenth-century stained glass. But it was the 'Adopt an Organ Pipe' table that really piqued my interest.

Here, you could adopt a pipe of the magnificent Harrison & Harrison organ, which was built in 1962 and contains more than 4,500 pipes. It costs £25 to adopt a 1–2 ft pipe, £75 for a 2–4 ft pipe and £150–1,000 for 8 ft plus. I paid £25 for the Great Quint 2/3 ft Treble D and gifted it to my brother, writing, 'Happy Christmas! I hope you visit St Albans one day, where you can meet your pipe!' It's a small – but crucial – way to support the cathedral. Each day, it costs a whopping £6,000 to keep St Albans Cathedral open and free to visit.

Refreshed and rejuvenated, I wandered the streets of St Albans, where Christmas shoppers were out in full force. Though a pleasant town today, St Albans has had its fair share of grisly history. During the Peasants' Revolt of 1381, John Ball, 'the mad priest of Kent', was hanged, drawn and quartered in the city, with King Richard II standing by. What's more, two battles of the Wars of the Roses took place in the vicinity.

In the heart of the town, I found the clock tower. It's a tall, impressive building from 1405, faced in flint and five floors high (during the Napoleonic Wars, it was used as a semaphore station). Here I found a handsome brown-tiled plaque, decorated with a foliate pattern. 'Near this site', it reads, 'stood The Eleanor Cross where the body of Queen Eleanor rested one night on its progress from Harby to Westminster.'

Unfortunately I had to wait a couple of hours to see the plaque, because a delivery lorry had taken the space. There wasn't much of a view of the cross, either. It was destroyed during the English Civil War and the rest of the monument was later demolished in 1701–02.

The tower in the centre of St Albans. You can see the red plaque to Eleanor bottom left.

That evening, I stayed in the White Hart Hotel, a timber-framed building with high-pitched tiled roofs and gabled dormers dating from 1470. During the Middle Ages, the original building was probably a guest house for the nearby abbey and, in the centuries that followed, it became a posting house, where post-horses were kept for messengers and coaches galloping up and down Watling Street.

The most remarkable moment in the White Hart's long and colourful history, however, was on 14 August 1746, when, for one night, the hotel played host to the most famous prisoner of the day: Simon Fraser, Lord Lovat, a Scottish landowner and head of Clan Fraser of Lovat (known to *Outlander* fans as 'The Fox', Jamie Fraser's grandfather). After being convicted of high treason in August 1746 for his role in the Jacobite Rising of 1745 – in some ways, a continuation of Edward I's wars with Scotland – Lovat was escorted to London to meet his end.

This news pricked the ears of the artist William Hogarth, who, on hearing that Lovat was staying the night at St Albans, galloped 25 miles from his home in Chiswick, London, to find the old chieftain settled into the parlour of the White Hart.

Lovat and Hogarth spent the evening in convivial company. Hogarth created an etching to mark the encounter, *Counting of Divisions*, which was later scaled up as an oil painting. Here Hogarth captured Lovat – this octogenarian – as a cunning man, counting his fingers as if marking his final hours.

Indeed, Lovat awaited a brutal punishment: execution by hanging, drawing and quartering. In the end, the sentence was reduced and, on 9 April 1747, at Tower Hill in London, Lovat became the last man in England to be beheaded. It would bring an end to the long list of powerful men who had died on that spot, including: Simon Sudbury, Archbishop of Canterbury during the Peasants' Revolt of 1381; Sir Thomas More, Henry VIII's Lord Chancellor, in 1535; William Laud, Archbishop of Canterbury, in 1645; and finally Lord Lovat, in 1747. At the last moment, much to Lovat's amusement, an overcrowded timber stand collapsed, leaving nine spectators dead. Lord Lovat's laughter, even as he was beheaded, is alleged to be the origin of the phrase 'to laugh one's head off'.

The view of the cathedral from my room.

That evening, as I sat in the front room of the White Hart, eating scampi and peas and sipping Sprite through a straw, I considered all this. I imagined the scene of Lovat and Hogarth, chatting and sketching on that summer's evening. Did Hogarth enquire of Lovat's fears of the death that approached? Did they drink punch together or share a pipe? Did they talk of the beauty of the cathedral? Or of travelling along Watling Street? Did they acknowledge that Lovat – this champion of the Jacobite cause, the great enemy of the kings of England – was journeying on the

241

same route traversed by King Edward, the 'Hammer of the Scots', all those years before?

My evening routines were now of military efficiency. Portable charger on charge. Check! Backpack packed. Check! Socks and boots ready to go. Check! My room was high in the eaves, with wonky floors and a slanted door to fit the crooked space, and out of the window was a wonderful view of the cathedral.

There was some comfort in imagining all the weary pilgrims who had stayed in these rooms, who slept to the toll of the cathedral bell. This soon strayed to mild alarm, however, when I was struck by a thought: could this have been the room that Lord Lovat had stayed in as he prepared to face his grisly death?

13. SACRED MONUMENTS AND ANTI-SCRAPES

'I loved her against reason, against promise, against peace, against hope, against happiness, against all discouragement that could be.'

Charles Dickens

ON WEDNESDAY 13 DECEMBER 1290, fifteen days after Eleanor's death, Edward split once more from the cortège, taking the most direct way from St Albans to London, continuing along Watling Street and entering the city through the north-west. Meanwhile, the cortège travelled east, 25 miles to Waltham Abbey in Essex, to travel the final 13 miles to Holy Trinity Priory, London, the following day.

Until this point, I had spent the whole journey feeling incredibly smug. Brand-new boots and not a single blister. An ambulatory miracle! Thank you St Alban! All the plasters I had bought remained untouched (and still unopened, as I write this), but something else was starting to give way. Shin-splints were setting in on my left leg – a sharp pain caused by repetitive action. Was the entire walk in jeopardy? Was I to fall – literally – at this hurdle, so late in the day? I called a doctor friend for a proper diagnosis. When, however, that diagnosis was problematic – 'Rest and avoid activities that cause pain' – I decided a doctor's opinion was not needed and set off to Waltham Cross, some 19 miles away.

The rhythms I was so familiar with repeated themselves once more. Sometimes I walked in silence, absorbing the world around me. Sometimes I had headphones in, transported to other worlds. I listened to an episode from the English Heritage podcast, 'A delicious history of the English pie', then the sonorous tones of Rob Brydon on Times Radio, as well as the entire *Phantom of the Opera* soundtrack (the benefit of windy weather is you can sing along and no one can hear).

First the village of Colney Heath, then North Mymms. Here I found a beautiful church, packed with all sorts of curiosities. On the outer wall, a mass dial, to mark the time of the services with the sun. On the inner door, a holy water stoup, a recess in the medieval wall where worshippers dipped their fingers into the water.

But it was in the churchyard that I found a friend. Here was a tombstone that read: 'In loving memory of Dorothy Colville . . . wife, teacher and local historian'. Dorothy sounded like my type of woman, a great champion of the humble churchyard. In an impassioned plea, written in a local magazine, she bemoaned how often they were overlooked by visitors, be they 'self-assured, poised American ladies' or 'softly spoken Australians'. All head straight to the church door and 'ignore the equally fine work that can be seen in the churchyards'.

In the case of North Mymms churchyard, Dorothy was right. There were plenty of wonders here. One headstone was adorned with a skull, cherub, hourglass, pick and shovel, dedicated to seventeen-year-old John Wood, who died in 1757. Another commemorated a victim of the Napoleonic Wars: 'Mr. John

Cobourne, serjeant in the North Mimms Company of Volunteers', who died on 2 January 1806, aged twenty-three. Both men, so young to go – only fifty years between them.

Some tombstones were ornate and richly decorated, others plain and neglected. As Dorothy once wrote, the graveyard was 'nothing outstanding, nothing to draw crowds, only memorials to the ordinary man and woman, but part of the history of the parish'.

But it was this ordinariness that I so admired. A moment please, for the understated, humble tombstone, strewn with ivy and moss and nestled in a graveyard. My favourite was that of James Goddard, who died in 1754. It read: 'Praises on tombs are trifles vainly spent; A man's good name is his best monument.'

Reading James Goddard's epitaph, it made Eleanor's memorials – stone crosses, bronze effigies, 200-mile processions – seem a little . . . flashy. Were these such 'trifles vainly spent'? Was this all a bit . . . tasteless?

Not if you're in the business of propaganda – the business of rewriting history. Edward was certainly grief-stricken after Eleanor's death, but was there more to it? Were the crosses – as some historians have speculated – some sort of scheme to rehabilitate Eleanor's reputation posthumously?

I considered this as I walked. If this really was the case – that the crosses were to rewrite Eleanor's reputation – it was a pretty extreme measure and would indicate that she was wildly unpopular. But with no concrete evidence for this, it all seems an overstretch. She was, after all, the queen of King Edward, who was a hero to his subjects. To me, the story of love rings true – that these crosses were a memorial prompted by Edward's broken heart.

There was, however, another burial that Edward arranged, which was pure theatre. He and Eleanor were superfans of the tales of King Arthur, as many across Europe were, but for them, this myth bore particular political currency. King Arthur – a British hero who first surfaced in Welsh writing – was the great hope for Welsh rebels, who believed Arthur might return to save them in their hour of need.

As a savvy bit of political propaganda, Edward hijacked the myth for his own advantage. In 1278, he and Eleanor visited Glastonbury Abbey to open what was believed to be the tomb of Arthur and Guinevere. John of Glastonbury described the royal visit of 1278, reporting how they 'found there in two separate chests, decorated with their portraits and arms, the King's bones, of wonderful size, and those of Queen Guenevere, which were of great beauty'.

You can see how Edward – this enormous man – would have delighted to see his hero king's bones, also 'of wonderful size'. The bones were wrapped in silk and placed in chests for reburial by King Edward and Queen Eleanor, whereupon they 'marked them with their seals and directed the tomb to be placed speedily before the high altar, while the heads and knee-joints of both were kept out for the people's devotion'.

By making such a big deal of burying Arthur's bones, it put to bed the Welsh belief that Arthur might return as their political saviour. Alongside this, Edward positioned himself as the new King Arthur – a great PR swing. He built great castles with symbolism of old. There were splendid round-table tournaments, with jousting, dancing and feasting. One object that has survived from these is the 'Winchester Round Table', which now hangs in Winchester Great Hall. Dendrochronological analysis dates it to 1275, a year after Edward and Eleanor's coronation.

What's more, Edward claimed to have 'recovered Arthur's crown' with his defeat of Llewelyn, the Welsh prince. So he used Arthur to legitimise his conquest of Wales, root the relatively new

Norman dynasty in the ancient history of Britain and associate his reign with a glorious and chivalrous past. A win for Team Edward, on all accounts.

The company of an Arthurian knight would have been most welcome as I weaved through the villages on 13 December. It was lonely, walking in the wintertime. The paths were empty and quiet. It was a surprise – sometimes a shock – to pass another walker. Equally alarming for the senses were the enormous, roaring roads. I crossed the A1 – the Great North Road, along which King Edward travelled to reach London. I passed Water End, a department of the Royal Veterinary College. Then Northaw village. Then a stretch along the Hertfordshire Way, towards the final destination: Waltham Cross.

But, with only 2 miles to go, I encountered a serious hitch. It was the third moment of great peril: Longhorn cows; the Dunstable lake; and now this. Somehow, OS had directed me to an enormous, thunderous roundabout, between the A10 and the B198. The traffic was two lanes thick in both directions and proved impenetrable. Credit to the roundabout designer – it was a constant flow of cars, none of which came to an absolute stop.

I stood on the grass kerb and considered the options. Should I retrace my steps and find a better crossing? Do I call a taxi, to transport me to the other side of the roundabout – or was that cheating? A woman rolled up beside me in a slow of traffic in a very comfortable-looking Land Rover Discovery.

'Are you all right?' she cried.

'Thanks very much!' I shouted. 'I'm absolutely fine! Cheers!' – which, considering I was limping, completely worn out and stranded on a monster roundabout, was probably unconvincing. It was a touching gesture from a stranger, nonetheless.

I waited for half an hour. It was a particularly dangerous

situation, for I stood to the left of the cars as they approached, so the drivers were unaware of me as they looked away to their right to spot a gap. Even if I crossed one side of traffic, there was a grass island in the middle, where I might find it even harder to escape. I could see the headlines now – 'Historian dead after trying to cross Britain's most dangerous junction by foot'. The comments would come flooding through: 'What an idiot!' and 'Why was she crossing a *roundabout* by *foot*!??!?'

In the end, I never reached a decision. Suddenly, there was a gap. The traffic stopped in both lanes and I went for it. I stepped out in front of a lorry, walking at first, and then – once all was clear – darted across to safety, my heart beating fast.

This miracle – The Miracle of the Historian and the Roundabout – was not the first to unfold at the town of Waltham Cross. It followed one of equal magnitude. At Waltham Abbey, Harold Godwin, Earl of Wessex, was miraculously cured of paralysis by praying before a Holy Cross. It is also, reportedly, where his son King Harold II (of Battle of Hastings fame) was buried.

There is another miracle, too, for here is another thrilling survivor: the third and final original Eleanor Cross. This one was built of limestone shipped from Normandy and had a hexagonal structure. It included the usual features – heraldic shields, geometric patterns, niches for Eleanor's statues and all sorts of twiddly bits of ornamentation – crocketed gables, pinnacles and leaf finials. Plus, there's an extra bonus feature: it's covered in wire mesh to stop the pigeons from roosting.

By all accounts, it's been pretty bashed about over the years. In 1718, the cross was already 'in much danger of being quite pulled down by carriages running against it', before, a decade later, a certain Mrs Robinson rebuilt part of her house and 'broke down a good deal of the Cross to make way for her roof'.

In light of this, perhaps it's no surprise that what you see of the Waltham Cross Eleanor Cross today (what a mouthful) is layers and layers of restoration. Touch-ups, here and there. Restoration to repair botched restoration. In the 1830s, parts were rebuilt with softer Bath stone, which quickly decayed and required more work. The original statues were removed for safekeeping in 1950 and replaced with replicas. They are now in the archives of the Victoria & Albert Museum.

The third surviving Eleanor Cross at Waltham Cross.

All three Eleanor Crosses – at Geddington, Northampton and Waltham Cross – are rare survivors of the medieval age. But that hasn't happened by chance. So what does this involve? What are the modern practices for keeping alive this ancient monument of *luuurve*?

Historically, there are two major approaches to caring for historic buildings: restoration and conservation. In the 1800s, a revived interest in Gothic architecture – as opposed to Classical styles – led to an enthusiasm for restoration of medieval churches. It was time to tidy up.

Under the instruction of architects such as George Gilbert Scott, old churches were 'rationalised' and reordered. Walls with faded medieval paintings were given a new lick of paint, old windows were hacked out and new tracery and sculpture put in, in accordance with what the Victorian architect reckoned looked best.

Though the intention was well-meant and efforts to keep buildings in good nick are commendable, this was often heavy-handed and there was little effort to record what stood before.

Gone were the quirks and charms of centuries past, replaced with something totally false: a Disneyfied faux-medieval style. It was like Botox. Yes, all the wrinkles are gone, but the beauty is lost, because it's obviously fake.

From 1855, John Ruskin, the famous writer and art historian, took a stand against these architectural facelifts. In 1877, William Morris and other members of the Pre-Raphaelite movement founded the Society for the Protection of Ancient Buildings (SPAB). Morris referred to it as the 'anti-scrape' society, being opposed to scraping medieval plaster from the walls.

The SPAB manifesto declared: 'We think that those last fifty years of knowledge and attention have done more for their destruction than all the foregoing centuries of revolution, violence and contempt.' Which is quite a statement, when you consider Morris was writing well after the Dissolution of the Monasteries, the English Civil War and the Great Fire of London had taken place.

In 1877, Morris wrote a letter to the *Athenæum* newspaper, stating:

> *What I wish for, therefore, is that an association should be set on foot to keep watch on old monuments, to protest against all 'restoration' that means more than keeping out wind and weather and, by all means literary and other, to awaken a feeling that our ancient buildings are not mere ecclesiastical toys, but sacred monuments of the nation's growth and hope.*

And so the conservation movement began. Championing minimal alteration to the fabric of the building, other than the need to keep it standing or keep the weather out, SPAB also made efforts to make it immediately clear what was original and what was new. So a stone wall would be patched up with terracotta tiles to make an 'honest' repair – where later additions were visibly different, rather than blended in.

Of course, there are limitations to this approach. All historic buildings are themselves products of restoration and change. Each one – be it a palace, cathedral, church or castle – has evolved and adapted over the centuries. Just think of the redesign work of Queen Eleanor at Leeds Castle, building an entire gloriette. So it is odd to prevent any further intervention entirely, without restoration – as if the natural course of change should come to an abrupt halt in 2025.

Another practical challenge is that little touch-ups here and there aren't always robust enough to confront rapid decay. Sometimes, major changes are needed to ensure the building stays up at all – even if that means some loss of historic fabric.

251

Nonetheless, the establishment of SPAB put the brakes on over-zealous Victorian restoration. By 1947, the Town and Country Planning Act marked the beginnings of the 'Listed Buildings' system, where a government organisation (now Historic England) keeps a master list that categorises historic buildings as Grade 2, 2* or 1. These buildings require official permission to alter (though through 'Ecclesiastical Exemption', churches are exempt, with their own system of maintenance). Today, there is some sort of restoration-conservation middle way.

So what of conservation of the Eleanor Crosses? The most recent such efforts were to the Northampton Cross in 2019, which was placed on the Historic England 'Heritage at Risk' register. It was the Northamptonshire Battlefield Society who led a campaign to conserve it. Stonework was bowing, iron fittings were decaying and ratchet straps were required to keep blocks in place. The whole structure was fenced off.

There was confusion, too, when Northampton Borough Council and Northamptonshire County Council each argued that the other was responsible. After a good deal of 'delay, dither and spin' from the local authorities and dramatic reports that Eleanor was 'turning in her tomb at Westminster Abbey', a plan was put in place.

In February 2025, I visited the team at Skillington Workshop, who led the conservation. They had worked on several of the structures I had walked past: the plaque on the Town Hall at Grantham, the Northampton Cross, the shrines of St Alban and St Amphibalus at St Albans Cathedral.

David, who runs the place, showed me around, along with others who had worked on the Northampton Cross, Emma and Theo. In the office, they talked me through the latest projects. We zoomed into images of cracked ledger slabs from Norfolk, expertly restored. David explained diagrams of church brasses, with scans to reveal a cross-section, and we browsed reports from a project in Derby, involving a seventeenth-century ceiling.

My favourite room housed the Sands and Aggregates Library: rows and rows of aggregate variations, stored in reused Nescafe Original Coffee Jars, used as references to match historic plasters and mortars. They were neatly labelled, to avoid confusion with the actual coffee station: 'Baston Fen, Plastering Sand, Lincolnshire', 'Mercaston, Building Sand, Derbyshire', 'Thornborough, Sharp Sand, Northumberland (Corbridge)'.

The conservation of the cross at Northampton took around six months of work. There were some major structural problems and a few loose pinnacles. Stonemasons such as Alan Micklethwaite (whose carving course I attended) were brought in to carve and install replacements.

When it comes to conserving structures like the Eleanor Crosses, everything is approached with care. Before work is undertaken, the structure is recorded for posterity, during which all kinds of technical wizardry are employed: photogrammetry, stereo paired photographs, rectified photographs. The stones are cleaned with nebulised water sprays and chemical poultices and condition reports are drawn up.

There are many problems to look out for: open joints where water might enter; ferrous fixings (a rusty iron tie between stones, which might expand and burst the stone); or defective stones, which have fallen out of place and become structurally unsound. Hard cement mortar, which was popular in the twentieth century, is often a big source of the problem. Unlike traditional lime-mortar mixes, cement is insoluble, forcing water to pass through the stone. So the important bit – the stone – becomes damaged while the cement remains intact.

A statue of Eleanor within the Eleanor Cross at Waltham Cross. This was the disapproving look she gave me as I ate my jacket potato.

When the work begins, loose areas are strengthened or reattached using non-ferrous metal rods. Replacement carvings are fixed in position. Lime-mortar is packed into cracks and voids. All of this is carefully recorded, too, and stored at the Historic England archive in Swindon, where future conservators can make sense of earlier alterations and measure the rate of decay.

It's worth noting that conservation isn't just about ensuring that structures don't fall down, impressive as that is. It's also a form of artistry, of thinking about the aim of the original creators and reflecting that in the decisions made today.

The Waltham Cross cross has been regularly patched up over the years. It is a beautiful structure, even though the setting is less picturesque: I struggled to photograph the cross without a Ladbrokes betting shop in view. Nonetheless, there was an excellent and very lively diner-style cafe nearby – The Breakfast Bar – where I enjoyed a hearty jacket potato with cheese and baked beans, washed down with a large cup of tea.

The light was fast fading and there were a couple of miles to tick off before I was warmed by the purple glow of a Premier Inn. A major milestone came when I walked through a dingy underpass. 'Hello!' I shouted, to test the echo. I was walking under the M25, a 117-mile ring-road that loops the city. So, by going through the underpass, I was officially within the vicinity of London. This was the home stretch!

After spending the night at Waltham Abbey, Eleanor's body was carried to London on Thursday 14 December 1290. Though the 13-mile route is built up today, in the medieval period, this was open countryside. Here's how William Fitzstephen, a cleric in the service of Thomas Becket, described the land through which the cortège passed:

To the north there are tilled fields, pastures and pleasant, level meadows with streams flowing through them, where watermill wheels turned by the current make a pleasing sound. Not far off spreads out a vast forest, its copses dense with foliage concealing wild animals – stags, does, boars and wild bulls.

Passing under the M25. An exciting moment!

As the cortège approached the city, they would have glimpsed an enormous wall. This was the famous London city wall, first built by the Romans around AD 200. It was 2.5 miles long, more than 2 metres thick at the base and 6 metres tall. The core was rubble-bound in a hard mortar and faced on either side by rough stone blocks.

256

SACRED MONUMENTS AND ANTI-SCRAPES

In the medieval period, Fitzstephen tells us, the wall was 'high and wide, punctuated at intervals with turrets and with seven double-gated entranceways'. At the east was the Tower of London: 'the royal fortress, of tremendous size and strength, whose walls and floors rise from the deepest foundations'.

By 1290, there were around 80,000 people living in the square mile within the city's walls. These were marked with gatehouses, which funnelled the roads out of the city: Ludgate, Newgate, Cripplegate, Bishopsgate, Aldgate, Aldersgate and Moorgate. Outside the wall was a protective ditch, which is still remembered in the names of streets like Houndsditch or Shoreditch.

To the south was the River Thames, 'which teems with fish', over which there was one bridge: London Bridge, completed in 1209. Back then, it was covered in houses on either side, several storeys high (similar to the Ponte Vecchio in Florence or the Rialto Bridge in Venice). At the outer end was a portcullis, for security. Across the river was Southwark, which, being outside city walls and thus free from city rules, became the home of theatres and brothels (hence Shakespeare's Globe Theatre was later located here).

The world inside the city walls was fizzing with life, populated by 'men of superior quality' and 'idiots who drink to excess'. At all times of the day, takeaway snacks of 'goose, guinea-hen or woodcock' were available beside the river.

Every Friday, at Smithfield, crowds gathered to watch horse-fairs: palfreys, high-bred young colts, packhorses, war horses, 'trotting gently around, the blood pumping in their veins, their coats glistening with sweat'.

Nearby were goods for sale: 'agricultural implements, pigs with long flanks, cows with swollen udders'. There were 'mares suited for pulling ploughs' and 'frisky foals who stick close to their mothers'. On the riverbank, ships arrived with goods from around the world: gold from Arabia, gems from Egypt, silks from China, dried fish from the Baltic, metal goods from Flanders, wine from southern France.

In the winter, when the river froze over, skating was popular. An array of skills were displayed by our medieval ancestors, as recorded with enthusiasm by Fitzstephen: 'Some, after building up speed with a run, facing sideways and their feet placed apart, slide along for a long distance. Others make seats for themselves out of ice-slabs almost as large as millstones and are dragged along by several others who hold their hands and run in front.'

At Easter, spectators packed out London Bridge, 'ready to laugh their fill' at the tournament on the water. This is how it worked: 'A shield being securely fastened to a mast fixed mid-river, a young man standing in the prow of a small boat, propelled by the current and by several rowers, has to strike that shield with a lance.'

Medieval London could be walked across, side to side, within an hour. A bit like walking within the Roman walls of York or Chester. It's hard to imagine for Londoners today, but anywhere outside the original city walls – Chelsea, Clapham, Covent Garden, Piccadilly, Bloomsbury, St Pancras, Waterloo, King's Cross, St James's, Mayfair, Soho, Hoxton, Shoreditch or Oval – was countryside, largely empty until the seventeenth or eighteenth centuries. It was valuable pasture (for animals brought in to market on the hoof), meadow (for hay to feed all the transport horses) and gardens (to grow vegetables for market).

When Eleanor's cortège entered in the north-east, they came into the city through Bishopsgate and processed past thousands lining the streets. The destination was Holy Trinity Priory, located close to Aldgate. Like the Hospital of St Cross in Winchester or St Mary's Abbey in York, it was a large religious complex with a church, dormitory and cloisters. This was a royal, sacred space: two children of King Stephen were buried here, Baldwin and Matilda of Blois.

My journey to Holy Trinity Priory was markedly different. Several days before, I shared a schedule with several friends, to join as they pleased. Here were the instructions on the WhatsApp group:

Start – Premier Inn Waltham Cross – 7 a.m.
Brimsdown station – 7.30 a.m.
Meridan Water – 9 a.m.
Stoke Newington – 10.30 a.m.
Dalston Junction – 12 p.m.
Hoxton – 12.30 p.m.
Finish – Leadenhall Street

Leaving behind the purple lights of Premier Inn Waltham Cross, I weaved through Gunpowder Park – so named because munitions were tested here. Then Enfield Island Village, situated on an island on the River Lea and once a weapons manufactory.

At Brimsdown station, I picked up two friends, Joanna and Lucy. At Meridian Water, three others joined: Lottie, Will and Alex. They emerged from the Underground like ants from bark – bleary-eyed and slightly fragile from the excesses of Friday night.

We were a merry band, jaunting along the canal path, disturbing the peace and tranquillity of rowers on the water. It was a varied stroll through Edmonton and Tottenham: canal boats, play-grounds, reservoirs, tower blocks, industrial units. As the sun rose, the sky turned a burnt orange, silhouetting cranes and smoking chimneys in the east.

At Stamford Hill, through the rows of terraced houses, we passed members of the Hasidic Jewish community. This area has long been home to a largely Jewish population. Today, it is the largest Hasidic community in Europe, referred to as the 'square mile of piety'. There are kosher supermarkets, bakeries, fishmongers and butchers, as well as eighty synagogues and thirty Orthodox schools in the wider area.

Early morning in London.

It was Shabbat, the Jewish Sabbath, a day of rest for Jews, observed from sunset on Friday to sunset on Saturday. We passed a group of young men wearing overcoats of silk cloth and the *shtreimel*, a tall, wide cap of fur.

Pushing south, the clothing changed once more and the quantity of one-size-too-small fisherman beanies increased at a rapid rate. I spent a small fortune on a very small coffee and an enormous, bigger-than-my-hand croissant. I was Alice in Wonderland – or, as most people know it, Hoxton.

SACRED MONUMENTS AND ANTI-SCRAPES

Here I picked up more pilgrims and our little group swelled to
ten. We practised a roll-call, numbering off, and pressed on. As
we walked along Shoreditch High Street, the familiar signs of
London life were appearing. First, Pret a Manger. Then, the sight
of looming office blocks, with glass sparkling in the sunlight. It
was here that the medieval cortège entered the city through
Bishopsgate.

We entered the shadowy maze of skyscrapers. Suddenly, after
days adjusting to the wilds of the countryside, I was in the heart-
land of the corporate world. In the week, this area was busy and
buzzy. But at the weekends, it is eerily quiet. Coffee shops shut.
Not a person in sight. We neared an odd, in-between space: Mitre
Square. A patch of grass, surrounded by walkways.

I brought the little group to a stop – a gradual stop, for some
(Lucy and Alex) had lagged behind, chatting. Once all were gath-
ered, I pointed at a plaque: 'Site of the Priory of the Holy Trinity
Founded 1108'.

An explanation was required. 'First up, you'll have to use your
imagination,' I asked of my fellow walkers. 'Though this might
look pretty unassuming, if we were here on this day in 1290, we'd
be standing outside a grand priory and there would be crowds
jostling to catch a glimpse of Eleanor's body as it arrived, carried
on a bier.' The more theatrical members of the group began to act
this out.

The tour continued on the other side of the square. Here we
gazed into the windows of a WeWork, at 77 Leadenhall Street.
'Have a look in there!' I declared, and the nine wanderers pressed
their noses up to the glass. Inside are the remains of the priory
– great stone arches, built into the modern structure, nestled
among metal staircases, office plants and glass surrounds. Do the
WeWork office workers realise, as they operate the coffee machine,

that they might be standing in the old cloisters where Eleanor's body was carried?

Arrival at Holy Trinity Priory.

When members of the medieval cortège arrived in London, discharged from duties, did they scamper off to London's taverns, telling stories of the epic journey? I concluded that this was indeed very likely. Keen to be rigorous in my research, I felt obliged to follow suit.

I led the troops to nearby Leadenhall Market, a beautiful Victorian covered market famed as a filming location in *Harry Potter and the Philosopher's Stone* (Harry and Hagrid walk through it before visiting the Leaky Cauldron). Still decked in walking boots, faces ruddy from the exertion, we settled into a very enjoyable, very merry afternoon in the pub.

14. WARERITE MAKES HISTORY

*'I would rather die in the adventure of noble
achievements than live in obscure and sluggish
security; since by the one I may live in a glorious
Fame, and by the other I am buried in oblivion.'*
Margaret Cavendish

AFTER ARRIVING AT HOLY TRINITY Priory on 14 December 1290, Eleanor's body was carried slowly through the city. Three days later, on the 17th, it arrived at Westminster Abbey, her final resting place. As discussed earlier with Rodney the funeral director, when we consider this leisurely pace through the city, it suggests her body had survived the journey in good condition, otherwise there would have been a great rush to bury her.

On 15 December 2024 – after a Christmas party I spent on a sofa, incapacitated by shin-splints – I returned to Mitre Square to complete the final steps (now, happily, no longer in walking boots and back in normal clothes). Alone once more, without the distraction of my fellow pilgrims, I explored the space where Eleanor had lay in vigil.

I carefully read the information board, when I saw the threads of history weaving a strange tapestry once more. The body of another woman had been here, overlapping with Eleanor's story in a surprising way.

The woman in question was Catherine Eddowes. Born in Wolverhampton in 1842, she was the sixth of twelve children. Her father was a tinplate worker and her mother was a cook at a local hotel – though, by the time Catherine was fifteen years old, both had died. Along with three siblings, she was admitted to a Bermondsey workhouse.

As an adult, Catherine was known to be 'a very jolly woman, always singing'. Nevertheless, like so many of the poor in Victorian Britain, she endured a life of grinding poverty, struggling to make ends meet. By the summer of 1888, forty-three-year-old Catherine faced dire circumstances, regularly returning to the workhouse. On 29 September 1888, she was arrested for drunkenness in Aldgate High Street, to be released hours later, in the early hours of 30 September.

No doubt the inspector thought nothing of it. That this poor woman would awake in lodgings some hours later, with a pounding head, her black bonnet dishevelled and little memory of the previous night's misdemeanours. But within the hour of Catherine's release, her body – still warm – was discovered in the corner of Mitre Square. The murderer had vanished, nowhere to be seen.

But, worse still, Catherine's body was horrifically mutilated. There was a 'great disfigurement of the face', her 'throat cut' and 'intestines were drawn out to a large extent and placed over the right shoulder'. The attack sent shockwaves around London: here was the latest victim of the notorious 'Jack the Ripper'.

But the horrors continued. Some weeks later, an anonymous letter was sent to the chairman of the Whitechapel Vigilance Committee. It was accompanied by part of a human kidney, presumed to be Catherine's. The author of this letter claimed to have 'fried and ate' the missing parts.

As I sat in Mitre Square, I imagined Catherine's final moments on this very spot and was sickened by the violence she endured. It was here, too, that Eleanor's body was brought – though in such different circumstances.

Both women's bodies were disembowelled and cut apart: Eleanor's filled with herbs, her organs placed in sacred spaces and a vigil held; Catherine's carelessly slashed open, her organs strewn across the street and her body parts – if the letter was true – eaten by her killer.

Both deaths were reported far and wide and, while tidings of Eleanor provoked solemn prayer, the news of Catherine provided sensationalist headlines for the tabloid press. Even today, photographs of her naked, mutilated body are freely available to see on Wikipedia. While Eleanor was buried in three elaborate tombs, Catherine was buried at City of London Cemetery, square 318, grave #49336.

By accident of birth, the world of these two women – in life and death – was so different, yet somehow, across the centuries, chance brought them both to this spot. How would either have fared in the other role? What would Catherine have been like, were she born a princess? Would Eleanor's virtues have stood firm in the brutality of Victorian London?

Catherine's story is a reminder that, as we flick through the history books, we only tend to glimpse the lives of an elite minority. The kings and queens, the fortunate and famous. Like most of us, the vast majority of our ancestors – ordinary folk, the *hoi polloi* – lived lives that are forgotten or only recorded when something extraordinary happens.

From Mitre Square, I weaved my way through the heart of

London – Cornhill, then Leadenhall Street. The grand columns of the Bank of England were wrapped in red Christmas ribbons. Here were a smattering of map-in-hand tourists, Lycra-clad joggers and church-goers in their Sunday best. The city was waking up, once more.

My destination was Westcheap, later known as Cheapside, a street to the east of St Paul's Cathedral. For centuries, Cheapside was one of London's most bustling, humming streets. Charles Dickens Jr – the eldest son of the famous writer – described it in 1879:

> *Cheapside remains now what it was five centuries ago, the greatest thoroughfare in the City of London. Other localities have had their day, have risen, become fashionable and sunk into obscurity and neglect, but Cheapside has maintained its place and may boast of being the busiest thoroughfare in the world, with the sole exception perhaps of London-bridge.*

The etymological origin of 'cheap' lies in the Old English word 'ceapan', which meant 'to buy' or 'to bargain'. This was a thriving marketplace, with roads today still betraying the original uses: Honey Lane, Milk Street and Bread Street. Its church, St Mary-le-Bow, features in the 'Oranges and Lemons' nursery rhyme – 'I do not know, says the Great Bell of Bow' – and tradition holds that only those born within the sound of the Bow Bells can truly call themselves a Cockney (a native of east London).

Had you interviewed a Londoner between 1300 and 1640 with the question, 'What first springs to mind when you think of Cheapside?' they would have probably replied: 'Busy market, with that old stone tower in the middle.' Or – for the more erudite members of society – 'A bustling thoroughfare, with a fine cross to the fair Queen Eleanor.'

For more than 300 years, the Cheapside Cross stood at the heart of London's busiest street – an enormous structure five storeys high, which cost a whopping £300 to build (about three times the cost of the earlier ones). Here the Eleanor Cross provided the backdrop for London life to unfold. Did soldiers, just returned from the Battle of Crécy, sit on the steps, recounting their adventures? Did Geoffrey Chaucer, as a small boy, pass the cross with his father and, on hearing the tales of the travelling cortège, was he fired up to imagine similar pilgrimages?

As a thoroughfare of the city, Cheapside was the setting for every kind of pageant and procession, during which the spectators would make merry on free booze: 'the conduit of Cheapside ran at one end white wine and at the other red'.

This was the red carpet of the medieval world – with Eleanor at the centre. Here, 'proud, warlike and beautiful faces showed, uncapped and unveiled, to the seething, jostling people'. Here, 'mayor and aldermen grew hottest, bowed most and puffed out with fullest dignity'.

During the victory parade of King Henry V, returning from Agincourt, a model castle was erected at Cheapside Cross, from which a choir of maidens sang out: 'Welcome, Henry the Fifth, King of England and of France.'

On 31 May 1533, Anne Boleyn processed through in preparation for her coronation, bouncing along in 'a rich chariot covered with cloth of silver' with a 'goodly company of lords, knights and gentlemen'. At the Cheapside Cross, the mayor gifted her 'a purse of cloth of gold'. Many years later, in 1559, this coronation route was replicated by her daughter, Elizabeth. In Cheapside, Elizabeth smiled to hear the words 'Remember old King Henry VIII!' cried out from the crowd.

But public favour only lasts so long. Cheapside Cross was no longer the darling of London. Over the years, other figures had been added – Edward the Confessor, St Peter, a pope and a cardinal – and to Puritanical reformers of the seventeenth century, Cheapside Cross was seen as the embodiment of royal, Catholic tradition.

Riots erupted as Puritans mustered to smash up the cross and Royalists rallied to stop them. This was no crumbling monument, forgotten and ignored. This was a powerful symbol standing tall in the heart of London and driving men to violence 300 years after it was erected. Ditties were written to condemn the attacks: 'To those that wronged the Crosse this is my curse/They never may have crosses [silver coins] in their purse.'

During the Civil War, London was a hub of Parliamentary support. When Charles I scarpered to raise an army, the snappily named 'Parliamentary Committee for the Demolition of Monuments of Superstition and Idolatry' set about pulling down offending monuments. Monuments deemed too Catholic or too royal or whatever the committee didn't like the look of. Cheapside Cross was one of the first on the list.

After three centuries of keeping watch over the people of London, Eleanor's monument was pulled to the ground on 2 May 1643, the careful work of medieval masons shattered in minutes.

When I visited the site on 15 December 2024, there was nothing to see on the street, though the west door of St Mary-le-Bow church has an inscribed stone, installed in 2015. The only surviving fragments – discovered in 1838 during works to construct a sewer along Cheapside – are cared for by the Museum of London, including a block showing the arms of England and Castile.

I was joined by the dean of St Paul's Cathedral, Andrew Tremlet, and Caroline Graham, its director of development. We stood in Cheapside, trying to visualise this being London's busiest street, full of all those people rushing past the Eleanor Cross. The dean read out a 'Pilgrimage Prayer' for the occasion: 'Guide Alice, as she walks with Christ in the footsteps of those whose love for Eleanor bore fruit in the crosses fashioned in her name.'

Cheapside, with the spire of St Mary-le-Bow Church.

After Cheapside, I passed St Paul's Cathedral and followed the steps of the funerary procession towards the Franciscan friary of Grey Friars. I imagined these same streets, 734 years earlier, when they marched solemnly through the walled precinct of St Paul's, then through winding lanes, with timber-framed buildings over-hanging the street.

From the windows were children leaning out, craning their necks to catch a glimpse of King Edward or even the Queen. If Henry III's funerary procession was anything to go by, Eleanor was dressed in fine robes – perhaps those from her coronation – and carried by honoured noblemen. Her face – now pallid – was visible from within a portable reliquary.

The cortège headed to Grey Friars to take mass. Today, nothing of the building remains, having been closed as part of the Dissolution of the Monasteries. An imposing, classical building stands on the site, at the intersection of Newgate Street and Warwick Lane, with a bright blue rectangular plaque: 'Site of Grey Friars Monastery 1225–1538'.

Another site I visited was that of the Dominican priory at Blackfriars – where Eleanor's heart was buried. Again, the priory doesn't survive, being another victim of the Dissolution. But in a small alleyway off Carter Street, named Church Entry, is a small garden, with a plaque, which marks where the entrance to the priory would have been. The nearby streets of Friar Street and Black Friars Lane are a nod to the ghosts of this monastic medieval past.

Onwards, I travelled along Fleet Street. Had I walked along here in the medieval period, I'd have passed out the city walls and walked west, parallel to the great River Thames. Here the riverfront was dotted with buildings. The rounded church at Temple, the HQ of the Knights Templar. The Savoy Palace, a mansion occupied by Peter, Count of Savoy from 1246 (and the namesake for the hotel on that site).

Eventually, I'd have arrived at Charing, a small cluster of houses near the river. The name derives from the Old English word *cierring*, meaning 'river bend', referring to the bend in the River Thames.

It was at Charing that Eleanor's body spent the final night of her journey, probably at the Hospital of St Mary Rounceval. It was here, too, that the twelfth and final cross was built. This was the work of the brothers Richard and Robert Crundale. Made of dark-coloured Corfe marble and limestone shipped from

Normandy, it was the most expensive of the crosses, costing an eye-watering £600 (six times as much as the earlier ones).

This part of London – a bend in the river, marked by the Eleanor Cross – is now known as Charing Cross. A legend tells us the name is linked to Eleanor's story through the etymology of *chère reine* ('dear queen' in French). Alas, this is not the case, as 'Charing' was already established over a century before Eleanor died – though it is a nice chance of fate.

Charing Cross followed the fate of its Cheapside sister and, by 1590, now 300 years old, it was so 'defaced by antiquity' as to have become 'an old weather-beaten monument'. In 1647, it was pulled down, by order of Parliament. According to a ballad, Londoners were lost without it – both spiritually and practically:

> *Undone! undone! the lawyers cry,*
> *They ramble up and down;*
> *We know not the way to Westminster*
> *Now Charing-Cross is down.*

Nothing physical remains of Charing Cross. The stone, it's said, was used to pave Whitehall. But its power continued for years to come. Even without the stone structure, the site – now a traffic island at the top of Whitehall – wasn't just some old crossroads. It retained the power of the Eleanor Cross, remaining a site of immense symbolic significance.

The grisliest of these were four days in October 1660, when King Charles II ordered the execution of a number of the Regicides – the group of fifty-nine men who had signed the death warrant of his father King Charles I in 1649.

The chosen location was full of symbolism, being the spot of the old Eleanor Cross, that ancient symbol of monarchy, which had been torn down thirteen years before. What's more, the site was in view of the Banqueting House – the location where King Charles I had been executed on 30 January 1649. Was this the last thing those Regicides saw as they suffered in those final moments?

First, on 13 October, was Thomas Harrison. He faced a horrific punishment, being partly strangled, disembowelled, castrated and made to watch his organs burn before being decapitated. The writer Samuel Pepys was present and noted how Harrison was 'looking as cheerful as any man could do in that condition'.

Next, on 15 October, was John Carew, who was recorded as dying with dignity: 'more steadiness of mind, more contempt of death and more magnanimity could not be expressed'. On the 16th, it was the turn of Hugh Peters and John Cook. On the 17th were four: Thomas Scot (who had initially fled to Brussels), Gregory Clement (who went into hiding, his identity only confirmed by a blind man who recognised his voice), John Jones Maesygarnedd (brother-in-law of Oliver Cromwell) and Adrian Scrope.

To hammer home the point, an equestrian statue of Charles I was erected in its position – which still stands today. It shows the King wearing armour, holding a baton in his right hand and the reins of the horse in his left. He faces down Whitehall – the site of his own execution – and to Parliament beyond.

The statue itself is a remarkable survival of the Civil War. It was commissioned by the Lord Treasurer in 1630 and created by the King's favourite sculptor, Hubert Le Sueur, when Charles I was still alive.

In 1649, when Parliament ordered its destruction, the statue was sold to John Rivet, a London metalsmith, who was ordered to break it down. Instead of doing so, Rivet hid it and produced a few broken pieces of brass as 'evidence'. He made a good business selling brass-handled cutlery as royalist memorabilia.

When the monarchy was restored to the throne, the statue was found, bought by Charles II and erected in the position where the Eleanor Cross once stood and where the Regicides had died. A frustrating day for souvenir hunters, no doubt.

Today, the Charles I statue stands on that small traffic island in front of Trafalgar Square. Nearby is a small plaque on the ground. 'On the site now occupied by the statue of King Charles I', it reads, 'was erected the original Queen Eleanor's Cross'. It also informs us that 'Mileages from London are measured from the site of the original cross'.

Indeed, if you put 'London' into Google Maps – try it right now if you can – it directs you to this very point. The site of Eleanor Cross. So to stand at this plaque – to stand on the site of the Eleanor Cross – is to be in the very heart of London.

But this is not the end of Eleanor's story. Remember – history is alive and constantly changing. In the 1860s, the hands of time were rewound. The destruction of the Civil War – or the 'Great Rebellion', as the Victorians put it – was undone. Plans were put into action to rebuild the Eleanor Cross 'as nearly as possible the same in size and feature' as the original.

The instigator of this historic revival was South Eastern Railway. While pouring money into a thrilling modern development – a new terminus for Charing Cross station – they also rebuilt a lost monument of medieval London, located at the street-side entrance.

The cross was designed by Edward Middleton Barry, whose father, Charles Barry, designed the Palace of Westminster. When it came to the cross at Charing, Barry scoured drawings in the Bodleian Library, the British Museum and the Royal Society of Antiquaries, visited surviving crosses and took inspiration from Eleanor's tomb.

So though the Victorians could sometimes be heavy-handed –

scraping away medieval wall paintings – they also had incredible vision for building from scratch. After 570 years, history repeated itself. Sweaty-browed masons returned to the site, chipping at stone. Statues of Queen Eleanor were hoisted and fixed into position.

Just as it was in the 1290s, the people of London were enraptured by the building works taking place. In that moment, as they looked on in bemusement – the scrawny medieval urchin loitering outside the city walls or the Victorian gentlemen in top hat and pince-nez – they stood shoulder to shoulder across the generations, all thinking the same thing: 'What's all this, then?'

Though the masons have long tidied away their tools, their spirit is very much alive today. Next time you pass the Queen Eleanor Memorial Cross, trot down the steps into the Underground. Here, at the Northern Line platform, is a hive of activity. As commuters wait for trains to arrive, they are joined by a small army of workers – quarrymen, rough-hewers, masons, layers, carpenters, thatchers, scaffolders and apprentices.

On the walls is a magnificent black and white strip cartoon telling the story of the cross's construction in 1290. Like the Bayeux Tapestry, every step is captured – sourcing stone, taking measurements, building scaffolding, burning lime, cutting blocks, statues of Eleanor swinging through the air and, finally, the cross fixed on top.

The mural was created in 1979 by the brilliant artist David Gentleman and, on 5 March 2025, three months after the walk, I visited him. I've long been an admirer of his work and can still remember, as a girl, sitting on the floor and tracing my hand over his illustrations, which adorned the book covers of the Penguin Shakespeare plays. The cover of *Richard III* stuck in my mind – the two princes sound asleep in the Tower of London, unaware of their doomed fate.

It was thrilling for me, therefore, that he had agreed to meet me in person. David lives in a beautiful white north London townhouse, with window boxes bursting with daffodils. As I pushed open the gate, I heard a cry from below: 'Hello! Over here!' This was David's wife, Sue.

Their front living room is a large space, with bookshelves floor to ceiling. Near the front window, pooled in a stream of sunlight, was David. He has bright white hair and sparkling eyes that betray a wry sense of humour. We began to chat – David, Sue and I – while sipping tea and munching on Bourbon biscuits.

We talked for forty-five minutes or so. David and Sue reminisced – and laughed a lot – about their life together. Sue told me about her idyllic childhood: 'There was no electricity or running water, so we used to get water from the well . . . it was wonderful.' Her mother was a headmistress, and her father, George Ewart Evans, was a writer. One of his books, *The Pattern Under the Plough*, a record of British agriculture, was illustrated by David. This is how David and Sue first met.

It was in the 1970s, in David's early career, that the Charing Cross commission came about. 'It was complicated, but very interesting,' he told me, 'and I can't remember any job I've liked better than that.'

Like the projects of Edward and Eleanor, this was a team effort. Though David did the engravings, Sue helped with the research, bringing piles of books home to understand the world of the medieval masons. 'I also did a lot of modelling with hammers,' she remembered, chuckling, arm up in the pose. 'It's actually me on the wall, doing the carving!'

The Charing Cross images were wood engravings, printed from seventy wood blocks, each no more than 4 inches high (now part of the collection of the V&A Museum). These were photographed, enlarged twenty times and screen-printed onto melamine sheets, which were fixed to the Underground walls.

As we headed upstairs, David's career unfolded before my eyes. The walls were adorned with a framed image of the complete Charing Cross design, followed by all kinds of posters and prints. In a glass cabinet were the original wooden blocks, from which many iconic designs were born: book covers of Penguin Modern Classics Shakespeare series, the National Trust's oak leaf logo, to name a few.

On the top floor of the house is David's studio. It is the most immaculate, ordered working space I've ever seen. Everything had its correct position. A hook to hang a watch, to balance a mug, to wind a cable. There were nails protruding from the wall, to display every variation of masking tape. Rulers and set squares, perfectly arranged. Pencils lined up and sharpened to a point, ready to go. This was – like the medieval masons – a man of utmost precision. I felt instinctively that Eleanor the business-woman would have heartily approved.

I was delighted that David showed me the iron printing press – a wonderfully heavy, robust machine – where blocks were inked up and his beautiful prints created. As David and I admired the mechanism, Sue cried up from downstairs: 'I've found the box!' In a storeroom – again, neatly organised – were piles of boxes containing letters and invoices from decades of past projects. This was David and Sue's very own archive.

One of these boxes related to the Charing Cross project. Clearing a space at a desk by the window, I spent the afternoon poring over the documents. First was a letter from the publicity officer of London Transport, Michael Levey, dated 19 June 1978. In the right-hand corner was a smart red Underground logo.

David in his studio.

The contents of the letter discussed the design idea for the three lines at Charing Cross station: 'The Northern Line medieval scene deals with the Cross. The Bakerloo platforms will deal with the National and National Portrait Galleries. The Jubilee Line seat recesses might very suitably deal with the Trafalgar Square aspect, e.g. Nelson, the Column or the lions.'

Next, in this dive through the mini-archive, were notes from friends, offering research recommendations. 'I saw five books yesterday that could be of interest to you,' wrote one Ellen Crampton. 'Unfortunately, three of them were in bookshops and only two in the Reference Library.'

Here and there were glimpses of Sue's role in all this – for she was the one processing letters and following up phone calls. One document had an intriguing scribble in green pen: 'Phoned to say in East Africa.'

There was another letter, dated 8 February 1979, from the Chief Public Relations Officer at London Transport:

Further to our telephone conversation yesterday, the date for the Press launch of the murals at Charing Cross will now be Tuesday, 13 March, at 10.30 hours, which was one of the dates convenient to you.

The other arrangements all stand, including lunch with the Chairman at 55 Broadway afterwards. I have passed on your suggestion about how to contact Melvyn Bragg to Ken Pope.

Among the documents was a press release, issued by Perstorp Warerite, a chemicals company. It was at their manufacturing plant in Aycliffe, near Durham, where David's designs were transferred to make the panels, using a new material called Warerite. Once again, Queen Eleanor was memorialised at the cutting edge of design.

WARERITE MAKES HISTORY

The press release was dated 13 March 1979 and titled 'WARERITE MAKES HISTORY IN NEW UNDERGROUND STATION':

> *The project presented one of the biggest challenges ever undertaken by Perstorp Warerite. Most of the figures in the design span the joints between the panels so a perfect match was vital. A total of 155 veneered boards had to be curved to an exact radius of 2.930 m so that they locked precisely into each other during installation. There is a 268 ft run on each of the north and south bound platforms.*

I found another press release, this one from London Transport, hyping up the new public artwork:

> *Passengers using the modernised Northern Line platforms at the new Charing Cross tube station, due to come into use with the opening of the Jubilee Line on 1 May, will see an exciting new concept in Underground station decor – and get a bit of a history lesson.*

A history lesson indeed! And what a surprise it would be for Eleanor to know that, a mile from her tomb effigy, her legacy was remembered in this wall mural in an underground tunnel and passed by thousands each day.

According to the London Transport press release, the cost of the Northern Line murals was about £50,000. It was all part of a bigger project – costing £450,000 – to modernise the platforms, where new floors were added, with speckled white terrazzo tiles. It was a peak 1970s colour scheme: platform ceilings had orange melamine panels and trackside walls were painted olive green.

The Charing Cross murals were – in David's words – a tribute to the original medieval masons – 'the skill and imagination of the people who in building it stretched their own capabilities to the utmost'.

But while sifting through these letters, I realised, too, the sheer number of people involved to put plans into action – all those conversations and letters, back and forth, those discussions at Warerite HQ – all considering how best to commemorate the memorial to Queen Eleanor.

In the late afternoon, I left David and Sue in peace. David gave me a warm hug on the doorstep, waving as I opened the gate. Sue stepped into the street to direct me to Camden Town Underground station.

As I sat on the tube, my mind whirred, thinking through all those incredible projects they'd worked on over the years. But I was also inspired by their relationship. David and Sue – so generous, so modest – were an incredible team. Through hard work, passion and devotion to one another, they'd achieved remarkable things. Like Edward and Eleanor, here we saw the mark of love – of teamwork – once more.

After nine minutes on the Underground, I stepped off at Charing Cross to come face to face with the murals. Within a couple of hours of seeing David operating his printing press, here I was, eye to eye with the result, still glorious in Warerite, forty-six years later.

I traced my finger across the curved surface, those lines set out by the wooden block, inked up and printed in David's studio. I found a stonemason wielding a hammer and thought of Sue, half a century earlier, posing as a model. Part of the mural includes King Edward, offering instructions to the stone carver – his 'action-focused grieving' captured in woodcut.

A statue of Eleanor is placed in position by the medieval masons, as depicted on the Northern Line platform of Charing Cross.

It is accompanied by an information panel, with a photograph from the opening in 1979, of David chatting to a young Prince Charles. Together they look at the scene of lime-mortar being made. Both men, in their different ways, have played such a part in keeping these crafts of Eleanor's world alive: David through this mural, which is seen by thousands each year; and King Charles through his charities, which run educational courses in stone carving.

Stepping out into the spring sunshine, I crossed the road to the top of Whitehall. Standing alone in the centre of the island, around which vehicles circle day and night, I considered the events that had unfolded here.

I thought of the medieval masons and carpenters who toiled away in that little hamlet of Charing and of the Eleanor Cross

281

they created, which stood tall for three centuries – a marker to welcome travellers from afar. It was here, too, that the Puritans came to tear it down; here that the Regicides suffered, taking their final, desperate gasp of air.

This plaque marks the spot of the original Charing Cross. The statue of Charles I is seen behind and, in the distance, the Palace of Westminster.

I looked up to pink sky, where Charles I was silhouetted, high on his horse. At my feet was the plaque, to commemorate this as the central point of measurement. I glanced around: the Houses of Parliament down one vista, Buckingham Palace along another. The National Gallery was behind me and Nelson was above, looking down towards me from his column.

There is something about this very spot – the site of the original Eleanor Cross – that has a magnetism. It is one of those 'thin places', where a thread binds us across hundreds of years. Everything has happened here, and London seems to spiral around it. Like the cross at Geddington, there seemed to be a force here, emitting an energy that kept the city in check.

As I stood at that traffic island on that sunny spring afternoon and gazed down to Westminster, where Eleanor's body lay, I felt her legacy was very much alive.

15. THE FORGOTTEN WOMEN

'The life of the dead is placed in the memory
of the living.'
Cicero

SOMEONE NEEDS TO SAY IT: Westminster Abbey is cluttered. It's like a hoarder's attic – the kind of place you put your glasses down and never find them again. An urn to commemorate a scientist here, a statue of a Victorian prime minister there. There are more than 3,000 people buried within its walls, all piled in together. When I look back at our journey from Lincoln, it seems rather a good metaphor for walking through England as a whole: a delightful jumble of monuments, plaques, signs, panels, public statues, public art, public sculpture.

For Edward and Eleanor, Westminster Abbey was a place of huge importance. Here they were crowned and here their children were married. Here was the shrine of the saint they prayed to, Edward the Confessor, and the tomb of Edward's father, Henry III. And they knew it was here that they would lie, side by side, in time immemorial.

On 17 December 1290, nineteen days after Eleanor died, her funeral took place at Westminster Abbey, the culmination of the journey from Harby. As mournful laments echoed around the abbey walls, Eleanor made her final journey. Adorned with 'royal vestments, crown and sceptre', she was carried, with solemn serenity, along the great nave. Either side, the nobility of England watched on in silence as they bade farewell to their Queen – this great pillar of England – for the final time.

Did the royal children weep to see their mother's body lying in front of the high altar, finally in her place of rest? What of King Edward, that tall, lonely figure? Did he hold back tears, to see his beloved Eleanor's body, surrounded by flickering candles?

As prayers were spoken and blessings given, did Edward think back to when it all started – that moment in Burgos, thirty-six years before, when he first laid eyes on Eleanor, then a twelve-year-old girl. In hindsight, did Edward realise that this was the moment everything had started, the moment his life began? And now, as he looked back to see Eleanor's body lying at the altar, he landed on a heart-breaking, stomach-churning truth: that his Eleanor would never come back to him and this was the final page of their fairy tale.

Two days later, in the final part of the Queen's elaborate triple-burial, Eleanor's heart was buried at the Dominican priory, at the site now known as Blackfriars. This was planned well in advance and Eleanor had paid for a chapel to be prepared herself. It was probably more of a reliquary than a full tomb, with decoration including an angel holding a heart and three small bronze statues. In a touching insight to her own grief, her heart was buried alongside her son, ten-year-old Alphonso, who had died in 1284.

After the funeral, Edward retired to the countryside, alone with his thoughts. On 4 January, he sent a letter to the Abbot of Cluny, in which he penned some of the most romantic words in medieval history, writing of his beloved Eleanor: 'who in life we dearly cherished and who in death we cannot cease to love'.

THE FORGOTTEN WOMEN

At Westminster Abbey, a beautiful tomb was created for Eleanor, where she was moved after her temporary burial. It is this tomb that was the end point of my journey. After nearly 200 miles and some half a million steps, finally, the end was near.

On Wednesday 17 December 2024, I set off from Trafalgar Square and headed down Whitehall. The final mile. This area, with Horse Guards Parade, 10 Downing Street, the Old Admiralty Building, the Houses of Parliament, Westminster Abbey and the Cabinet War Rooms, is – and has been, for more than a thousand years – a seat of command. Here, political and ecclesiastical power plays out and the royal prerogative – the same prerogative once wielded by Eleanor herself – is exercised.

But the area around Whitehall and Parliament Square is also a memorial to the dead. Here is the Cenotaph, designed by Sir Edwin Lutyens; here are the statues of great wartime leaders – Field Marshal Montgomery and Sir Winston Churchill.

It was a bronze monument, adorned with sculpted uniforms and helmets, which piqued my interest: the Monument to the Women of World War II. This was unveiled in 2005, in recognition of women's contribution to the war effort – those who were called up as mechanics, engineers, munitions workers and air-raid wardens and the 640,000 women in the armed forces.

Like the Eleanor Crosses, this monument served an important purpose – to keep alive the memory of forgotten women of the past. It made me consider, as we had been so focused on Eleanor, the women who surrounded her, the women who are so often overlooked.

There were the maids and laundresses in Eleanor's household. There was Belaset, the Jewish woman from Lincoln. What of the wives who held up the 'Home Front' – who managed the households and estates of crusading knights and lords – as Eleanor embarked on the Ninth Crusade? What of Eleanor's daughters who never made it – the little girls who died in infancy or who died in the womb and were never given a chance to know the world?

Then, I considered all the women who had played a part in my own journey. In Grantham was the statue of Margaret Thatcher – our first female prime minister. In Geddington, we met Reina, the curious little girl on the steps of the cross. There was Celia Fiennes, the travel writer, who made pains to record the crosses in her own day.

Dora Barrett, the artist who created the Dunstable statue. Dorothy Colville, the determined historian who campaigned for the protection of her local churchyard. The unknown woman who offered to help at the Waltham Cross roundabout.

The list goes on. Catherine Eddowes, who was brutally murdered at Mitre Square. Sue Gentleman, who worked on the Charing Cross mural. The judge, Sara Cockerill, who was so compelled by Eleanor's story, she spent years researching Eleanor in her spare time and wrote a detailed biography, which I used as a reference source for my journey.

All these women are connected to Eleanor in some way. As I stood at Whitehall, I considered this for the first time. The Eleanor Crosses are things of utmost beauty and craftsmanship, but here Eleanor is passive, silent and created through the commission and hands of men. Was this really the best way to remember Eleanor the Feisty, to think of Eleanor the Formidable? Perhaps it was this strange thread of women that proved a greater legacy and a truer testament to Eleanor's fiery spirit.

At 11 a.m., I arrived at Dean's Yard, an enclosed courtyard at the back of the abbey. Here I prepared to meet a serious VIP of clergy and the third dean of my journey. First, the dean of Lincoln, then the dean of St Paul's and now the dean of Westminster Abbey.

This is a big job, as Westminster Abbey has been a sacred site for more than a thousand years. The original church (which was part of an abbey complex) was located on Thorney Island, an area of marshy land where two branches of the River Tyburn flowed into the Thames.

In the mid-eleventh century, King Edward the Confessor rebuilt the abbey church in the Romanesque style, and the new church was consecrated on 28 December 1065. The following days must have been a PR nightmare.

The star celebrity guest – King Edward the Confessor – was too ill to attend the opening and, a week later, on 5 January 1066, he died. The next day – 6 January 1066 – the late King was buried before the high altar and his successor, King Harold, was crowned. An opening party, a funeral, a coronation – all in the space of ten days. A busy start for the church team.

King Edward's body rested in limbo for almost 100 years until, on 13 October 1163 – now known as St Edward – his remains were translated to a shrine. It is this shrine that remains the heart of the abbey today.

The next big Westminster Abbey redevelopment happened under Eleanor's father-in-law, Henry III, an extremely pious man who was devoted to Edward the Confessor. Things kicked off in 1245, as it was recorded by the chronicler Matthew Paris:

The King . . . commanded that the Church of St Peter, at Westminster, should be enlarged and the tower with the eastern part overthrown to be built anew and more handsome, at his own charge and fitted to the residue or western part.

Hundreds of craftsmen flocked to the site, hauling Kentish ragstone, Purbeck marble, lead from Derbyshire and timber from the surrounding countryside. Soon, there was a chapter house, a cemetery and bell tower, and all kinds of royal buildings nearby. In 1269, the new abbey was consecrated. It was in the nick of time, for just five years later, in 1274, it hosted the glitziest event of the century: Edward and Eleanor's coronation.

Edward is also connected to the abbey in another way. Some years after Eleanor's death, he commissioned a magnificent oak chair, decorated with birds, foliage and animals and designed to enclose the Stone of Scone (a heavy stone, which is symbol of royal authority in Scotland). It was this chair that became 'King Edward's Chair' or the 'Coronation Chair', which is on display in the abbey to this day and is still used by monarchs when they are crowned.

Westminster Abbey is a royal peculiar – a church that reports directly to the monarch (rather than the diocese). I was welcomed to the office of David Hoyle, the dean, a cheery man with a keen interest in history – who has played his part in it too, as it was he who conducted the state funeral of Queen Elizabeth II on 19 September 2022. It was a great honour to be welcomed to the private rooms – furnished with sofas, hundreds of books and a healthy display of Christmas cards – so I was on my very best behaviour.

He guided me through the winding corridors of the deanery, where robes were hanging and clergy moved to and fro. Then we descended into the nave, passing the famous King Edward's Chair, and made our way towards the chancel. Suddenly, the hand of history felt heavy. Walking along this nave, I followed in the footsteps of monarchs past. Along these very stones, ermine cloaks and velvet slippers have passed, as Tudors, Hanoverians and Windsors processed. The final steps before a life-changing, historic moment, years in the making.

Here, future queens – young Elizabeth Windsor and Catherine Middleton – took steps to marry their beloved. Here, Elizabeth I and Victoria walked to their coronation. And now – after half a million steps – I, too, followed the dean of Westminster Abbey to complete my journey.

This was the cumulation of all those miles of endeavour – mounting rickety styles, trudging through boggy fields, wading through deep puddles. Slipping and sliding across motorway bridges, pavements, railway crossings. Passing under railway arches, along canal paths and past signposts and village notice-boards. All was building up to this moment.

The coronation anthem, Handel's 'Zadok the Priest', began to play out in my head, with its rising string arpeggios and immense building momentum. As royals past prepared to marry their bride- or groom-to-be or begin their life as monarch, I also prepared for something monumental: I was to come face to face with Eleanor herself.

As David unclipped ropes for us to pass through forbidden areas (which felt very VIP), we paused to look at the Cosmati Pavement. This is one of the highlights of the abbey: a beautiful mosaic floor commissioned by King Henry III in 1268 and created by specialist workmen brought over from Rome.

The technique was '*opus sectile*', meaning 'cut work', and the result is a hypnotic whirl of polychrome, where triangles, squares, circles and rectangles intersect. Some are made of dark onyx, others of purple porphyry or green serpentine or yellow limestone. There is coloured glass, too, of red, turquoise, cobalt blue and bluish white, all laid upon a bed of dark limestone.

It was quite something to think that, some 700 years before, Eleanor stood in the same spot, admiring the pavement as I was now. Did she point out details to her daughters: 'Look, Joan, see how beautiful those swirls are. Your father and I saw lots of these when we were on Crusades, when I was pregnant with you.'

As well as being a thing of beauty, the pavement is also riddled with *Da Vinci Code*-esque mystery. David explained the hidden meanings: 'Within these mosaics is a hidden message, a count-down of the world coming to an end.' It was another sign, once more, that all the threads had come together in this moment, in this sacred space.

The Cosmati Pavement at Westminster Abbey.

My feelings were immediately confirmed as I looked up from the pavement to come face to face with Edward I himself. 'Oh! Hello!' I said instinctively, quite surprised. 'I didn't expect to see you here.' Here was the King, with short, curly hair and a scruffy, unshaven chin. He wore a golden coronet, red tunic, blue robe and white, embroidered gloves.

But Edward wasn't looking at me. Instead, his eyes were fixed to his right and – with a long, slender finger – he was pointing towards the altar, towards the very door that led to Eleanor. I couldn't believe it. It was as if he'd been waiting to show me the door, to say: 'We've been expecting you, Alice. This way, please!'

Following King Edward's instructions, I finally stepped foot in one of the most sacred spaces in all of England: the chapel of St Edward the Confessor. A space where – for centuries – the sick made pilgrimage, the faithful knelt in prayer, and kings and queens were buried.

This is a space Eleanor had visited – her robes sweeping across the floor, as my velvet coat did now. I glanced around at the many wonders. The shrine of Edward the Confessor. The tomb of Henry V. The tomb of Henry III – Eleanor's father-in-law, whose body Eleanor had seen reburied, in this very space, in the final months of her life.

I followed the instructions of King Edward I.

Then, in the far corner, I glimpsed a flash of bronze shimmering in the sunlight, which streamed through the stained glass. Instinctively, I knew this was it. I took the final steps, counting them down in my head: *five . . . four . . .* 'Zadok the Priest' reaching its pinnacle . . . *three* . . . that magnificent build-up of strings . . . all those moments of doubt, of difficulty . . . *two* . . . overcome, forgotten . . . *one*.

Here she was. Here we were, meeting at last! After 734 years, the fates had brought us together at this exact moment. How strange it was – how thrilling – to be with Eleanor herself. Inside this tomb chest were her very flesh and bones. The remains of her body, which once moved and breathed, just as I did now. The fingers that once signed great papers. The lips that once kissed those of Edward. The torso that had been carefully filled with herbs.

'Hello,' I said. What else are you supposed to say? Then I added, 'I've come all the way from Harby!' I looked at her bronze effigy. No response. I had a moment where I imagined, in some twist of fate, Eleanor's effigy stirring, coming to life. What would she say to me? Perhaps she would thank me: 'No one pays much attention to me nowadays – they all prefer the tomb of Elizabeth I, around the corner.' Then we would laugh together, the ice broken.

Of course, Eleanor understood people would visit her tomb, just as she had visited that of Henry III. So, in this moment, I realised she had probably imagined this exact scene. She had been expecting me: a young woman many years later, in awe of Eleanor's achievements, who made a pilgrimage to pay her respects. Wasn't this all part of her plan, which I was fulfilling?

Naturally, there was no response from the effigy. But I like to imagine she was smiling down on me in that moment (hopefully not still in purgatory). I lit a candle and the dean said a prayer.

The bronze effigy is an artwork of real beauty. It is easy to take objects such as these for granted in the manufactured age, but to consider this was made my hand, with rudimentary tools, is quite astonishing. It was the work of William Torel, made in 1291, not long after Eleanor died. It is the best surviving contemporary image we have of Eleanor, though probably heavily stylised. Here she lies, meditative and thoughtful and dressed in flowing robes. Her right hand (which would once have held a sceptre) rests beside her.

The left hand is raised over her chest, pulling at the cord of her mantle – or is this a sacred gesture, reminiscent of the blessings given by saints? Her hair flows freely, as it did for her coronation, and she wears a full circlet crown. To add to the splendour, all of this would have originally been gilded with glittering jewels. Her head rests on pillows, with a personalised diamond pattern of alternating castles and lions – the symbols of Castile and León.

The effigy lies upon a heavy stone chest, 3 metres long, 1 metre wide and 1.65 metres high. It is adorned with an arch-and-gable motif and shields of Eleanor's pedigree – the arms of Castile, León and Ponthieu – and the royal lions of England. And all of this would have been vividly coloured – the rich red and gold of the English shields, blue and gold diagonal stripes of Ponthieu, the golden castles of Castile and León. A Norman French inscription surrounds the tomb chest, which, translated, reads:

Here lies Eleanor, sometime Queen of England, wife of King Edward son of King Henry, and daughter of the King of Spain and Countess of Ponthieu, on whose soul God in His pity have mercy. Amen.

Eleanor's effigy is far from the prying eyes of visitors to the abbey, however. If you visit today, you'll only see a distant glimpse of the tomb chest, which is positioned high above the ambulatory, the visitor route. What's more, Eleanor's effigy is encased in a carved iron grille, so delicate, so intricate, it is reminiscent of a garden trellis covered with weaving climbers. Like the princesses of medieval romances, Eleanor lies trapped forever, in creeping ivy.

At the tomb of Eleanor, in Westminster Abbey.

The dean escorted me from the shrine and treated me to a lunch in the Refectory (I told you deans were a decent sort). I bade goodbye and thanked the team who had looked after me.

If I had been running a marathon, this was the equivalent moment of passing the finishing line. I'd be breaking through the ribbon. Champagne corks flying in the air. Instead, I wandered the cloisters and perused the gift shop, unaccustomed to being at such a loose end. 'Where have you come from today?' the lady at the till asked. 'Lincoln', I replied. She smiled and nodded – then looked slightly surprised when I added, 'by foot'.

I bought some Cosmati Pavement socks, made my thanks and stepped into the December sunshine. The Eleanor pilgrimage was complete.

16. IN DEATH WE CANNOT CEASE TO LOVE

'It appears to me impossible that I should cease to exist
or that this active, restless spirit, equally alive to joy
and sorrow, should only be organised dust – ready to fly
abroad the moment the spring snaps or the spark goes
out which kept it together. Surely something resides in
this heart that is not perishable – and life is more
than a dream.'
Mary Wollstonecraft

WITHIN SIX MONTHS OF ELEANOR's death, the Archbishop of York reported that 47,000 masses had already been said for her soul. There was an incentive, of course: anyone who said a paternoster and Ave Maria for the Queen was given a forty-day exemption from penance – meaning time off your own stay in purgatory.

On the first anniversary of Eleanor's death, there were glorious memorial services. Westminster Abbey was ablaze with light, with each member of the congregation holding a candle and Eleanor's tomb surrounded by flickering flames. Edward granted Westminster Abbey seven of Eleanor's properties, the profits of which were to be used to commemorate Eleanor's memory.

Eleanor's coffin was surrounded by thirty large candles, at all times. Two candles were to be always lit, the other twenty-eight only during feasts. Prayers were recited, alms given to the poor, bells rung on certain days. But most extraordinarily, the abbey was required to perform these rituals in perpetuity – and they did so, until the Reformation, when such Catholic practices were brought to a halt. This means that, for 250 years, there was a candle flickering by Eleanor's tomb, day and night.

At the same time, services were held across the country, at her old estates – including at places like Leeds Castle and Langley. At Harby, Edward endowed a chantry chapel and lands made over to Lincoln Cathedral to pay for a priest to continue to pray for Eleanor's soul.

But what of the royal family, after her death? Just over two months after Eleanor died, Edward travelled to Amesbury to visit his daughter Mary and his mother, Eleanor of Provence. Away from the pomp and procedure of the mourners' parade and Eleanor's funeral, was this the moment where Edward finally sunk into his grief? Did he find solace in the arms of his mother, knowing he could rely on her unconditional love?

But Edward would have also been concerned to see his elderly mother, sixty-eight years old, looking increasingly frail. Indeed, in June that year – just seven months after the death of his wife, Eleanor of Provence died. She was embalmed by nuns, like her daughter-in-law, and buried at Amesbury – where I like to imagine young Mary would often visit her.

It had been a dramatic fifteen months for the family. Two sisters married. Joan had become a mother, while Mary was on the verge of becoming a nun. The two matriarchs, Eleanor of Castile, then Eleanor of Provence – the mother and grandmother – had died. A maternal vacuum opened. Did Eleanor, the eldest daughter, assume the spot?

Eleanor's effigy at Westminster Abbey.

As the years passed, Edward and his children pressed on with this new chapter. History books will focus on the big events that unfolded – wars with Scotland, ever-worsening debts, a strained relationship with Parliament – but behind the scenes, their pain at the loss of Eleanor remained.

When we think of grief, sometimes people make the mistake of believing that the pain slowly fades, as time passes. But remember the words of William of Malmesbury – that grief 'knows no limit and is ignorant of a steady course'.

Those who have lost a loved one may not be outwardly grieving, but the grief is always there. I've heard people compare their grief to a pot of glitter: you think you have cleared it all up, but it sticks to everything and, all of a sudden, there it is again. You can never get rid of it. Sometimes people talk about grief as an anchor – a weight you get used to, holding you in place.

I wonder what it was like for the royal family, in the years that followed 1290. Did they feel deep sorrow on 28 November each year, the day Eleanor died? When the princesses watched their children grow up, did they wish Eleanor was still alive, to see their first steps?

Edward remarried again to Margaret of France, nine years after Eleanor's death. Clearly, he was in no rush and not urgently concerned about having just one son. Had the King accepted – should Prince Edward follow the fate of his brothers – that his crown might go to Eleanor, his eldest daughter, who bore the name of her formidable mother and grandmother?

The marriage to Margaret of France (King Philip IV's half-sister) was a political necessity. Edward had been at war with France and this was part of the bargain for peace. But Eleanor still held firm in Edward's mind. When Margaret gave birth to a daughter in 1306, she was named Eleanor.

How did little Edward fare, just six years old when his mother died? After King Edward I's death in 1307, when he was buried in Westminster Abby beside Eleanor, Prince Edward took the throne as Edward II. I'm afraid to say it was one of the most disastrous reigns in English history – barons revolting, failed military campaigns (including the Battle of Bannockburn) and, eventually, his capture, forced abdication and death, in 1327.

What of Queen Eleanor herself? How did her reputation fare? In 1327, an account from St Albans recorded Eleanor as a 'most pious, modest and merciful woman . . . a pillar of the entire realm'. She remained in high esteem throughout the medieval period and into the Tudor age. In 1605, William Camden referred to her as 'good Queen Eleanor', who 'daily and nightly sucked out the ranke poison' of Edward's wound in Acre, so that 'well worthy was she to be remembered by those crosses'.

But after the Reformation – as Catholic Spain became increasingly unpopular – a counter-narrative arose. In an indirect attack on the half-Spanish Queen Mary I and her husband, Philip II of Spain, Eleanor was used as a battering stick. In the 1550s, a popular ballad, *The Lamentable Fall of Queene Elenor*, began:

> *When Edward was in England king,*
> *The first of all that name,*
> *Proud Ellinor he made his queen,*
> *A stately Spanish dame,*
> *Whose wicked life and sinful pride*
> *Thro' England did excel:*
> *To dainty dames and gallant maids,*
> *This queene was known full well.*

The ditty goes on and on, with Eleanor committing all kinds of fictitious atrocities. On her deathbed, she confesses to murder and committing infidelity with a friar. All of this was hugely popular in the Elizabethan anti-Spanish political climate.

In 1593, George Peele's *The Famous Chronicle of King Edward the First* added fuel to the fire, wherein Eleanor was painted as a Lady Macbeth-esque villainess capable of unspeakable cruelty and depravity, who only sought to push the cause of the Spanish people.

Stories were elaborated with soap opera-esque betrayal. In one, Eleanor confesses to adultery with her brother-in-law. And Joan of Acre – in a shocking twist – discovers her father is not King Edward I, but a French friar, causing her to drop dead in shame.

These songs were performed and reprinted throughout the seventeenth century. *The Lamentable Fall of Queene Elenor* was reprinted in 1628, 1629, 1658 and 1664. When we consider that most of the crosses were destroyed between 1643 and 1646, did these ditties play a part in painting a hostile portrait of Eleanor and encouraging the mob?

There were positive accounts of Eleanor, too. Sir Richard Baker's *A History of the Kings of England*, published in 1643, hyped up the myth of Eleanor sucking poison from Edward's wound at Acre, which clearly made its mark, since in 1654, the writer John Evelyn summarised her as 'Queen Eleanora, the loyal and loving wife who sucked the poison out of her husband's wound'.

In 1739, James Thompson penned the play *Edward and Eleonora: A Tragedy*, in which Eleanor was portrayed as a heroic, devoted figure, 'a Princess distinguish'd for all the Virtues that render Greatness amiable'. Being a thinly veiled critique of contemporary politics and corruption, the play was banned under the then-recent Licensing Act. In the 1840s, Agnes Strickland's publication *Lives of the Queens of England* presented Eleanor as the perfect queen. So it seemed Eleanor's legacy had come full circle.

But Eleanor was neither a wicked villainess nor a saintly model of perfection. She was – like everyone – more complex, and it is up to you to make your own judgement on Eleanor's character and legacy. She had her flaws, of course, and there are black marks to her name, even taking the standards of medieval England into consideration. Yet she also faced immense pressure and overcame challenges in ways many of us will never know. Think of her as that vulnerable teenage girl first arriving on the shores of England – a land of strangers, soon to be thrown into the tumult of civil war. Navigating the politics of thirteenth-century England was sink or swim: where many others might have drowned, Eleanor fought to stay afloat. She was fiercely intelligent, an important advisor to King Edward and a patron of the arts. She grew to become a caring mother and a devoted wife – and a woman who refused to be a passive, background figure whose only duty was to bear children. It's a shame that some writers in the past have found it implausible that Eleanor could be a powerful, headstrong woman who enjoyed professional success without being a monster.

What of the legacy of the Eleanor Crosses? For some 300 years, they were a major feature of England's towns – the waypoints for those travelling to and from London – and care was taken to keep them in good nick: Cheapside Cross was regilded several times in the 1500s. As we've discovered, most were destroyed in the Civil War and only three survive today.

It's strange how these legacies ebb and flow. By the eighteenth century, an appreciation for the crosses began to gather momentum once more. The Society of Antiquaries commissioned a survey of the Geddington, Hardingstone and Waltham crosses. The beautiful engravings that resulted brought them to the attention of historians, landowners and architects.

It was in the Victorian period, when another royal love story between Queen Victoria and Prince Albert played out – again leaving one overcome by grief – that the Eleanor Crosses experienced a blossoming architectural revival.

It was perfect timing, for the Gothic Revival movement – constructing modern buildings in medieval styles – began to hold sway. Soon, Eleanor Cross-like structures began popping up here, there and everywhere. A major figure in all this was the architect George Gilbert Scott. As a young man in the 1830s, he worked in Northampton, where it seems he was greatly inspired by the Northampton Eleanor Cross.

In 1843, Gilbert Scott channelled this inspiration to produce the Martyrs' Memorial, in Oxford – which looks strikingly similar to its Northampton mother. It was built to commemorate Bishop Hugh Latimer, Bishop Nicholas Ridley and Archbishop Thomas Cranmer, who were burned in the mid-1550s for their Protestant beliefs (not long after some of Eleanor's memorials were also smashed to pieces).

The actual site of this terrible event was Broad Street, just around the corner and nestled within the city, where it is marked by an iron cross sunk in the road. But the chosen location is a better one, for – like the Eleanor Crosses – it can be seen by travellers on the approach to the city. It was mentioned in 1853 in the novel by Cuthbert Bede, *The Adventures of Mr Verdant Green*:

> [H]e who enters the city, as Mr Green did, from the Woodstock Road, and rolls down the shady avenue of St Giles', between St John's College and the Taylor Buildings, and past the graceful Martyrs' Memorial, will receive impressions such as probably no other city in the world could convey.

The build-your-own-Eleanor-Cross trend soon picked up and many of them were built to mark the loss of a loved one, as Edward had all those years before. In the village of Ilam, in Staffordshire, the wealthy soap manufacturer and landowner Jesse Watts-Russell commissioned a replica cross to remember his wife, Mary. Designed with the help of Gilbert Scott, it is almost indistinguishable from the designs of the 1290s.

The Glastonbury Market Cross in Somerset was erected in 1846, while the Banbury Cross in Oxfordshire went up in 1859, to commemorate the marriage of Victoria, Princess Royal (eldest daughter of Queen Victoria) to Prince Frederick of Prussia. In 1865, Edward Barry's Charing Cross replica was standing in place. In 1868, the Ellesmere Memorial at Walkden, in Lancashire, was completed, to commemorate Harriet, wife of the 1st Earl, who died in 1866.

But the greatest of all was the Albert Memorial of 1872, located opposite the Royal Albert Hall in London – a memorial to the beloved consort of Queen Victoria, again designed by George Gilbert Scott. Though Albert's memorial was far larger than any of the original medieval crosses and different in design, Gilbert Scott explained that he adopted 'the style at once most congenial with my own feelings and that of the most touching monuments ever erected in this country to a Royal Consort – the exquisite "Eleanor Crosses".

Then came the Loudoun Monument in the market town of Ashby-de-la-Zouch, in Leicestershire. Designed once more by Gilbert Scott and completed in 1879, this one was commissioned by Charles Rawdon-Hastings to remember his late wife, Edith. There was also the Sledmere Cross, in Yorkshire, completed in 1898, and the Queen Victoria Monument, in Birkenhead in Merseyside, unveiled in 1905.

*The Queen Eleanor Memorial Cross in the forecourt of
Charing Cross railway station.*

In the twentieth century, stone crosses enjoyed another renaissance, following the First World War. Commemorating the war dead, hundreds more crosses were built in churchyards, streets and railway stations across the country. Sometimes the Victorian Eleanor Cross replicas (such as the Sledmere Cross) were repurposed as a war memorial after the First World War, blurring the lines of remembrance.

So although many of the originals no longer stand, the Eleanor Crosses live on in other monuments – in other tributes to those we've loved and lost. And that number may very well increase. As I write this book – now three years on from the death of Queen Elizabeth II – we are in the process of considering her memorial. On 9 November 2022, a statue of her was unveiled at York Minster, where she stands in a niche on the minster's west front. It was unveiled two months after the Queen's death, originally intended to mark her Platinum Jubilee.

And a national memorial is coming, we're told, to be located in St James's Park, near Buckingham Palace. The final design will be unveiled in April 2026, coinciding with what would have been the Queen's 100th birthday. It's interesting to consider the timeframe. By this point after Eleanor's death, most of the crosses were nearly complete. Perhaps the Eleanor Crosses should be taken into consideration, as the memorial for Elizabeth II is discussed? Perhaps it's being discussed by the design committee, as I write.

And so, as we reach the modern day and look to the future, the great tapestry of Eleanor's legacy grows once more, the threads weaving through time. It is a legacy that is alive and ever-changing. It comes in all shapes and forms, blossoming and blooming in the most unexpected of ways. Think of the creation of the mural in Stony Stratford by Luke McDonnell, in 2019. Since then, Eleanor catches the eye of everyone who strolls along the high street. 'It's the opposite of the burning of the books,' Luke explained to me. 'It's keeping that history alive.'

Every year, the Queen Eleanor Cycle Ride sees a group of thirty cyclists retracing the route from Harby to London. It takes place over the August bank holiday weekend, across four days. The cycle raises money for the work of the Connection at St Martin's, an organisation based next to Charing Cross, which works to combat homelessness in London.

Or what about at Leeds Castle, where Eleanor is coming to life with artificial intelligence? More than 700 years after her death, visitors will be able to talk to her, in English, Spanish and French, and meet her in the (virtual) flesh, once more.

All of this is evidence of an Eleanor revival in the works. And you – as someone who has made it this far in the book – are now part of it, alongside stonemasons, artists, conservators and campaigners. By reading this book, you are extending the branches of Eleanor's legacy. You have your place in the Eleanor Queue, if you like. And this is just the beginning.

I hope you might consider a day trip to the beautiful Leeds Castle and meet AI Eleanor face to face. Pay a visit to Glastonbury Abbey, where Edward and Eleanor reburied King Arthur's bones. Or Caernarfon Castle, where King Edward II was born. Or Queen Eleanor's Garden at Winchester, where you can tick off Edward's round table too. Next time you pass through Northampton's Queen Eleanor Interchange, take twenty minutes to park up and have a look at the Hardingstone cross.

When you next walk through the countryside, you might notice ridge and furrow patterns and think of the medieval world to which Eleanor belonged. If you are a Londoner, on a night out in Soho, take your friends on a detour to the plaque in Trafalgar Square. Perhaps you are a student at Oxford, who will now stroll past the Martyrs' Memorial with a deeper knowledge of its links to Eleanor of Castile. Maybe you will consider a stone-carving course.

Or perhaps it's Eleanor's spirit you might channel. Perhaps you've been experiencing imposter syndrome at work and reading about Eleanor has inspired you to be more assertive or start your own business or build a property company. If you are facing flak for being a hard-nosed woman in business, take comfort that Eleanor of Castile faced the same problems, seven centuries before. 'What Would Eleanor Do?' you might ask yourself in tricky moments.

As we come to the end of our journey together, let me share a moment of doubt I faced while writing this book. While walking the 200 miles, I felt a great pressure to feel radically transformed in some way. As I neared London, I waited for some sort of zap of spiritual lighting, some great event that would shine a new light on my sense of self.

The whole thing was an absolutely thrilling experience and I felt an immense sense of achievement at the end – the type you get from running a marathon or passing a tricky exam. But there was no major personal transformation. This concerned me for a while. Until I realised it didn't matter.

Not every walk can possibly be transformative or life-changing – or else keen walkers would face a lifetime of endless upheaval. It is fine to complete a walk of any length and enjoy it for the sake of it – for this simple experience is wondrous in itself and transformative in the long run. A habit to weave into your daily life. So, if there is a lesson to take away, it is this: to walk in the fresh air and be curious to your surroundings is one of life's greatest and most restorative pleasures. And that, I believe, is the most valuable gift of all.

For, when we are curious, the world becomes an exciting place. And a comforting one, too. Everywhere are shadows of our ancestors' lives and remnants of their love. Think back to the obelisk in the grounds of Deene Park, a tribute to the fifty-nine-year marriage of Edmund and Marian Brudenell. Or Celebration Avenue in Northampton, that long line of rowan trees, each of which was dedicated to a loved one. And, of course, the Eleanor Crosses themselves – monuments to the love of a grief-stricken husband, as well as to centuries of dedication from those who have taken care to protect them.

Perhaps – like me – you will take comfort to know you are part of this tapestry, woven across the centuries. In your hours of grief or heartbreak or whatever challenges you may face, you can remember that you are not alone. You follow in the footsteps of millions of people past, who have felt your joy or endured your pain.

This book is a tribute to those we've loved and those we've lost. And, as we think of Eleanor, more than seven centuries after her death, and her role within one of England's greatest love stories, perhaps the best way to remember her is through something universal. Whether it be as grand as a stone cross or as simple as a word of kindness, it is all the same: an act of love.

A NOTE OF THANKS

THERE ARE MANY PEOPLE TO thank for this book. Caroline Hardman, my wonderful agent, and the team at Hardman & Swainson. Enormous thanks to the brilliant team at Pan Macmillan – Mike Harpley, Melissa Bond, Ríbh Brownlee, Charlotte Dixon, Poppy North, Emma Pidsley and Josie Turner. Thanks to Helen Purvis and the wonderful team at Knight Ayton Management.

Along with the support and encouragement of my wonderful family and friends and many who have helped along the way, thank you to Sara Cockerill, Nick Holder, David and Sue Gentleman, the Revd Gillian Gamble, Maria Garbutt-Lucero, Caroline Graham, Luke McDonell, Louise Wilkinson, Jim Harker, the Revd Canon Dr Simon Jones, the Very Revd Andrew Tremlett, the Very Revd Dr David Hoyle, Simon and Amanda Burn, John Goodall, Clive Aslet, Alan and Tracey Micklethwaite, Gillian Stern, David Holtam, Jack Hodsall, Charles Wood, Sylvia Bland, Guy Hayward, Ruby Gray, Lucy Davidson, Daniel McKay, Benedict Ryan, Lottie Mattocks, Susannah Duck, Patrick Pomeroy, Jack Guffogg, Will Klintworth, Sophie Lucas, Margaret from Geddington, Claire Arrand, Dr Andy King, Anna McDonald, Jane

Cowan, Jack Dunn and the team at Weldon Stone, and David Carrington and the team at Skillington Workshop.

Thanks to those who made the walk possible. The countless farmers, landowners and local councils who have cared for the land across which I walked, keeping the stiles, fences, signposts and footpaths in good nick. Thanks to all the staff who welcomed me at the many hotels, Premier Inns, bakeries and village shops.

My thanks to the support from the teams at Lincoln Cathedral, Westminster Abbey, St Paul's Cathedral, the Queen Eleanor Cycle Ride, Viking UK, Geddington Church, the British Pilgrimage Trust, Northampton Battlefields Society, English Heritage, the National Trust, Chalke History Festival and many others. Thank you to the many historians who have been so supportive, welcoming and friendly.

Thanks must go to Eleanor herself and to King Edward, who – though he might have been a bit of a brute – did have pretty good taste when it came to architectural commissions.

Books would be nothing without booksellers. Thanks to the team at Blackwell's on Broad Street in Oxford, Waterstones, Hatchards and all the independent bookshops, for all your hard work and for always being so enthusiastic and helpful.

Finally, thank you to *you*, dear reader, and everyone who has ever read my books or watched a video on social media. Your enthusiasm for history knows no bounds and it is a delight to have your company. I look forward to many more historic adventures together.

Until next time.

Alice Loxton
Wednesday 30 April 2025
The Lamb and Flag, Covent Garden

MORE TO EXPLORE

Thanks so much for reading *Eleanor*. Here are some recommendations for those hoping to find out more.

Books about Eleanor and her medieval world:

Eleanor of Castile: The Shadow Queen by Sara Cockerill
'The Eleanor Crosses: A Journey Set in Stone' by Nick Holder, on
    the English Heritage website (www.english-heritage.org.uk/visit/
    places/eleanor-cross-geddington/history)
Daughters of Chivalry: The Forgotten Children of Edward I by Kelcey
    Wilson-Lee
The Time Traveller's Guide to Medieval England by Ian Mortimer
Medieval Horizons by Ian Mortimer
She-Wolves: The Women Who Ruled England Before Elizabeth by
    Helen Castor
Normal Women: 900 Years of Making History by Philippa Gregory
Medieval Women: Voices and Vision edited by Eleanor Jackson
    and Julian Harrison
Eleanor of Castile by Jean Powrie
Eleanor of Castile by John Carmi Parsons

The Eleanor Crosses by Decca Warrington
Going to Church in Medieval England by Nicholas Orme
A Cross for Queen Eleanor by David Gentleman
A Great and Terrible King: Edward I and the Forging of Britain by Marc Morris
Edward I by Andy King
Power and Thrones: A New History of the Middle Ages by Dan Jones
Sceptred Isle: A New History of the Fourteenth Century by Helen Carr
Pilgrimage in Medieval England by Diana Webb

These might be handy for exploring the country:

Britain's Pilgrim Places by Nick Mayhew-Smith and Guy Hayward
London: A Guide for Curious Wanderers by Jack Chesher and Katharine Fraser
Hidden Histories: A Spotter's Guide to the British Landscape by Mary-Ann Ochota
Rice's Architectural Primer by Matthew Rice
Rice's Language of Buildings by Matthew Rice
Restoration Stone Carving by Alan Micklethwaite
Church Going: A Stonemason's Guide to the Churches of the British Isles by Andrew Ziminski
Pilgrimage: Journeys of Meaning by Peter Stanford
The National Trust Members' Handbook
English Heritage Members' Handbook
Historic Houses Handbook
An Ordnance Survey map or – my preference – the OS Maps app

Some other helpful research resources:

Historic maps produced by the Historic Town's Trust

MORE TO EXPLORE

The London Library
History Today
BBC HistoryExtra
British History Online
English Heritage website
Oxford Dictionary of National Biography
British Newspaper Archive
British Library website
National Trust Collections
Historic England Research Records
Bibliography of British and Irish History
JSTOR
Oxford Art Online
The Sunday Times Digital Archive
The Telegraph Historical Archive

And for a general pick-me-up:

The latest edition of *Stamford Living*

THE JOURNEY CONTINUES

Here are some activities you might like to consider and some places to visit. Don't forget suncream.

The Queen Eleanor Cycle Ride

www.queeneleanorcycleride.org

The Queen Eleanor Cycle Ride is a great way to get involved. It is a four-day sponsored cycle ride which takes place over the August bank holiday weekend every year. The 200-mile route follows quiet roads from Harby to London and links the locations of the twelve Queen Eleanor Crosses. It is organised by the Friends of the Connection at St Martin's and raises money to end homelessness in London.

British Pilgrimage Trust

www.britishpilgrimage.org

The British Pilgrimage Trust was founded in 2014 to 'advance British pilgrimage as a form of cultural heritage'. One of the co-founders was Dr Guy Hayward, who features in Chapter 11. The British Pilgrimage Trust website has a free and comprehensive collection of more than 250 routes and places to visit in Britain, with digital maps to guide you. The Trust also organises guided walks. I joined one of these (led by Guy), which took us around Oxford for the day and we walked 5 miles in total. We started at St Frideswide's Well in the secluded grove around Binsey Church, before heading into the city, exploring Oxford Oratory, climbing the tower of University Church and visiting Merton Chapel, among many other delights. It wasn't just a guided tour, nor a history lesson, but opened my eyes to what pilgrimage means, both historically and today. It is a wonderful thing to do – either alone or with a friend.

The Society for the Protection of Ancient Buildings (SPAB)

www.spab.org.uk

SPAB was founded by William Morris in 1877, as discussed in Chapter 13. Today, they run all sorts of training schemes and conservation courses, where you can learn about historic processes including pargeting, lime plastering and working with mortars. Every summer there is a working party that lasts for several days and – as well as being great fun – is a wonderful way for beginners to try out new techniques. There are lots of learning resources on the website, too.

The King's Foundation

The King's Foundation offer an array of education and training programmes, many of which teach skills that keep Eleanor's medieval world alive – natural yarn-dyeing, working with wood and stained-glass techniques.

Charing Cross

At the Northern Line platform of Charing Cross Underground station, in London, are the murals designed by David Gentleman.

These give a great idea of how the crosses were built in the medieval period. Outside Charing Cross railway station is the Queen Eleanor Memorial Cross. Though it is a replica, it gives a good impression of the original medieval crosses. It's also worth visiting the Charles I statue, located at the top of Whitehall. This was the original site of the Eleanor Cross, as recorded by the plaque on the ground.

Lincoln Cathedral and Castle
Once the tallest building in the world, Lincoln Cathedral is a triumph of Gothic architecture and one of the most impressive buildings of the medieval age. This is home to a replica of Eleanor's visceral tomb and there are small statues of Eleanor and Edward on the outer south wall, too. At Lincoln Castle, which is nearby, you can see part of the original Eleanor Cross in the grounds.

Harby village
Harby village is where Eleanor died. Head to the church and walk to the back of the churchyard. Beyond the rickety fence is a field with strange lumps and bumps in the ground. This is the remains of Sir Richard de Weston's house, where Eleanor took her final breath. The church has some wonderful Eleanor details, including a statue on the outer wall and a beautiful stained-glass window, installed in the millennium. When you visit, make sure you go to the correct Harby (NG23 7ED) as there is another Harby village nearby!

St Albans Cathedral
St Albans Cathedral is home to the shrine of St Alban, which Edward and Eleanor would have visited. Eleanor's body was also here as the cortège passed through the city. Make sure to visit the

clock tower in the centre of the town, as there is a plaque commemorating this.

Geddington village

Geddington is a beautiful little village in Northamptonshire and home to the best surviving and most elegant Eleanor Cross. Sit on the steps of the cross, walk across the original medieval bridge, visit the church where Eleanor's body lay and – most importantly – pay a visit to the Star Inn.

The Eleanor Crosses

The three crosses to visit are located in Geddington village, Northampton (NN4 8AX, there is parking opposite) and Waltham Cross. When you visit, take some time to make a sketch of the crosses – it's a great way to force yourself to look at and understand the structure.

Leeds Castle

Located in Kent – not Leeds! This is a wonderful, fairy-tale-like castle, which Eleanor and Edward were heavily involved in developing. It's also worth visiting the falconry display, as this was a sport that Eleanor adored.

Westminster Abbey

Located in the heart of London, this is where Eleanor is buried. She is located in the heart of the abbey, beside the shrine of Edward the Confessor. To get a close look at her effigy, book a place on the guided tour.

Stony Stratford

In Stony Stratford, at the intersection of New Street and the high street, is a magnificent mural of Eleanor, designed by Luke McDonnell. Make sure to pay a visit to The Cock or The Bull – of 'cock and bull story' fame.

Caernarfon Castle

Caernarfon Castle was built by Edward I to assert his authority in Wales. The structure is monumental in scale and incredibly imposing – but makes for a lovely day out nonetheless!

Winchester Great Hall

This magnificent medieval hall displays a beautiful round table, believed to have been used by King Edward in the thirteenth century. Make sure to pop outside and visit Queen Eleanor's Garden, a recreated medieval garden dedicated to Eleanor of Provence and Eleanor of Castile.

The Church of St Bartholomew the Great

Though not a key part of Eleanor's story, this is London's oldest church, founded in 1123. It's a great place to get a sense of the kind of buildings Eleanor would have known. Another London church to visit, not far away, is Temple Church, which was once the HQ of the Knights Templar.

MORE PHOTOS

Following in the footsteps of the Ancient Romans.

Excited to arrive in Ancaster . . . but still 8 miles to Grantham.

6 a.m. selfie with the new Eleanor Cross in Stamford.

The Geddington Eleanor Cross at night.

A village sign in Hardingstone, showing the Northampton Eleanor Cross.

A close-up of the Northampton Eleanor Cross.

Eleanor's heraldry and several books are prominent on the cross.

Delapré Lake in Northampton.

Travelling in style.

Chutneys available at Milton Bryan.

The monastery in Burgos where Eleanor and Edward were married.

A statue of Eleanor at the 'Medieval Women' exhibition at the British Library.

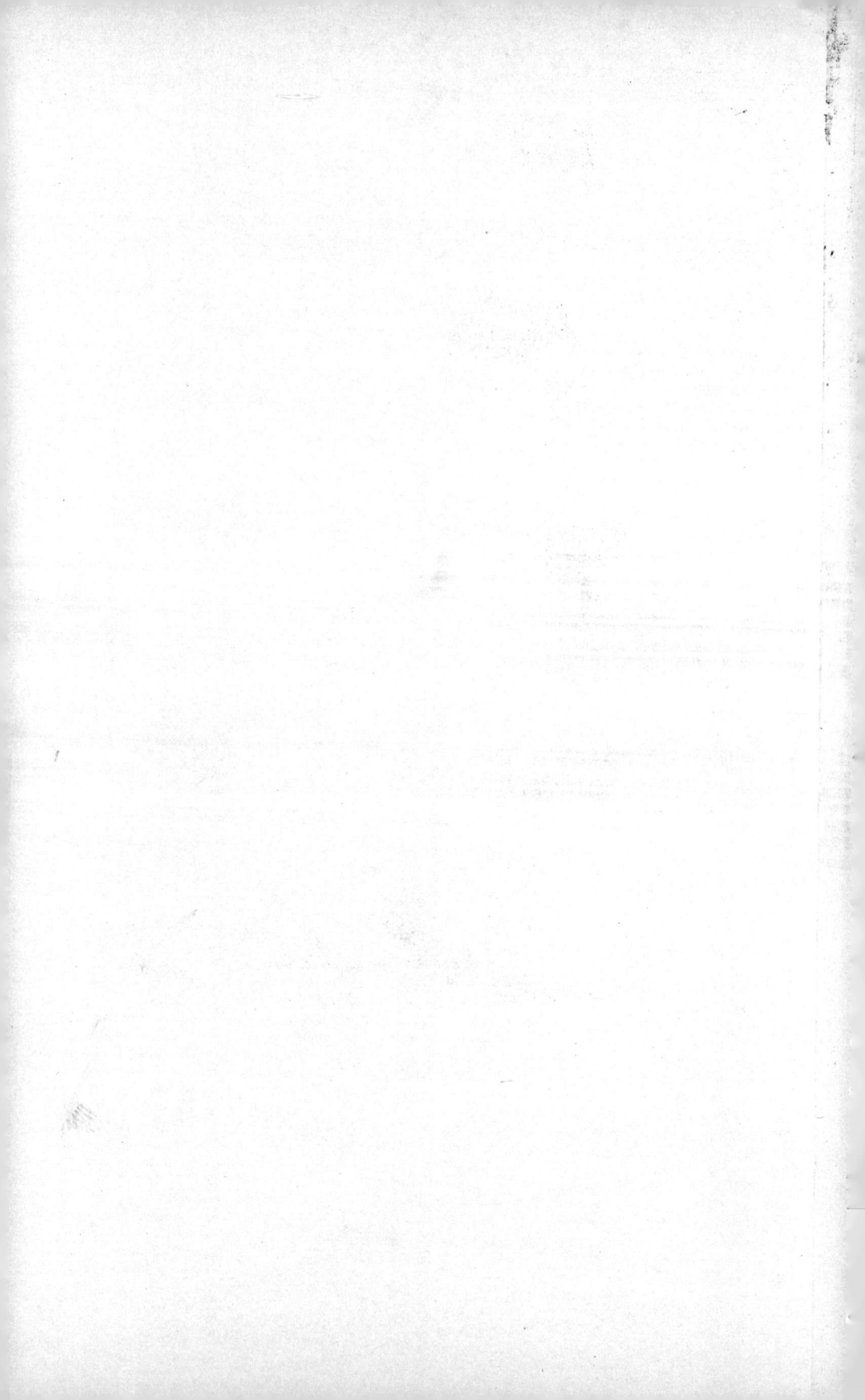